THE SHOPPER'S GUIDE TO
Washington, D.C.

From the *Hometown Guides* series, books that offer lively and original regional history and travel guides for in and around Washington, D.C. Other titles include:

Dirt Cheap, Real Good: A Highway Guide to Thrift Stores in the Washington, D.C., Area
by CHRISS SLEVIN AND LEAH SMITH

Quest for the Holy Grill: 50 Crummy But Good Restaurants Within Rambling Range of Washington, D.C.
by DONOVAN KELLY

Walk and Bike the Alexandria Heritage Trail: A Guide to Exploring a Virginia Town's Hidden Past
by FRIENDS OF ALEXANDRIA ARCHAEOLOGY (FOAA)

The Middleburg Mystique: A Peek Inside the Gates of Middleburg, Virginia
by VICKY MOON

Washington, D.C., From A To Z: The Look-Up Source for Everything to See & Do in the Nation's Capital
by PAUL WASSERMAN AND DON HAUSRATH

Breaking Away to Virginia and Maryland Wineries
by ELISABETH FRATER

Historic Hotels and Hideaways
by TRISH FOXWELL

A City of Gardens: Glorious Public Gardens In and Around the Nation's Capital
by BARBARA SEEBER

Save 25 percent when you order any of these and other fine Capital titles from our Web site: www.capital-books.com.

THE SHOPPER'S GUIDE TO
Washington, D.C.

WHERE TO FIND THE BEST OF EVERYTHING

Karen Ertel
and
Stephen Koff

A Capital Hometown Guide

CAPITAL
BOOKS, INC.
Sterling, Virginia

Copyright © 2004 by Karen Ertel and Stephen Koff

All rights reserved. No part of this book may be reproduced or utilized in any form or by any means, electronic or mechanical, including photocopying, recording, or by any information storage and retrieval system, without permission in writing from the publisher. Inquiries should be addressed to:

Capital Books, Inc.
P.O. Box 605
Herndon, Virginia 20172-0605

ISBN 1-931868-84-0 (alk.paper)

Book design and composition by Susan Mark
Coghill Composition Company
Richmond, Virginia

Library of Congress Cataloging-in-Publication Data

Ertel, Karen.
   The shopper's guide to Washington, D.C. : where to find the best of everything / Karen Ertel and Stephen Koff.
       p. cm.
    Includes bibliographical references and index.
    ISBN 1-931868-84-0 (alk. paper)
    1. Shopping—Washington Region—Guidebooks.   I. Koff, Stephen.
II. Title.
TX335.5.W2E78   2004
640'.73'09753—dc22
                                                        2004007868

Printed in the United States of America on acid-free paper that meets the American National Standards Institute Z39-48 Standard.

First Edition

10 9 8 7 6 5 4 3 2 1

For Anna, who has the coolest truck and is wise beyond her years.

For Sam, who fills our lives with wonderful music. The meals will get better now, and we can play. Book's done.

For all the independent shop owners who struggle to bring us something new, different, and personal in a world of one-size-fits-all, big-box retail. You make shopping fun.

Walmart, W2438, 07/28/04

cc5356, cc5356.50

ACKNOWLEDGMENTS

We want to thank these people for their ideas, tips, expertise, companionship, hand-holding, sharing, merchandise testing, and/or patience while we busied ourselves shopping and writing. We've inevitably left someone important out, so to all who lent a hand or an ear, please know we are grateful.

Dorothy Altmiller
Lisa Ambrusco
Noemi C. Arthur
Peter Bortz
Dennis Brack
Tom Brazaitis
Eleanor Clift
Susan dee Cohen
Ronnie Costello
Jon Danforth
Cindy DiBiase
Tom Diemer
Kathy Doherty
Sandra Duraes
Sandro Duraes
John Edgell
Joseph Egerton
The Free Radicals
Carrie Grabo
Kim Hall
Birgit Henninger
Esta Johnston
Kathie Kroll
Margaret Laurenson
Elisabeth Leamy
Daniel Lee
Ken Lee
Philip Levy
Joan E. Lisante
John Lymangrover
Jay Mallin
Jake McGuire
Judy Miller
Madeleine Mitchell
Evelyn Montgomery
Luis Peraza
Jermaine Randall
Lorene Rider
Judy Ryan
Nancy Schuhmann
Travis Smith
Theresa Sottler
Paula Casale-Spitler
Joann van Lunteren
Ian Weitzman
Paul Wood (best of luck, Phaser)
Mike Young
Norm Yow
Shiva Zargham
Peter Zia

CONTENTS

CHAPTER 1: Introduction — 1
So Many Stores, So Many Choices—and
   How We Made Them — 1

CHAPTER 2: Top Ten Stores — 5
Our Favorite Things — 5

CHAPTER 3: Food and Drink — 19
Gourmet and International Food Stores — 19
Wine, Beer, and Spirits — 30

CHAPTER 4: Fashion and Accessories — 35
For Men and Women — 35
Strictly for Women — 40
Ten Fashion-Forward Boutiques — 46
The Scoop on Shoes — 50
Strictly for Children — 51
Jewelry and Accessories — 53

CHAPTER 5: Music — 57
CDs and Records — 58
Musical Instruments — 61
Sheet Music — 66

CHAPTER 6: Bookstores — 69
The Best in a City Full of Greats — 69
A Note on Newsstands — 80
Strictly for Children — 80

CHAPTER 7: Toys, Games, and Hobbies 83
Toy and Game Stores, Magic Shops, Hobby Stores 84
Video Games 93

CHAPTER 8: Home and Garden 95
Basic Goods: Hardware, Fireplace, and Patio 95
Home Furnishings and Accessories 101
Pottery, Glassware, and China 109
Linens and Fabrics 110

CHAPTER 9: Electronics and Cameras 115
Cameras and Photo Gear 115
Stereos and Televisions 119
Computers 123
High-Volume Computer Dealers 125

CHAPTER 10: Health and Beauty 127
Cosmetics, Perfumes, and Beauty Supplies 127
Vitamins, Nutritional Supplements, and Organic Produce 131

CHAPTER 11: Bargains 135
Discounts, Closeouts, and Off-Price Stores 135
Consignment Boutiques 139

CHAPTER 12: Sporting Goods 141
Selected Specialty Goods by Location 150
Golf and Tennis 150
Skates and Skis 151
Bikes 151
Running and Walking 152
Camping and Hiking 153

CHAPTER 13: Potpourri 155
Shops So Good, We Had to Find a Place to Tell You 155

CHAPTER 14: Getting to Great Shopping, A Neighborhood Guide 161
Georgetown 162
Old Town Alexandria 162
Wheaton 163
U Street and Adams Morgan 163
Capitol Hill, Eastern Market, and Eighth Street 164

Dupont Circle	164
Clarendon	164
Chevy Chase and Bethesda	165

CHAPTER 15: Where to Find It — 167
The Best of Everything by Location — 167

CHAPTER 16: A Directory of Even More Noteworthy Stores — 185

Accessories	185
Arts and Crafts	186
Audio Equipment	187
Bicycles	187
Books	188
Cameras	191
Camping and Hiking Gear	191
CDs and Records	192
Clothing	193
Computers	199
Cosmetics	199
Costumes	200
Curtains	200
Discount	200
Dollhouse Supplies	200
Fabric	201
Fireplace	201
Food	201
Furniture	202
Games	204
Golf	204
Hats	205
Hardware	205
Hobby Shops	205
Home Furnishings and Accessories	206
Jewelry	208
Lamps	209
Linens	209
Magic Shops	209
Musical Instruments	210
Shoes	210

Sporting Goods	211
Toys	212
Vitamins	213
Wine and Beer	214
CHAPTER 17: To the Mall	215
A Directory of Area Shopping Malls	215

CHAPTER 1

Introduction

SO MANY STORES, SO MANY CHOICES—AND HOW WE MADE THEM

If shopping is a chore, there's a good chance you've been doing it all wrong. Done right, shopping can be a form of recreation and exploration, not to mention a great way to get to know the community. That's what this book is about.

It can help you find the best of everything in Washington and its suburbs, whether you're looking for toys, wine, high-fashion or trendy clothing, Brazilian candy, German chocolate, Italian groceries, hard-to-find records and CDs, vintage musical instruments, hats, housewares, books, magic tricks, hardware, and much more. And it can guide you to pleasant detours—neighborhood side trips, if you will—that are not only fun but sometimes delectable as well: a local bakery, ice cream shop, diner, sushi bar, even a French video store.

Think of it as shopping as adventure.

This book was born out of necessity and a little frustration. We lived here in the mid-1980s, when we attended graduate school and moved back in the 1990s. The retail world was changing, and big-box stores seemed to be gobbling up more and more homegrown businesses. Not that there's anything wrong with big-box—but have you ever tried putting together a Ping-Pong table on a holiday eve and found you're missing a $2^1/_2$-inch lag bolt? A good hardware store could have helped. Instead, we had to improvise with a package of three-inch bolts from Home Depot, and they weren't exactly right.

Good hardware stores are out there, though they're becoming fewer and farther between. Good stores of all kinds exist throughout the region; you just have to go find them. So, realizing that this town needed a good insider's guide, we did.

We started by exploring, using our knack for discovering the interesting and unusual. It's not bragging to say that one of us—Karen—is so good at it that her friends regularly come from hundreds of miles away to visit Washington, but not its monuments. They want her to guide them on a shopping escapade.

We then broadened our reach with an ever-growing network of sources and tipsters. In some categories, we reached out to world-class professionals for advice—one of the advantages of living in Washington. Some of the advice was terrific. The only way to know was to go shop.

We visited stores and more stores, hundreds if not more. We always went anonymously and unannounced. "Just browsing," we'd say. We rarely dressed up; more often, we'd go in jeans. Those few merchants who treated us shabbily are not in this book. We'd like to say, "You know who you are," but the fact is, they probably don't.

If a store impressed us—generally, a result of its merchandise, with a splash of service for good measure—we considered it a potential "find" and went back. We didn't keep an exact count, but the majority of stores did not warrant a second visit and are not included in this book. But if we thought the shops worthy, we talked to proprietors or managers, salesclerks, and customers. Many of the best stores had fascinating stories, some of which we've included. Most had a loyal base of patrons who did a better job of talking up their favorite shops than even the owners could.

A single constant stood out, whether the store sold imported beer or specialized in expensive clothing for hip-hop stars and NBA players: the owners took joy in what they did. Some were frustrated with the challenges of competing against better-heeled, national chains, but their love for their businesses keeps them going. As the owner of a specialty guitar store said, if he merely wanted to move merchandise, he might as well be selling any commodity. He sold guitars, not widgets, to discerning players.

Ideally, you'll approach these stores with that same level of appreciation, whether you're looking for tennis and golf supplies, western ware, cosmetics, or the best hobby shops around. If you need something that's not among our picks, you're still likely to find it in this book, because in the later chapters we've provided more sweeping directories of area shops, malls, and neighborhoods worth exploring. You might discover your own "finds" and secrets of Washington and its suburbs, and you'll know the city as you've never quite known it before.

More than anything, we wish you much fun and adventure as you shop.

Karen Ertel and Stephen Koff

P.S. Let us know about your own shopping discoveries at findsdc@aol.com. Send us your e-mail address, and we will give you periodic updates on store openings, closings, relocations, and other news.

CHAPTER 2

Top Ten Stores

OUR FAVORITE THINGS

You think it's easy shopping in all these stores, talking to merchants, trying out this item or buying that? Well, no—but it sure can be fun when the planets align and that perfect combination of unique, interesting, and exciting pops out from the cluttered aisles and racks. We think the stores in this second chapter stand out the most.

Each store represents the best quality and selection in its niche; each offers good customer service (remember, we visited anonymously before deciding whether any store was worthy of your visit); and each was delightful to shop at.

The top ten was a collaborative effort between the two of us, Karen and Stephen, with some input from our daughter, Anna, and our son, Sam, both teenagers. All four of us ultimately agreed on most, but a couple of stores were really individual picks: Old Luckett's Store was Karen's—Steve just plain likes his stuff new. And it probably won't shock you to find out that Southworth Guitar was a Steve pick, given that Karen could die happily without ever going to another guitar store.

Our son protested the inclusion of Backstage, mainly because he is still unhappy that his dad bought funny sunglasses there and then walked around Eighth Street with them on. (Steve still wears them proudly when his recreational geezer rock band, The Free Radicals, plays "Secret Agent Man.")

But in the end, there was family harmony. We all agreed that there is something really special about each and every one of the shops we chose, and we hope you will, too.

~~~

EINSTEIN MIGHT not approve, but at Artcraft you can buy a "people cabinet" shaped and painted in his likeness (even holding a chalkboard stating, "$e = mc^2$"), appropriate for storing your old dissertation on quantum physics, a bottle of Scotch, or even your socks. You can also get something as large as a dining table and chairs finished with a colorful, geometric purple border, or as small as a uniquely shaped candle or a ceramic tile with the sun and the moon. We picked this store for the top ten because it's festive looking—even the outside is painted in bold purples and blues and has a really cool sign. Of course, the inside isn't too shabby either, as you find yourself standing in a sea of brightly colored, nonstodgy contemporary crafts, furniture, even jewelry made by more than four hundred American artisans. Unless you're the world's biggest curmudgeon or really disdain the craft/folk art thing—and a little *can* go a long way—this store is irresistible.

> **ARTCRAFT COLLECTION**
> 132 King Street
> Alexandria, VA 22314
> (703) 299-6616
> www.artcraftcollection.com

Artcraft came about after owners Sharyn and Jay Winer turned their hobby of scouring unique American art galleries during family vacations into a business. In her pre-Artcraft life, Sharyn sold used clothing and was even a private detective for a while. Construction manager Jay's family owned the Historic Savage Mill shopping center in Maryland, and in 1992, they opened the original and largest Artcraft Collection store (in the Savage Mill center). Since then, they have expanded with two more stores, one at Reston Town Center and one in Old Town Alexandria, which their son Adam manages.

The Winers are relentless in their pursuit of a great artisan. Case in point: they loved Texas artist David Marsh's multicolored pine armoires, which they found on a buying trip to Boston, but Marsh was unable to sell to Artcraft because he had already reached the limit of galleries he could accommodate. Over the next four years the Winers called Marsh every once in awhile, "just in case." Then, one day, Marsh called *them*. Another dealer had a flood;

would they like to buy a truckload of furniture? They would and did, and that sealed the deal with Marsh.

Other furniture artists include Ralph Garrett and Sticks, a Des Moines company that does a lot of custom work and prints messages in the wood. Local artist Paul Carbo does those amazing "people cabinets" we mentioned earlier, cut in the shape of the people he depicts. Besides Albert Einstein, you can get Sherlock Holmes, Groucho Marx, and "a terrific Katherine Hepburn." Carbo can even do a piece of furniture that looks like *you* if you give him a good picture.

But furniture is just a small part of the inventory. Artcraft has items from every medium: glass, ceramics, wood, metal, and on and on. Earrings and jewelry, oddly shaped clocks, whimsical carved chess sets, brightly colored and patterned silverware, intricate wooden cutting boards and boxes, human-size metal animal sculptures, wooden perpetual calendars that truly are works of art, and teapots that look like they came out of a Disney movie, to name a few. When Aerosmith was in town, frontman Steven Tyler spent a lot of time in the Alexandria store. Local political celebrity and very patient wife of James Carville, Mary Matalin, has been know to pop in as well.

Other Locations: 11960 Market Street, Reston, VA (703) 964-0145; 8600 Foundry Street, Savage, MD (410) 880-4863.

In the neighborhood: In Alexandria, check out the eclectic collection of home furnishings a few doors down at **Rugs to Riches**, 116 King (www.rugstoriches.com), or walk several blocks up the street for antiques and home furnishings at **Random Harvest**, 810 King.

The Reston Town Center location is next to **South Moon Under** (see our write-up in chapter 4, Fashion and Accessories, for details).

~~~~

WANT TO humiliate your teenage children? It was easy for us to do after visiting Backstage on Capitol Hill. We bought a pair of large, oddly shaped, black sunglasses "fashionably" larger on one side than the other—and wore them on the street! While the kids were more than a little horrified at the public spectacle, they were grateful that we refrained from buying the huge Afro wig that bought back memories of high school, circa 1973.

Backstage is the store to visit if you are an actor, and many professionals stop by when they are in town. Kelly McGillis has come in to buy makeup, and Lynda Carter, Stacy Keach, and Robert Goulet have been customers. Members of the a touring ballet company from Russia purchased ballet slippers, and a dancer from Croatia went home with several pairs of tights because she said she couldn't get the same quality in her country.

> **BACKSTAGE INC.**
> 545 Eighth Street SE
> Washington, DC 20003
> (202) 544-5744
> www.backstagebooks.com

If you want a seriously great Halloween costume, Backstage has more than two thousand for rent and a seamstress on the premises. And if owners Sandra and Sandro Duraes ask for details about the party you are attending, they are not being nosy. They want to protect you from the humiliation of having an identical twin at the party. Two Cinderellas in the exact same costume! They have been invited to the White House to fit staff and waiters in colonial outfits, and Chelsea Clinton rented a costume once. The store always does a lot of business when a former senator from Virginia holds his annual Mardi Gras party. It also can help you set up a mystery party, offering directions for the game, invitations, and other essentials, in a box.

Backstage doubles as a theatrical bookstore, the only one in the area, and some of its scripts are signed by the authors. Originally it was a bookstore at Dupont Circle; the current owners bought the shop in 1996, moved to Capital Hill in 2000, and expanded it to carry costumes and theatrical supplies.

In the neighborhood: Near the Navy Yard, Backstage is not far from **Eastern Market.** The Eighth Street area has a growing variety of interesting little stores and restaurants, including **Hoopla Traders**, **Alvear Studio**, and **Plaid** boutique.

TOUR GROUPS from Europe and out-of-state vacationers traveling on Interstate 95 who make a stop at Boot Hill Western Store in Woodbridge may know something you don't: Northern Virginia has one of the very best western wear stores in the United States.

> **BOOT HILL WESTERN STORE**
> 13231 Gordon Boulevard
> Woodbridge, VA 22191
> (703) 490-0090

Greet country and western star George Strait at the entrance (well, it's not really George, it's one of those life-size cutouts, just like the cardboard presidents you can pay to pose with near the White House), as you inhale the smell of leather and wood in this sixteen thousand square feet of pure western bliss. If you are hunting for fancy footwear, two-step your way across the gleaming hardwood floors to find perhaps the largest selection of name-brand boots on the entire East Coast. If you want the very best and have the funds, head to the elevated platform reserved for the high-end handmade boots, which can cost as much as $1,600 (for a pair of supple Texas, handmade Lucchese classics made of alligator skin). Even if you're into New York chic, it's hard to go into Boot Hill without falling in love with at least one pair of luxuriously soft leather boots.

Ladies who want a great outfit for a night of country and western dancing can choose from long skirts and western-style shirts, such as a red, white, and blue, starred and striped blouse by Crazy Cowgirl. Other brands include 1849 Authentic Ranchwear (bearing the label "100% pure American"), Cowgirl Up, and Brooks and Dunn. (Yup, the country duo has its own clothing line.) Men can buy Wrangler jeans and shirts, too, as well as beautifully detailed leather belts adorned with ornate buckles, some with tooled designs such as scorpions. Personally, we're mighty impressed with the rugged and super-heavy oilskin coats made by Outback Trading Company.

It is nearly impossible to describe everything Boot Hill has to offer: kids' clothes, cowboy hats on a high rack (grab a pole to take one down), genuine eelskin briefcases, Montana Silversmith sterling silver belt buckles emblazoned with the word, "Bodacious," hot pink and orange bandanas, and souvenir statues of a horse named Elmer (a pun on Elmer's glue) in various poses ("Patriotic Elmer" wears red, white, and blue, for example).

Bad joke: Why did the cowboy die with his boots on? Because he didn't want to stub his toe when he kicked the bucket!

In the neighborhood: There's not much in the immediate vicinity, but **Potomac Mills**, the outlet mall, is only a few miles south. Or head north a short way on Route 123 for an afternoon of gift shopping and gallery browsing in the charming riverside village of **Occoquan**.

WE SAID it spontaneously the first time we walked through the door of CDepot: "Wow!" If you listen to a lot of music—rock, punk, jazz, musicals, or R & B—you have to check this place out. The only section that didn't impress us was classical. CDepot is not only large, it is also complete, selling a mix of about 60 percent new, 40 percent used. Here's proof:

Dead Kennedys—alongside a section for Jello Biafra's solo work. Robert Fripp—nine different titles, and that's not even counting the King Crimson selection. Grateful Dead, naturally, but also separate listings for the solo recordings of Jerry Garcia, Bob Weir, Phil Lesh, and Mickey Hart. Likewise, not only the Rolling Stones, but a separate stock of Mick Jagger, Keith Richards, Charlie Watts, Ron Wood, and Bill Wyman solo CDs. Flipping alphabetically through the Ps, you'll find Graham Parker, Van Dyke Parks, Alan Parsons, Gram Parsons, Partridge Family. . . .

> **CDEPOT**
> 9039 Baltimore Avenue
> College Park, MD 20740
> (301) 982-3472
> www.cdepot.com

Speaking of bubblegum, when was the last time you saw a new copy (two of them, actually) of *The Best of the Ohio Express: Yummy, Yummy, Yummy?* It's not our cup of tea, but at $8.99 it's worth the price of a gag. (Which is the only reason we can imagine why the label bothered to remaster this from vinyl to CD.)

Then there's an entire row packed with Al Green, and a row and a half of Marvin Gaye. If blues make you happy, you can find Big Bill Broonzy to Sonny Boy Williamson and everything in between. Jazz lovers likewise won't be disappointed. Store owner Sandy Williamson says it best: "We have more Miles Davis CDs than many stores have jazz altogether."

There's even a political section, with Noam Chomsky, Timothy Leary, and Pope John Paul II. Hmmm . . . is the pope political? We'll let others decide.

In the neighborhood: Atomic Music, a jam-packed used guitar-and-amp bazaar, is next door, but otherwise you can't walk from CDepot to other shops. But **downtown College Park** and the **University of Maryland** are a short drive, as is **Ikea,** in the opposite direction. **Barefeet Shoes,** 9300 Baltimore Avenue, just up the street, is worth a stop if you like stylish footware.

WE'LL LET you in on a government secret, one that's closely held by the whip-smart (or so we'd better all hope) engineers and wizards at the white office tower/fortress of the Nuclear Regulatory Commission on Rockville Pike. When they're not giving advice to the president or averting a meltdown, they're plotting how to get away to eatZi's, next door. As a sign on the door says, "Pinch yourself. This was not a dream."

The intoxicating smell of baking bread hits you as walk into this twelve-thousand-square-foot gourmet food emporium/deli/carryout. Samples of cake, appetizers, dips, breads, even wine on Saturdays, tempt you as you maneuver from the salad area to the sandwich area to the hot entrée area to the dessert area. Then there's the center station—where you can get anything from scalloped potatoes to crawfish quesadillas to Thai chicken and cellophane noodles to crab cakes and fresh fish. Although eatZi's is part of a Dallas-based chain, it's the closest thing Washington has to the Macy's gourmet basement in New York's Herald Square or Eaton's in downtown Toronto.

> **EATZI'S**
> 11503-B Rockville Pike
> Rockville, Maryland 20852
> (301) 816-2020
> www.eatzis.com

eatZi's is not a restaurant, though it has tables and hot specials of the day at the grill—half a chicken, or perhaps seared salmon, ribs, or a pesto shrimp pasta—with two sides. You can pick up several kinds of pasta (add your choice of sauce after choosing the noodles), Asian dishes, comfort food like twice-baked potatoes, curried noodles, chicken salad, and even, on one visit, sweet noodle kugel. Zap it in one of the microwaves if you're eating in.

This is also a good place to stock up on the latest salsa, a bottle of wine, a beautiful bouquet of flowers, terrific produce, and gourmet cheese. Maybe you want to take home a premade dinner—what the store calls a "chef-crafted" meal. Chicken Parmesan with pasta, beef stew with carrots, or sushi? Take your time with a cup from the coffee bar while you're deciding.

We were wowed by eatZi's the first time we went in, and our enthusiasm hasn't wavered the numerous occasions we've gone back.

In the neighborhood: eatZi's is just a block from **White Flint Mall** and close to just about any chain store you can imagine. Check out **Amazing Savings**, 4816 Boiling Brook Parkway, for candles, cutlery, makeup, and other items at savings that are, in fact, pretty amazing. (See chapter 11, Bargains.)

DANISH MODERN furniture was all the rage when we were growing up in the 1950s. There were tropical green, palm tree print curtains, "blond" wooden glass-top coffee tables you could put magazines inside, and those huge ceramic ash trays with rows of indentations for multiple cigarettes to rest in. And then our parents couldn't get rid of that furniture fast enough! When the trend was over, it was over—or so we thought.

Fortunately, some of the people who bought the "good stuff" when they purchased what is now called "mid-century modern" furniture kept it around. And when those folks decide it's time to move to smaller quarters, they call Travis Smith and Skip Przywara from Good Eye to come buy their hip, stylish pieces.

> **GOOD EYE**
> 4918 Wisconsin Avenue NW
> Washington, DC 20016
> 202-244-8516
> www.goodeyeonline.com

If you remember Dino, Sammy, and the Rat Pack and the days when cars had fins and highball still referred to liquor, you'll find Good Eye one of the coolest stores in D.C. No junked-up bins of old, dusty discards here. Instead, enter to find color-coordinated, retro living rooms, in browns and beiges, a reupholstered Bauhaus-style sofa and chairs with chrome arms, coupled with a '60s classic chrome and glass cocktail table—with wicker tiki-style freestanding racks to hold your cocktail glasses. And check out the checkout stand—at least until it's sold (the decor changes frequently): it's a tiki bar surrounded by cases of vintage tiki glasses and modern, bright orange and blue vases and bowls.

Our first visit was at Christmastime, and a pink revolving tree caught our eye right away, because it was exactly like the one our glamorous childhood neighbor, Kitty, was lucky enough to have (Kitty was a bleach-blonde divorcee, as the whole neighborhood knew and discussed, of course, at length). We, on the other hand, had square parents and were stuck with a "real" tree. During the holiday season, Good Eye got in more small things, such as calendars and coasters by popular artist Shag (www.shag.com). In fact, the store filled a vending machine, made to hold candy, with Shag merchandise, including cocktail napkins. Other super-duper items included a robot waiter that looked like it could serve cocktails, and a freestanding bubble terrarium on a white pedestal.

Downstairs, Good Eye's walls are painted in different colors and patterns to accommodate various furniture groupings. One week, a vintage Eames orange armshell chair has been coupled with a '60s Saarinen "Tulip" cocktail table and a '40s modern orange and black floor lamp, collectively forming a "Swinging London Bachelor Pad"—complete with orange walls. Another area, painted in a yellow diamond pattern, once held a "Luxe Living Room," with a two-piece gold sofa (with reversible blue cushions) for $595 and a '70s teak coffee table for $295. Our favorite so far (and the merchandise is different each time we stop by) is a former gas station lobby set consisting of a two-person sofa and two chairs, reupholstered in red, black, and white.

Good Eye is a store to check out if you're redoing your basement or, especially, if you're thinking of giving your home a retro look. The owners have a terrific flair for decorating. Travis has designed and furnished several area restaurants and bars, including two CarPool Clubs and the Evening Star Café in Alexandria. Prices are very good, and if items don't sell within eight weeks, they are reduced substantially. An adorable red and white chair that our teenager loved was on sale for $150 one day, while some terrific pink and turquoise lamps were under $100. Unfortunately, pink and turquoise clash with our current décor.

In the neighborhood: Good Eye has limited hours, so call ahead. During the holiday season we have found it open on a weekday, but usually it's open only on weekends and Fridays. After you shop, head to the **Outer Circle Theatre** to catch a flick or to **President Cigars**. There are a lot of restaurants in the same block. Good Eye is five blocks south of **Mazza Gallerie** on Wisconsin Avenue, which has a **Neiman Marcus** department store, **Villeroy & Boch** fine china shop, and the upscale women's store, **Harriet Kassman**.

IMAGINE YOURSELF minding your own business, driving down an isolated country road north of Leesburg, Virginia. You pass some big old colonial farms, a farmer's market, and an aging motel on the way to a bridge that'll take you over to Point of Rocks, Maryland. As you approach a town of sorts, you see a three-story, white and green house surrounded by what appears to be junk sitting all over the side porch: old bathtubs and wooden doors, rusty lawn chairs, a green, wooden bed frame. No, this isn't some crotchety old hermit's house. You have just arrived at Old Luckett's Store, a bargain hunter's paradise and one of our frequent country destinations.

If you don't believe us, just ask the hoards of people who line up "all the way back to the shed" to get in during the once-a-year sale on Groundhog Day. Or the high-end antique dealer who allegedly slips in to buy Old

OLD LUCKETT'S STORE
42350 Luckett's Road
(Route 15)
Leesburg, VA 20176
(703) 779-0268
www.luckettstore.com

Luckett's merchandise only to jack up the prices threefold when she resells it. And we've heard a very well-founded rumor that a green, wooden folding chair identical to the $29 job we saw at Old Luckett's was priced at $160 at an upscale chain store near Tysons Corner specializing in shabby chic.

Once a general store, post office, and home of the Luckett family, this 1910-era home now houses more than twenty dealers (almost all women) in over six thousand square feet of space. A few items in the store are new—candles, soap, sachets, etc.—but most is of the shabby chic, country primitive, or retro vintage variety.

Not long ago, we took two good friends who were visiting from Ohio on an excursion to Luckett's Corner, as it is called. We all figured we'd spend a short time there and then head back to Leesburg for lunch and antiquing at the high-end stores. About three hours later, we were dragging our friends out of the store, but not until one of them had purchased a tufted footstool for $35 (which she planned to recover). They headed to another store across the road, where the same friend bought a very large wooden tray painted with some ugly orange paint for $29. We never made it to Leesburg; instead, we headed home, drank wine, and stripped the paint from the tray, which revealed gorgeous wood underneath. Needless to say, a good time was had by all.

In the neighborhood: The charming yellow house with the red and white dotted shutters next door, the **Beekeeper's Cottage** (www.beekeeperscottage.com), (703) 771-9006, carries Rachel Ashwell linens and upholstery, vintage hand-painted furniture, spa products, and small home accessories. On your way through Leesburg (about five miles away), stop at **Mom's Apple Pie Bakery**, 220 Loudoun Street SE, (703) 771-8590 (www.loudouncounty.com/food/pie.htm). It's our favorite bakery in the area, with delectable single-serving-size pies providing a perfect excuse for an afternoon snack. If you tire of scouting for knick-knacks but still are in a bargain-hunting mood, visit **Leesburg Corner Premium Outlets**, just off of Route 15, which has all the usual outlet stores as well as some not so common ones such as **Pottery Barn Furniture Outlet** and **Williams-Sonoma Marketplace** (good deals on stemware).

BIGGER THAN some library branches, Second Story's Rockville store is a mecca for anyone who likes books—art books, literature, sports (we picked up a great hardcover fishing guide recently for $8 and some change), history of all periods, religion, military, biography, science (from anatomy to zoology) . . . well, just about every subject imaginable. The other location is good, especially if you're a collector, but the Rockville headquarters knocks us out with volume and depth. We have a friend, a retired academic and physiologist from the National Institutes of Health, who hates to shop but gladly braves the streets of strip center Rockville for trips to Second Story. Owner Allan Stypeck, an expert appraiser of antiquarian volumes, has put the store on the map, not only because of his inventory but also because of his public radio program, *The Book Guys*.

> **SECOND STORY BOOKS**
> 12160 Parklawn Drive
> Rockville, MD 20852
> (301) 770-0477
> www.secondstorybooks.com

Stypeck cares deeply about books, not decor. "We're not looking to embellish the buildings with a lot of accoutrements," he says. "We sell books." And so in a warehouse-like building—look carefully for the sign or you'll miss it—stand row on row of gray metal and wooden cases filled with volumes that can keep you browsing for hours (furniture, popular music, fighting ships, photography, child care . . .). Most of the books are in good condition, some like new, making this not only a magnificent find for any reader, whether it's mysteries or philosophy, but, especially, a fine outlet for anyone in the market for coffee-table-quality art books, whether Matisse, Picasso, Seurat, Miró, or Grandma Moses.

The other location, incidentally, on P Street just off Dupont Circle, while not wow-worthy, isn't chopped liver, either. On a random visit, we were unable to resist an apparently never-read (it still had the Borders sticker on the back), on-the-road chronicle by trumpeter Wynton Marsalis. This is a small town, no matter what they say; we ran into a lawyer/activist we know when visiting the P Street store, and our conversation moved from presidential politics to the nuclear power industry to Charlie Parker's live Stockholm recording sessions. He worries, though, that this book will give away his favorite shopping secrets. As Joe Lieberman would say, is Washington great or what?

Second Story also carries a selection of old phonograph records.

Other location: 2000 P Street NW, Washington, DC 20036, (202) 659-8884.

In the neighborhood: The warehouse location of the main store is not conducive to strolling to other shops, but it's a short drive to **Springriver Corp.**, 5606 Randolph Road (see chapter 12, Sporting Goods), a great find for anyone into water sports, and **Joe's Record Paradise,** 1300 E. Gude Drive (see chapter 5, Music). In fact, a day at Second Story and Joe's Record Paradise, with lunch at **eatZi's**, might be considered perfect for anyone whose idea of a good time is music and books.

~~~~~

SOME GUYS have midlife crises and buy Porsches. Others satisfy their urge at Southworth Guitars, one of the most amazing used guitar stores this side of New York's West 48th Street.

> **SOUTHWORTH GUITARS**
> 7845 Old Georgetown Road
> Bethesda, MD 20814
> (301) 718-1667
> www.southworthguitars.com

Southworth doesn't merely sell vintage; it sells instruments that inspire awe. How about a rare 1959 blond Gibson ES335—for a mere $45,000? A late '51 Gibson Les Paul prototype—for $12,500? A '65 left-handed, tangerine-colored Fender Stratocaster—for $26,000? A '66 Fender Precision bass, gold and in impeccable shape—for $12,000? And lots more, for less.

Customers include UK and Japanese investors and American doctors and lawyers who played guitar in high school and wish they had never gotten rid of that old Strat or SG—and are willing to pay top dollar to get the same ax now. Of course, the clientele also includes Tom Petty (who recently got an old red Marshall stack here as well as a black Gibson ES 335 from the '60s), John Mayer (a '65 charcoal-frost Strat), and collectors from across the country. Eric Clapton and the late George Harrison are among those who have traded with store owner Gil Southworth.

Toward the back of the showroom is Gil's amp museum: dozens of blond and tweed Fender amps he picked up along the way, in new shape and generally not for sale. "Mind you, I'm dying to sell every guitar in there," says Gil, who started buying equipment in 1972, when he was in tenth grade. (His first guitar was a two-pickup solid body, for which he paid $24.95.) "But twenty years ago, everybody was real excited about the vintage guitars but not about the amps, so I just bought up every vintage, mint blond and tweed amp I could find." Now they're collector's items, too.

If you can't convince him to sell you one of them, there's still plenty you can buy here, and plenty more you wish if only you didn't have that mortgage payment, car payment, kids' tuition. . . .

In the neighborhood: Southworth is on the edge of **downtown Bethesda**, with lots of window-shopping and restaurant-hopping options. Stop by **Hinata**, a nifty Japanese grocer with a first-rate sushi bar at 4947 St. Elmo Avenue, for lunch or just to pick up some seaweed-wrapped crackers or the Japanese candy, Pocky.

~~~

WALK INTO this fairyland of bright blue, spike-headed robots, green Mister Peanut figures, and die-cast mini trucks around lunchtime any weekday and you're more than likely to find a bunch of men and women standing around, shooting the breeze about trains, trucks, and maybe The Three Stooges. Retirees, toy collectors, and friends love to hang out with Perry Mohney, owner of The Toy Exchange in Wheaton, and you, too, will want to pay this store a visit. You'll be wowed by the sea of gleaming silver robots, '50s rocket ships, Matchbox cars, and all the X-Men, Star Wars, and Ninja Turtle action figures you can dream of. Even the ceiling is covered with brightly packaged toys.

> **THE TOY EXCHANGE**
> 11265 Triangle Lane
> Wheaton, Maryland 20902
> (301) 929-0690
> montgomerycountymd.com/
> shopping/toyexchange.htm

Mohney started his store in the early 1990s, when he turned a hobby of collecting robots and space toys from the '50s and '60s into a vocation. Those toys are confined to a case—a '50s robot called Zoomer and another made by Ideal Toys command anywhere from $800 to $1,800. But Mohney has very affordable merchandise, too, including replicas of some of the expensive items—they look like the real thing and cost only $20 instead of $200 or $2,000. Vintage Matchbox cars can be had for $5 and up. Even the younger set can start collecting figures that were missing from their own caches of Power Rangers and Care Bears.

If you wonder what your toys would be worth if your parents hadn't taken them to Goodwill, GI Joe offers a good lesson. The regular old Joe you and your friends all had might not be worth much, because so many were made. But something that wasn't popular, such as an Intruder Joe German fighter, might go for as much as $600 because it's hard to find—parents didn't want to buy bad guys for their kids. And a female nurse Joe figure is valuable, too, because parents didn't buy girl dolls for their boys.

Mohney has something for everyone. He carries electric trains and even some used video games for great prices. Our son bought "Dark Cloud 2," a used video game, for $15, the best price he had seen.

In the neighborhood: Other fun stores in the area include **Barry's Magic Shop** (street entrance on Georgia Avenue—see chapter 7, Toys, Games, and Hobbies) and **Barbarian Comics**, 11234 Grandview Avenue, (301) 946-4184 (in the shops behind Barry's). There are multiple international food stores and eateries in the area. Mohney recommends the subs at **Marchone's Italian Deli**, 11224 Triangle Lane, in the big strip of shops in front of the metered parking lot. One cautionary note: At midday on Saturdays, parking is next to impossible in that lot. We've had to park in a Metro lot and walk across the footbridge, which is usually fine—if it's not ten degrees outside.

CHAPTER 3

Food and Drink

Being an international city, Washington is a food-lover's paradise. While there are good specialty food shops in virtually every neighborhood, we chose to highlight the following stores because they are real standouts. So rev up your appetite, get out your corkscrew, and prepare for some gourmet delights.

GOURMET AND INTERNATIONAL FOOD STORES

A LITTERI is not in the best shopping neighborhood, but if you like authentic Italian stores, you'll be very happy you went out of your way to find this one. Once the aroma of Italian sausage and cheese hits you, and you see the one hundred different kinds of olive oil and good assortment of Italian wines, you'll forget about all the forklifts you dodged in the parking lot.

A third-generation family business, open since 1926, A Litteri is popular with students and faculty from Galludet College (right across the street), who

> **A LITTERI INC.**
> 517-519 Morse Street NE
> Washington DC 20002
> (202) 544-0184
> www.litteris.com

line up at the deli daily for Italian subs and other goodies. Says owner (and grandson of the founder) Mike DeFrancisci: "We are a complete store here, not just a specialty shop. You can get whatever you need in one stop."

It's true. Pasta alone decorates one full wall, and Italian tomatoes, jars of peppers, and big, wonkin' containers of basil and oregano (not those wimpy little bottles like they have at Safeway) take up another large area. A Litteri also has plain old Progresso soup, bags of roasted chickpeas, and big tubes of BelAria® polenta. And it has Papoutsanis soap from Greece—made with olive oil and a favorite of ours.

While it doesn't make its own pasta, A Litteri carries a good supply of frozen from several vendors. If you're going directly home, you can pick up a 2.5-pound container of frozen lasagna for a bargain: $10.99 for cheese, $11.99 for meat. The prices in general at A Litteri are excellent. For a total of $10, we recently got four twenty-eight-ounce cans of Sun of Italy tomatoes, a package of thick Anna brand pasta, a large, crusty loaf of freshly made bread (supplied by **Catania Bakery**, 1404 N. Capitol Street NW, [202] 332-5135), and two bars of Papoutsanis.

In the neighborhood: It can be an adventure to find this place, as A Litteri is in an area of warehouses that supply stores and restaurants, although some do sell souvenirs. Search for the red, white, and green Italian flag colors on the front of the store—it's easy to miss. If you're in a food-hunting mood, make the **Eastern Market** on Capitol Hill part of this excursion; it's less than two miles away.

~~~

THE BEST way to discover a great store is by surprise, as was the case at Bradley Food and Beverage—a shop well worth having to wait for a space in the too-small parking lot where you'll joust with BMWs and Land Rovers for a spot. On a scouting mission to check out a hardware store recommended by a friend, we discovered this deli/specialty store/coffee bar in Bethesda's Bradley Shopping Center. It was a welcome place to get a $1.49 slice of fresh tropical yellow cake with moist peaches and pineapple and to sneak down free samples of guacamole and tortilla chips, ginger cookies with cherry sauce, and spicy pretzels.

> **BRADLEY FOOD AND BEVERAGE**
> 6904 Arlington Road
> Bethesda, MD 20814
> (301) 654-6966

While the store carries the requisite jarred salsas, jellies, and sauces of any good gourmet shop, much of the stock at Bradley is local: coffee is from Baltimore Coffee, and spices are from Vann's, another Baltimore company. Gift baskets are a huge seller here; the Fiesta basket includes gourmet tortilla chips, salsas, dips, and freshly made guacamole, combined with a six-pack of Corona Beer and a lime. The Maryland Basket holds Eastern Shore goodies. Bradley's ceiling is littered with empty baskets waiting to be filled, and the holiday season keeps the staff busy keeping up with demand. Other seasonal gift items are abundant; in November, we found solid chocolate dreidles for Hanukkah and boxes of shiny Christmas ornaments that looked so real you wouldn't know they were really foil-covered chocolate balls.

Are you a glutton for punishment? Check out the big hot sauce selection, including the aptly-named Lawyer's Breath and super-scorching Deathwish. Bagels come from the famous H & H Bagel of New York, sent "parbaked" from the Big Apple but finished off in ovens at Bradley so they're fresh daily. Turkey is the deli section's biggest seller, browned on the premises to make it taste almost as fresh as the bird at your Thanksgiving table. Deli salads are made in the kitchen upstairs.

Baked goods come from different suppliers, but Bradley's buyers choose carefully for freshness and quality. The store is designed for carry-out, but you can sip espresso, fresh juices, and smoothies at its "Oasis" drink bar.

In the neighborhood: **Strosnider's Hardware** (see chapter 8, Home and Garden) is in this strip shopping center, as is **Bruce Variety**. Downtown Bethesda is a couple of blocks away.

~~~~~

IF YOU can't get to Rio, try Wheaton, Maryland, instead. We aren't able to guarantee sunshine, but you can have a little Brazilian cheese or a Garoto chocolate or two. Go on Saturday and you're likely to find the food counter packed with Brazilian natives drinking small cups of sweet, strong café Pilao. Shop for treats such as Lacta candy and pao de queijo (cheese bread), or pick up some more utilitarian sundries: Phebo soap, Skala hair products, and Risque nail polish. Ready for a night of dancing? Get a dress for your night out at the **By Brazil Boutique** next door. The shop also carries Brazilian jeans by companies such as Zoomp—more flared

> **BY BRAZIL**
> 11335 Georgia Avenue
> Wheaton, MD 20902
> (301) 962-6686

and cut lower than typical jeans made in the United States—and lots of fashionable Brazilian shoes.

In the neighborhood: Wheaton is a wonderland full of international groceries and eateries.

Wheaton: An International Food Lover's Paradise

Adventurous eaters in search of international culinary delights will rejoice over Wheaton's gold mine of small specialty food stores, representing more cultures and ethnic groups than any other neighborhood in the metro area. Inhale the scent of Pollo a la Brasa (rotisserie grilled chicken) while you check out Ethiopian, Brazilian, Caribbean, West Indian, Jewish, Asian (of all kinds), Filipino, and Italian supermarkets. Going to Wheaton is pure, no-frills joy.

You can get there by car or Metro. If driving, take the Beltway to the MD-97 N/Georgia Avenue exit (31A) and stay on Georgia Avenue (toward Wheaton) for a little more over a mile and a half. Street parking may be tough, but there is a metered lot off of Georgia Avenue. (To get there, turn left onto Reedie Drive when you see Dunkin Donuts.) If you choose to use Metro, take the Red Line to the Wheaton exit and walk across the footbridge.

Start by window-shopping along the row of shops that runs parallel to the parking lot. If you're hungry, you might pick up an Italian sub at the half-century-old **Marchone's Italian Deli**, or try goodies from the Filipino, Caribbean, and Japanese eateries and groceries that line the strip. If baking is more your thing, check out **The Little Bitts Shop**, a haven for cake and candy makers. Just for kicks, hunt for your favorite Spiderman comic at **Barbarian Comics**, or get a real live action figure of Spidey at **The Toy Exchange** (See the full write-up in chapter 2, Top Ten Stores).

After you've taken in the lower level, head up the stairs to Georgia Avenue. Sample a couple of shrimp summer rolls and homemade dipping sauce at **An–Binh Oriental Market** or watch amateur and professional magicians practice their tricks at **Barry's Magic Shop** (see chapter 7, Toys, Games, and Hobbies). Look for out-of-print books at **Bonifant Books** or check out Jewish gifts at **Abe's Jewish Book and Gift Store** ("If it's Jewish we have It"). Cross busy Georgia Avenue and you'll find even more, includng the **Ethiopia Plus International Food Mart** and the **Wooden Shoe Pastry Shoppe**, a haven for those seeking vegan or kosher pastries.

This is only a partial listing for this remarkable area—check out the adjoining strip centers and have fun exploring.

A WASHINGTON institution built in 1873, Eastern Market is the only market in the District of Columbia in continuous operation since the nineteenth century. History lovers and architects will appreciate the building itself—it's a good example of commercial architecture built during the 1870s. But the real draw is the stalls filled with produce, cheese, meats, baked goods, and fresh flowers. And there is always a line at the no-frills eatery, **Market Lunch**, renowned for its crab cakes, fried fish platters, full early-morning breakfasts, and low prices.

EASTERN MARKET
225 Seventh Street SE
(near Capitol Hill)
Washington, DC 20003
www.easternmarket.net

Saturday is the busiest day—the market expands to include outdoor stalls as well; on Sunday, the whole enterprise becomes a flea market.

Eastern Market is closed on Mondays. Hours are: Tuesday–Friday, 10 a.m. to 6 p.m.; Saturday, 8 a.m. to 6 p.m.; and Sunday, 8 a.m. to 4 p.m. Both the Orange and Blue line Metro trains stop at Eastern Market.

In the neighborhood: Check out the many little shops in the area, including the **Bird-in-Hand Bookstore and Gallery** 323 Seventh Street SE, (202) 543-0744, which has art and design books and exhibition catalogs.

THE INTOXICATING smell of baking bread hits you as walk into this twelve-thousand-square-foot gourmet food emporium/deli/carryout. Samples of cake, appetizers, dips, breads, even wine on Saturdays, tempt you as you maneuver from the salad area to the sandwich area to the hot entrée area to the dessert area. And then there's the center station with its dozens of fresh offerings: pasta, Asian dishes, comfort food, curried noodles, chicken salad, even, on one visit, sweet noodle kugel. We were wowed by eatZi's the first time we went in, and our enthusiasm hasn't wavered since. That is why this store made our Top Ten favorites. (See the full write-up in chapter 2.)

EATZI'S
11503-B Rockville Pike
Rockville, Maryland 20852
(301) 816-2020
www.eatzis.com

TUCKED IN a tiny strip on an unglamorous stretch of Lee Highway is a little oasis—an inviting Bavarian structure decorated with circular wooden German and Swiss flags and a yellow sign advertising, "Hot Brats to Go." Although it has moved from its original location and is on its third owner, German Gourmet seems not to have lost any consistency in its selection of great German sausage, cheese, wine, noodles, and European chocolate. This store has been an area institution for the past forty-five years.

> **GERMAN GOURMET**
> 7185 Lee Highway
> Falls Church, VA 22046
> (703) 534-1908
> www.german-gourmet.com

Just ask customer Jasmine Okail, whom we overheard praising Michael Haene, one of the owners, for a beer he recommended for cooking. "Thank you. I finally made goulash that actually worked." Turns out she has been coming to the store since childhood, when a previous owner would sneak her candy when her mom wasn't looking.

We don't blame her for coming back. The candy really rules—bins of individual foil-wrapped chocolates in shapes such as bugs, cars, and dice; marzipan pigs; boxes of chocolate playing cards, Dutch shoes, and liqueur-filled confections.

There is often a line of customers at a deli case full of German sausages, cheeses, homemade bratwurst, liver dumplings, sauerkraut, spatzle, and cheese salad. The shop offers catering with choices of a "picnic platter" of sausages to a seafood platter featuring peppered fish, smoked oysters, and smoked mussels. It has all kinds of German wines and beer, including more choices of minikegs than we've seen at the best beer stores.

From the bakery, try the delicious "hat" pastry stuffed with almond filling and a cylindrical roll filled with hazelnut crème. In addition to the German and Austrian natives who come for the food, the ambience, or the German magazines and greeting cards, the German Gourmet attracts a lot of military or former military personnel who were stationed in Germany. As owner Haene says, "It's a one-stop shop for German items."

In the neighborhood: Before or after you get your fill of German sausage or chocolate, put on your bowling shoes for a game of duckpin bowling at **Falls Church Bowling Center**, 400 S. Maple Avenue, Falls Church (703-533-8131).

IT STARTED with games. One of us is an addict of "Turbo 21," a free game offered on the game Pogo.com game Website. Each game seems to have a running conversation, and one of the participants was an Italian-American woman from New Jersey, Cindy DiBiase. We'd play a round or two, congratulate the winner, and learn a thing or two—namely, how to cook amazing Italian food, thanks to Cindy. She's not one to allow compromise on her recipes, and when she commanded us to buy Auricchio provolone cheese for our sauce, we headed straight to The Italian Store in Arlington.

> **THE ITALIAN STORE**
> 3123 Lee Highway
> Arlington, VA 22201
> (703) 528-6266

We found the cheese, all right, but that was no longer our priority after we discovered the freezer case brimming with homemade ravioli stuffed with lobster ($11.99 for a box of sixteen large ones), porcini mushrooms ($7.99 per box), spinach ($6.99), and many other choices. It's all made by the Italian Store itself and comes in a tidy box stuffed with a handful of cornmeal. Now, before you write us off as Chef Boyardee amateurs, know one thing: we make our own pasta, from scratch. And without some fancy pasta maker (though we bow down before our Kitchenaid® stand mixer every day, for its ability to knead dough.)

Okay, back to the Italian Store. The delicious smell made us hungry for sandwiches and pizza from the deli, and a take-a-number system allowed us to shop while waiting, along with the thirty or so other people, in line one busy Saturday. We discovered Italian pastries from Brooklyn; freshly prepared take-out containers of chicken Parmigiano ($6.99 pound); Gorgonzola or alfredo sauces ($4.99 pound each); boxes of anise-flavored pizelles made by Little Pepi company; Lavazza coffee; illy espresso; and the granddaddy of all Italian cheeses, Parmigiano-Reggiano for $12.99 pound.

Although the Italian Store is in a strip mall, it's hard to miss once you spot the mint green Vespa and pale blue scooter-like delivery truck flanking the outdoor tables, livening up the exterior. We've been loyal customers, despite the twenty-five-minute drive, ever since our first visit.

In the neighborhood: In the **Lyon Village Shopping Center**, along with **Giant, CVS Pharmacy**, and one of the largest of the area's four **Big Wheel Bikes** shops.

Cindy DiBiase's Mother's Homemade Tomato Sauce

Since we started making Cindy DiBiase's mother's basic pasta sauce, we have turned our backs on jarred sauce. Here's Cindy's recipe:

2 cans crushed tomatoes (about 26–28 ounces, depending on the brand used)
1½ cans to 1¾ cans water
¼ cup oil (personally, we never use the oil)
Spices, according to taste:
    garlic powder
    salt
    pepper
    fresh or dried parsley
    fresh basil

Bring the tomatoes and water to a boil, then lower to a simmer. Add garlic powder, salt and pepper, parsley, and basil. ("How about some onions or peppers or wine in there?" we asked Cindy. "NO," she said. "They don't go in this particular recipe." "How many shakes of the spices?" we asked. "Shakes?" replied Cindy. "No, no, throw away those plastic shaker lids and throw the spices in with your fingers.") It's advisable but not mandatory to add some of the rind from that Auricchio provolone cheese at this point. Simmer for a couple of hours. Don't boil, just simmer, and don't let it get too thick. When the sauce is done, remove the provolone rind and discard it. This sauce is remarkably easy, and family members get really happy when they smell it cooking.

SOMETIMES YOU'VE just got to have a fettoosh—that is, a scrumptious Middle Eastern salad, delectable thanks to its parsley, cucumbers, tomatoes, and crunchy pita chips. And when we get a Jones for a fettoosh—or for freshly made dolmas (stuffed grape leaves), hummus (a purée of chickpeas and tahini sauce), or baba ghanouj (an eggplant dip)—there's one sure-fire way to get a fix: head to the Mediterranean Bakery.

MEDITERRANEAN BAKERY
352 S. Pickett Street
Alexandria, VA 22304
(703) 751-1702

Part bakery, part deli, part fresh market, and part world-class grocery for other-world staples, the Mediterranean Bakery is a mecca for anyone who enjoys gourmet cooking or eating. It is run by the family that owns the popular Middle Eastern/Lebanese restaurant in Georgetown, Fettoosh. (Which, like the misnamed "bakery"—it is so much more—serves a fine fettoosh.)

The exotic selection of vinegars and olive oils alone is impressive; we counted twenty-nine kinds of vinegar, including twenty kinds of balsamic, and more than sixty different olive oils from Italy, Spain, Lebanon, and Greece. A 250-milliliter bottle of Columbia sherry wine vinegar from Spain, aged fifty years, sells for $15.49, Manicardi balsamic vinegar from Italy, aged twenty-one years, is $29.95. Exotic spices, unique hot sauces, and jams and jellies, including Cortas fig jam, line the long shelves. Imported cooking supplies from Japan, Thailand, India, and Italy are available as well.

A cookware area has clay bowls for making hummus, and $6.95 will buy you a mold to make your own falafel, a vegetarian "burgerlike" treat. Intricately designed tea sets line the back wall, with an array of prices befitting the selection: a Russian Lomonosov cobalt blue tea service for six at $365, but demitasse cups ranging from $2.95 to $18.

The Mediterranean Bakery and Café actually does have a bakery and a café, serving breads, baklava, pistachio cookies, date-filled confections, and Key lime tarts. Several varieties of cheese and spinach pies are displayed in glass cases, and there's the full-service carryout, serving pizza, gyros, and other culinary delights—including fettoosh.

~~~

THE METRO area is fortunate to have a vast array of Asian food stores, ranging from tiny mom-and-pop operations to large chains. Of these, the best we have found is the Korean-based Super H Mart in Fairfax. Super H is actually part of the HanAhReum franchise, which has many stores in the area, but Super H, which took over a space formerly occupied by a Superfresh, is a full-size superstore. It has items from every Asian country, a limited number of imported European and Latin American products, and items you can buy at the regular supermarket, such as cheese, soda, cereal, and pasta.

SUPER H MART
10780 Lee Highway
Fairfax, VA 22030
(800) 427-9870
www.superhmart.com

Even if you don't cook with Asian products, it's worth a trip to Super H just for produce. We have never seen such a variety at any store—ever—and the prices are so great that we hate to buy certain produce anywhere else. A good-size container of already peeled garlic is $1.47, a large bag of fresh bean sprouts is fifty cents. Herbs that might sell for as much as $1.99 for a small container are available here in small bundles for a fraction of that price. The produce department is so large and diverse (we don't even know what a lot of the stuff is, especially that big, hard, spiky brown thing) that we have taken several non-Asian out-of-town guests to this store just to impress them. Hey, the Washington Monument is great and all, but *our* guests don't go away hungry.

There are novelties too—entertainment, if you will. Next to the bakery, an employee makes seaweed wrappers, while another presses sweetened rice cakes flat. The bakery offers lovely confections in unique shapes, many of them with colorful fillings. The store has a large fresh fish market, and some of its offerings are swimming in tanks. Most meat is attractively cut and packaged, and the deals on shrimp are sometimes unbelievable.

Super H Mart also sells cooking items, electric rice cookers, humidifiers, small, colorful refrigerators that are unlike those used in the United States, and several brands of Asian cosmetics. Our son, fascinated by Japanese treats, has bought plenty of Pocky (a Japanese cookie/candy that is fairly easy to find) in other stores and cities, but Super H carries an extra-large version, one we hadn't even seen in Manhattan. Super H often offers free samples, though not all of them will appeal to less adventurous Western palates. Green tea ice cream was not to our liking, and what appeared to be a sweet roll sample in the bakery was stuffed with a substance that tasted like fish.

In the neighborhood: Head next door to **Petco** for your dog or cat supplies, or **Party City** for a great Halloween costume.

Also Noteworthy:

APHRODITE
5886 Leesburg Pike
Falls Church, VA 22041
(703) 931-5055

Jam-packed with Middle Eastern goodies, vinegars, and such, this store—according to our sources—has "the best" olives and homemade Turkish delight (a rolled jelly confection). It also has Greek pastries such as baklava and kataifi (a walnut and honey-filled Greek pastry that looks like it's covered in shredded wheat; it's actually shredded phyllo or pastry dough).

BESTWAY
3109 Graham Road
Falls Church, VA 22042
(703) 560-2101

This regular-size grocery store specializes in Latin American products. Pick up packs of thick corn tortillas, beans of all kinds, and creamy Salvadoran cheese; shop for hard-to-find produce; or stick with the huge selection of Goya and Adobo products.

Other location: 690 Elden Street, Herndon, VA (703) 668-0323.

DEAN AND DELUCA
3276 M Street NW
Washington, DC 20007
(202) 342-2500

Soho, New York, may have the flagship of this high-end specialty gourmet (and kitchenware) store, but the Dean and Deluca in Georgetown is all Washington. Offering regional specialties, such as rockfish and Maryland-style crab cakes, it also pays tribute to the region's southern roots with corn chowders and pudding, buttermilk-fried chicken, sweet potato casseroles, and even succotash. Enjoy a latte at the outdoor café as you people watch—you might just see Georgetown resident George Stephanopoulos walking his dog.

MONTGOMERY FARM WOMEN'S COOPERATIVE MARKET
7155 Wisconsin Avenue
Bethesda, MD 20814
(301) 652-2291

This co-op originated in 1932 as a community-based effort the help save family farms during a terrible drought. Farmers' wives sold eggs, produce, and baked goods out of the same white frame building on Wisconsin Avenue (right in busy Bethesda) where it operates today. Note: Operates seasonally only from June–October, and only open on Wednesdays and Saturdays (7 a.m.–3 p.m.)

RODMAN'S
5148 Nicholson Lane
Rockville, MD 20895
(301) 881-6253
www.rodmans.com

Good regular prices and great sales make this a popular stop for imported cookies, candy, cheese, crackers, wine and beer, and vitamins. Rodman's also has shops at 5100 Wisconsin Ave NW in Washington and at 4301 Randolph Road (at Viers Mill) in Wheaton, Maryland.

THE RUSSIAN GOURMET
1396 Chain Bridge Road
McLean, VA 22101
(703) 760-0680

This is the area source for Russian, Polish, and other Eastern European food, including wine, beer, and caviar. Check out the Ukranian rye bread and admire the bright colors and exotic designs of the wrapped candies, for sale by the pound.

SUTTON PLACE GOURMET/BALDUCCI'S
3201 New Mexico Avenue NW
Washington, DC 20016
(202) 363-5800
www.suttongourmet.com

A large purveyor of gourmet food, chocolate, coffee, produce, and restaurant-quality take-out items—salads, soups, entrées, baked goods, and desserts—Sutton Place once broke our hearts: its Bethesda store served superb, fresh ice cream by the scoop, then stopped. Some locations feature pizza cooked in a wood-burning oven. And they still sell ice cream by the carton. (Other locations include Bethesda, Alexandria, Reston, and McLean.)

TRADER JOE'S
(Multiple locations; check the phone book or Website for the one closest to you.)
www.traderjoes.com

We don't think we could live without this national purveyor of inexpensive and healthy fresh goods and frozen, prepared items. Shop for bargain wines, vitamins, imported cheese (with fabulous prices), nuts, chocolate, and Mexican entrees. The Maple Pecan Crunch cereal is addictive, and our dog can't go long without Trader Joe's Peanut Butter Flavored Dog Biscuits. Before the chain, which started in California, opened stores in Ohio, our friends from that state would load up their cars here with Trader Joe's goodies before heading home.

WINE, BEER, AND SPIRITS

The Washington area is a wine lover's dream come true. There are so many fine, even remarkable, wine stores here, we could write another book about them alone. Cheers!

CHEVY CHASE Wine and Spirits is rumored to have the largest beer selection east of the Mississippi, and to be one of the top three in the continental United States. "A beer snob's paradise," a friend says. But Chevy Chase Wine is more than a beer store. Family-owned since 1986, it's a full-service store that carries a large selection of hard liquor, too.

> **CHEVY CHASE WINE AND SPIRITS**
> 5544 Connecticut Avenue NW
> Washington, DC 20015
> (202) 363-4000

Walk in the front entrance and you feel as if you are in an old European wine shop, with blue-gray walls and white distressed paneling, full-scale (albeit fake) street signs, and hanging grapes. Enter through the back, and you find yourself in sheer beer heaven. With more than twelve hundred beer offerings, two hundred from Belgium alone, the selection can only be displayed by single bottle rather than six-pack. Scan the shelf for the beer you want and a clerk will retrieve it from a walk-in cooler.

Owner Buddy Weitzman claims to have been selling liquor "since repeal." Not for a minute do we believe Buddy is that old, but he certainly has been around long enough to know his Bordeaux from his Burgundy. You won't find recommendations from wine reviewers, such as *The Wine Spectator*, hanging from the shelves. Instead, Buddy's staff personally tastes new wines before they are chosen, and they are always on hand to give you a recommendation. But be warned: Figure out exactly what you're serving before you ask for advice. Telling Buddy chicken is on the menu isn't good enough. He needs to know the sauces and side dishes, too. "Have you ever tasted plain chicken? It tastes like cardboard. It's the sauce that matters!"

Chevy Chase Wine and Spirits has wine tastings for customers on Saturdays. Because it has a hard-liquor license, the shop is closed on Sunday.

In the neighborhood: You're in luck if you're in a movie-viewing mood. The **Avalon Theatre** is right up the street, and the nearby **American City Diner** has a "Reel Food" dinner (with movie) at 7:30 or 8:00 every night. **Potomac Video** has a phenomenal selection of foreign films (and American, too) in its downstairs section, and even, um, films of the adult variety.

WHAT APPEARS on the outside to be a small wine shop actually houses one of the best beer selections

> **NORM'S BEER AND WINE**
> 136 Branch Road SE
> Vienna, VA 22180
> (703) 242-0100

Food and Drink   31

in the metro area. Norm's Beer and Wine in Vienna is one of those "finds" that was sitting in our own backyard, but it took a local Internet beer guide to tell us what we'd been missing.

Owner Norm Yow started the shop about six years ago, because he liked to drink high-quality beer. "Craft" beers are his specialty—that is, premium beers that are made with better ingredients and use fewer fillers and no filters. He carries over four hundred kinds, ranging from Budweiser to Almaza, a Lebanese brand.

We were on the lookout for a beer of our youth, Little Kings Cream Ale, made by the old Hudepohl-Schoenling Brewing Company. Sadly, we learned that Norm used to carry it but can't anymore. To sell beer in Virginia, he has to get it from a distributor licensed in Virginia, and Norm's distributor no long carries Little Kings. But our disappointment lessened when we looked at the other choices: Birra Moretti from Italy, Utenos from Lithuania, Okocim from Poland, and Arrogant Bastard Ale from California.

Norm's also has a nice selection of wines. And what is Norm's personal favorite beer? Sierra Nevada, made in good old California.

In the neighborhood: After you pick up that six-pack, check out **Cenan's Bakery** (www.cenansbakery.com), (703) 242-0070, just a few doors down from Norm's. Take home a loaf of bread or go for a sandwich dressed with Cenan's special sauce, a blend of seeded mustard, homemade mayonnaise, and horseradish.

~~~~~

TOTAL WINE is so good that we couldn't exclude it—even though it's part of chain with about thirty stores. Each Total Wine superstore carries more than eight thousand selections, from every grape-growing region in the world. The chain even produces its own guide, the 338-page *Total Guide to Wine*, available for free.

> **TOTAL WINE AND MORE**
> 1451 Chain Bridge Road
> McLean, VA 22101
> (703) 749-0011
> www.totalwine.com

This store is so large that French wines alone take up several long rows. Each wine is displayed under a decorative map of the region where it is produced. You can spend a fortune here—a Château Latour Pauillac 2000, for instance, for $479.99—or get *vino* for the masses, like the wine in a paper carton or a four-liter bottle of Inglenook Chablis for $11.99. Local Virginia wines, hard to find in smaller stores, are well represented here. They don't call it "total" wine for nothing; the store sells cheese, soda, coffee by the pound, and gourmet snacks such as Romanoff caviar, Lindt chocolates, and Virginia peanuts. It also has imported and microbrewed beers. And, of course, it sells wine accessories, cutting boards, coasters, speed pourers, stoppers, ice buckets, and even a bit of stemware, ranging from a six pack of Riedel Vinum Syrah Rone for $122.99 to a six pack of Luminarc Vale goblets for $7.99.

Other locations: Total Wine and More has many stores. Check your local yellow pages or www.totalwine.com to find the one closest to you.

Also Noteworthy:

CALVERT-WOODLEY LIQUORS
4339 Connecticut Avenue NW
Washington, DC 20008
(202) 966-4400
www.wineaccess.com/store/calvertwoodley

Abundance of wine and beer, plus 250 cheeses, deli meats sliced to order, and freshly ground coffee by the pound.

MACARTHUR BEVERAGES
4877 MacArthur Boulevard NW
Washington, DC 20007
(202) 338-1433
www.bassins.com

Known for its great selection of wines, and its annual fund raisers: the **California Barrel Tasting and Vintners Dinner**, held annually since 1984, which benefits The Addy and Bruce Bassin Memorial Cancer Research Fund at George Washington Medical Center, and the **Heart's Delight Wine Tasting and Auction** annual benefit for the American Heart Association.

PEARSON'S
2436 Wisconsin Avenue NW
Washington, DC 20007
(202) 333-6666
www.pearsonswinewebsite.com

Stop by "plain old Pearson's," just north of Georgetown, for a bottle of pinot noir—"the world's most sensual wine (never opaque, dark, and brooding)"—

and a lesson in history. This family-owned former pharmacy has been around since 1933, and rumor has it that Harry Truman's bodyguard was a regular—purchasing pints of Jack Daniels for the President's weekly poker game.

SCHNEIDER'S OF CAPITOL HILL
300 Massachusetts Avenue NE
Washington, DC 20002
(202) 543-9300
www.schneiderswine.com

A family-run business since 1949, this store has wines from a 1961 Chateau Petrus 1.5 liter for $10,000 to a 1999 Chateau Gaillard Touraine at $5.99 and at least twelve thousand choices in between. Old and rare wines are housed in a 7,500-square-foot, temperature-controlled warehouse.

CHAPTER 4

Fashion and Accessories

To look at us, you wouldn't know we're clotheshorses. Well, actually, we're not; our method of shopping is usually to run into L.L. Bean, Ann Taylor, Joseph Banks, or any place that sells Levi's and get out as quickly as possible. Of course, we make an exception for formal parties, because everyone could use help dressing up—and greater Washington is full of excellent independent clothiers glad to lend a trained eye for an unfashionable guy or gal. We chose the stores in this chapter, ranging from casual to formal to überfashionable, because they grabbed us in some way, because the customer service was outstanding, or because our advisers with terrific taste recommended them.

FOR MEN AND WOMEN

TOUR GROUPS from Europe and out-of-state vacationers traveling on I-95 who make a stop at Boot Hill Western Store in Woodbridge may know something you don't: Northern Virginia has one of the very best western wear stores in the

> **BOOT HILL WESTERN STORE**
> 13231 Gordon Boulevard
> Woodbridge, VA 22191
> (703) 490-0090
> www.boothill.us

United States. Whether you're in the market for fancy footwear, great outfits for a night of country and western dancing, Wrangler jeans, or beautifully detailed leather belts adorned with ornate buckles, Boot Hill has it all. That's why it made our Top Ten list (see chapter 2.)

~~~~~

LOUD MUSIC, metallic floors, metal and leather belts, and lots of cool, urban streetwear make Commander Salamander a must-visit destination store for the preteen set on up. Even if you don't dig the duct tape skirts or the black metal-studded look, you can still find pink and blue pastel monkey shirts by Paul Frank, Hello Kitty bath sets, or cylindrical metal purses made of bent license plates from New York, Italy, and Germany.

> **COMMANDER SALAMANDER**
> 1420 Wisconsin Avenue NW
> Washington, DC 20007
> (202) 337-2265

Follow the red, orange, and yellow swirly patterned tile floor back to find clothing by Fetish, Tripp, and Dog Pile. In need of a black vinyl jumper with a metal-studded, pleated shirt to wear under that black metallic-zipper jacket? This is definitely the place to buy it, and you can get some boldly patterned or fishnet stockings to accessorize. If you aren't quite that daring, sporty pants and tops by Nike and Puma are also for sale.

Cautionary note: Some parents may find the expletive-laden T-shirts, spiked metal collars, and "Jesus is my homeboy" hats to be irreverent or even offensive.

In the neighborhood: Georgetown, where shopping and dining abound.

~~~~~

VIRTUALLY EVERYONE knows about the L.L. Bean catalog company, but there are only a handful (four to date) of Bean retail stores (not counting the numerous outlet mall stores). Metro DC is lucky enough to have one of them. The quest for Bean is one of a scant few excuses many have for venturing to Tysons Corner Center, but the two full floors of everything Bean makes a trip to traffic-clogged Tysons worthwhile (during nonrush hour, of course).

> **L.L. BEAN**
> Tysons Corner Center
> 1961 Chain Bridge Road
> McLean, Virginia 22102
> (703) 288-4466
> www.llbean.com

Coats, backpacks, women's and men's clothing, and shoes are upstairs, while children's clothing, home furnishings, and outdoor items are on the first floor. Everything sold is made of high-quality, low-glitz, outdoorsy Bean construction. The Bean store also has a pond, two-story waterfall, and kids' climbing wall. Personally, we don't think you can beat the quality of anything by L.L. Bean.

In the neighborhood: Tysons Corner Center (between Vienna and McLean, Virginia) is one of the largest in the United States. L.L. Bean is next to **Bloomingdale's**. See chapter 17, To the Mall, for more information about Tysons Corner Center.

WORLD-CLASS hip-hop and R & B entertainers, prominent figures from the NBA and the NFL, and normal folks like us have been known to shop at the super-fashionable Outline Inc. in Prince George's Plaza. But be sure and take your credit card, because Outline carries only the best names in designer clothing: Moschino, Versace, Gucci, Dior, and Dolce & Gabbana, to name a few.

OUTLINE INC.
Prince George's Plaza
3500 East-West Highway
Hyattsville, MD 20782
(301) 559-9000

Outline Inc. was born in Baltimore in the mid-1980s, evolving from what was originally Kazin Shoes. The two cutting-edge Baltimore Outline stores were so successful that the chain expanded to the Metro DC market in 2003, opening in Prince George's Plaza with a professionally modeled fashion show and a DJ from Radio 93.9 WKYS.

The styles are what draws the stars. The sales are what attracts the mortals. While we were deciding whether to try on a top by the Australian company, Coogi (50 percent off, mind you), a wistful girl made her weekly visit to see if the $700-plus red and black patterned drop-dead gorgeous leather coat was maybe—just maybe—on sale. No dice, that week anyway, and she went away empty handed. But she'll be back—and so will we.

In the neighborhood: If you can't afford high-end designer wear, PG Plaza has some great lesser-priced clothing stores, including **Last Stop** jeans.

VINTAGE JEANS are the ticket at this ultracool store across from the Wisconsin Avenue entrance to the Georgetown Park parking garage in Georgetown. You might also find some 1950s bowling shirts, an old Izod Lacoste alligator shirt or two, or a big pair of pink and yellow plaid golfers' pants—the kind you once saw in your father's closet and, amazing though it is, now can pass for hip. But mostly, this store is about old Levi's.

> **RAGE CLOTHING**
> 1069 Wisconsin Avenue NW
> Washington, DC 20007
> (202) 333-1069

Unlike other vintage stores, you won't find junky racks of old clothing thrown together here. The jeans are so neatly folded, stacked, and labeled (by decade) that you have to look twice to see that they are actually "used." They don't necessarily look new—some are ripped or frayed—but so much the better. Prices vary, depending on the style and year made, but the average pair seems to be about $59. At the other end of the cost scale, 1950s-era Levi's, locked in a cabinet, can command as much as—gasp—four grand. "Four grand, as in four thousand dollars?" we asked. Yep, said Reiko, the employee on duty (they go by first names only), who sold a $3,000 pair to a Japanese tourist once. Don't even think about trying to buy the tiny pair of World War II-era jeans hanging on the wall—they're too valuable even to be offered for sale.

Lest you think you can haul your old jeans from the Gap to Rage and make a mint, here's some sad news: Rage is very selective and only buys from a distributor, which helps explain that sorted, stacked, and categorized look. But, there was *some* disarray upstairs in the "bag sale" area. For only $19.99, you could have all the "upstairs" clothing you could fit into a medium-size bag: tunics, sequined vests, really big sparkly dresses that make you wonder about their origin—Halloween, theatrical, disco, rock star? The real prize was an assortment of company logo jackets that still had the employee name tags sewn on. Our favorite was a brown number bearing the words, "The Quality Name in Virginia Concrete," and the name, "Ed."

NOTE: Rage carries new swimsuits during the summer season.

In the neighborhood: Wear your vintage jeans and Ed's old jacket over to **Johnny Rockets**, 3131 M Street NW, (202) 333-7994, for a burger and shake, and a hit of "Mac the Knife" on the juke box.

PREPPY HATERS who danced in the streets when the 1980s fad was finally over, beware. They're ba-aack. Three former employees of the Polo shop in

Georgetown Park got tired of just fantasizing about opening a store during lunch breaks, so they took some action. The result is Sherman Pickey, a twenty-first-century shop full of tweeds, lobster pants, and Izod Lacoste alligator shirts for men and women.

> **SHERMAN PICKEY**
> 1647 Wisconsin Avenue NW
> Washington, DC 20007
> (202) 333-4212
> www.shermanpickey.com

Armed with knowledge about clothing retailing, the owners find designers who are not necessarily "known" but produce high-quality jackets, dresses, shirts, and pants. Professorial-looking tweed sport coats and khakis are well constructed and lower priced than "name brand" of the same quality. We were similarly impressed with a silk brocade evening jacket that could be worn with the collar up or down, giving it two totally different looks, for $450.

In the nonclothing line, a personal favorite was a huge pink and white beach bag designed by CJ Laing, with hula girls wearing realistic-looking grass skirts of embroidery thread, for $150. Pants printed with whales, lobsters, and other nautical artifacts are available for women as well as men. You have to wonder: do these guys keep copies of the 1980s bestseller, *The Preppie Handbook*, lying around? Sure enough, they gleefully whipped out several copies—vintage ones at that, because the book is out of print.

Whimsy aside, we love this store and find it ironic that a "traditional" shop is a real standout in an area of trendy stores. Men's sizes range from 38 to 48, women's sizes, from 2 to 12, and like many of the shops in Georgetown, Sherman Picky is dog friendly—so much so that co-owner Ethan Drath's Burmese mountain dog (a rescue dog), Sherman, often accompanies him to work. A bowl of complimentary dog biscuits sits at the checkout counter.

In the neighborhood: You can't go wrong in any of the shops on upper Wisconsin Avenue in Georgetown. Drop a line to your old pal, Biff, and his girlfriend, Muffy, with stationery from **Rooms with a View**.

WHAT BEGAN as a funky surf shop in Ocean City is now a hip six-store chain selling men's and women's clothing, accessories, and limited home decor items. We polled the college crowd who work at other area boutiques, and nearly everyone mentioned this store as a favorite. Pretty pink rib-

> **SOUTH MOON UNDER**
> Bethesda Wildwood Center
> 10247 Old Georgetown Road
> Bethesda, MD 20814
> (301) 564-0995
> www.southmoonunder.com

Fashion and Accessories 39

bony dresses and skirts by Ruth; jeans by Paper Denim, Citizens of Humanity, and Seven; and bright floral swimsuits by Raisins and Radio Fiji are just a few of the lines. Larger than most other boutique-style stores, South Moon also has men's clothing, such as G-Star and Diesel jeans, DKNY dress pants, Quicksilver sweaters, and tropical swimwear by Billabong.

Other Locations: Reston Town Center, Annapolis Harbor Center.

In the neighborhood: The Wildwood Center is home to a **Sutton Place Gourmet/Balducci's** gourmet grocery store or grab a bite at **Hamburger Hamlet** across the street.

STRICTLY FOR WOMEN

BOLD-STRIPED hand-knit hats, one-of-a kind purses cleverly crafted from silk neckties, and fleece snow-flake scarves are but a few of the small items available at this women's cooperative in Fairfax. For more than a decade, this terrific shop has been run by a group of local artists. The result is a unique mix of carefully selected designer clothing from national and international companies and fashions handmade by local artisans.

> **ART TO WEAR**
> (703) 691-9000
> **Editor's note:** As we went to press, this store was looking for a new location in Fairfax. Call for details.

Case in point: Artistic jackets made from sweatshirts by a local crafter hang on a rack next to romantic casual skirts by BELMA, brightly colored jackets by Sacred Threads, and cotton casual wear by Sangam Cotton, a big seller. When the artisans aren't taking turns running the shop, teaching watercolor painting classes (in the back room), or making their drawings of old town Fairfax into silk-screened T-shirts, they're going to New York to pick lines of clothing and gifts.

It's difficult to define this shop's exact specialty. Cruise wear? Clothing for social events? Items you can take on a trip because they don't wrinkle? Bold African print jackets or dressy separates by A Touch of Class? Casual jacket-shirts by Color Me Cotton?

Or how about our favorite, a so-called magic dress by Soussan Designs ($140)? It can be transformed into eleven distinctive looks, from "hippie" dress to elegant gown fit for the prom. These dresses are big sellers and look good on everyone.

You can pick up some real bargains in this store, particularly one-of-a-kind accessories such as adorable evening bags by Adini (under $15) and handwoven headbands ($4.95). We even found a beautiful handwoven scarf that was at least eight feet long for $65. Besides the pins and hats and jewelry and other wearables, Art to Wear has infants' and children's items, thimbles, ceramics, and handmade cards.

In the neighborhood: For a good lunch, try the pad thai at **Cattleya**, 3981 Chain Bridge Road, (703) 934-8880.

IT'S NO surprise that Imagine Artwear has been named one of the Top 100 Retailers of American Craft by *NICHE* magazine (the magazine of progressive retailers) for several years in a row. The clothing that owner Carol Supplee carries is truly art—the really high-end items are made from handwoven, hand-died, and hand-painted fabric—and the price tags often reflect that.

> **IMAGINE ARTWEAR**
> 1124 King Street
> Alexandria, VA 22314
> (703) 548-1461
> www.imagineartwear.com

The pieces Carol chooses are classic, not faddish, but the fabrics and textures are contemporary. Every item is one-of-a kind or of very limited production. On-the-rack sizes generally range from extra-small to extra-large, but women of all sizes can shop because most of the artists will customize their clothing to size.

Our favorite item was a coat for a little less than $500, almost cartoonish-looking in cut, in bright red with black topstitching. Scarves were $35 and up, and jewelry started at $10; we found an amazing pair of blue and black square earrings with a cool geometric design for $20. However, those handwoven, hand-died, hand-painted items start around $600 and can go up to $1,400 or even more.

Metro residents have the savings and loan crisis of the 1980s to thank for Imagine Artwear's birth in our community. A former vice president of marketing for a savings bank, Carol became enthusiast for artwear when she started going to craft shows during "a hiatus" after the S&L's tanked.

Important note: Carol's elderly black lab, Hobbes, hangs out in the store and has a birthday party there every year.

In the neighborhood: Cross the street to find some wonderful home finds. Hand-painted French ceramics from **Quimper Faïence**, 1121 King Street, (703) 519-8339, Italian items from **My Place in Tuscany**, and real-looking (but not) flowers from **J Brown & Co.**, 1119 King Street, (703) 548-9010.

≈≈

> **THE PHOENIX**
> 1514 Wisconsin Avenue NW
> Washington, DC 20007
> (202) 338-4404

"I'VE BEEN shopping here for twenty years. This is the best store!" A stranger went out of her way to tell us this as we stood in this popular boutique with its festively colored mobiles, hanging stars, masks, and folk art. Given the crowds shopping here on weekdays, a lot of folks share her sentiments. The Phoenix sells contemporary lines by Eileen Fisher, Flax, and Cut Loose, and hand-knit sweaters by Margaret O'Leary. Some customers are drawn to the unique jewelry, gold from Italy, and accessories. This is the kind of place where you shouldn't be surprised if you see, swaying to the tune, "Volare," a woman in a fashionable but dull-colored gray coat wrapping a super-long yellow and orange knit scarf around her neck, transforming both her outfit and her disposition. We saw it happen.

Open since 1955, The Phoenix began when a married couple and their two young sons made their annual three-month-long trek to Mexico, stuffing the family station wagon full of folk art, jewelry, and other cool stuff along the way. Moving into the twenty-first century, The Phoenix is now a three-generation family business, and there still are trips to Mexico—just not by station wagon.

In the neighborhood: Cross Wisconsin Avenue and pop in at **Proper Topper**, where you'll find hats, some clothing, accessories, bath supplies, and an eclectic assortment of gifts. Originally a hat store in Union Station, the shop has a vintage feel, but almost everything in it is new.

≈≈

> **JUDY RYAN OF FAIRFAX**
> 9565 Braddock Road
> Fairfax, VA 22032
> (703) 425-1855

HOT CHOCOLATE on an icy day cinched Judy Ryan's inclusion in this book. Assuming that we were just ordinary shoppers, she and a co-worker greeted us at the door with this kind offer as soon as we entered her charming boutique in a strip center on the fringes of Fairax. Judy's personal knowledge of her customers—which one is traveling to Italy next summer, whose kid is graduating from college in California, and so on—allows her to recommend appropriate clothing choices. She recalls helping one woman, now a Fairfax County judge, to dress for her very first appearance in court when she was a brand-new lawyer. She also counts at least one high-ranking county official as a regular client.

A former psychiatric nurse turned "color-me-beautiful" analyst, Judy opened a tiny shop in Fairfax in 1988, coding each item of clothing by color. Her store is different now, in a larger space with parking, but she still groups her clothing by collection or "color" stories.

She carries many labels that are hard to find at a mall: Windridge, Willow, Russ Berens, and 600 West, to name a few, and jeans by French Dressing, a company that gives a percentage of its profits to breast cancer research. Sizes range from extra small on up to 16, and prices go from about $20 for a T-shirt, maxing out in the $275 range (except for leather jackets, which can be more). The store also has purses, belts, accessories, gifts, and shoes by Brighton.

In the neighborhood: In a strip mall with a **Book Nook** bookstore, **Outback Steakhouse** and **McDonald's**.

~~~~

NEXT TO a Dairy Queen in a small Vienna strip of shops, Trousseau is a real gem in the rough. While the lingerie display in the window sometimes make you wonder exactly what lurks inside, this shop is neither a Fredrick's of Hollywood clone nor an intimidating collection of overpriced thongs for size-1 beauties. Yes, those with buns of steel can buy great imported French bras, panties, and gowns, but so can a woman who wears a 3X nightgown or a 42 GG bra (yep, you got that right!). And if the 42 isn't big enough, Trousseau will alter it free of charge.

TROUSSEAU
306 Maple Avenue West
Vienna, VA 22180
(703) 255-3300
www.trousseaultd.com

The customer service in this store is the best you'll find anywhere, with staff more than willing to help whether you're buying a Felina bra for $27 or high-end French numbers for $165. Alterations at Trousseau are always complimentary for the life of the garment. Say what? Say you gain twenty pounds and your bra won't fit. The folks at Trousseau will put an extender in there for free.

Trousseau carries wedding supplies: veils, invitations, and the like. It also sells Moonstruck chocolates, handmade in Oregon and more than 70 percent cocoa—a hot seller here ever since Oprah gave them the seal of approval on her show. The Moonstruck motto: Chocolate is not simply candy but an experience to be enjoyed by all the senses.

Trousseau started as a bridal shop and expanded after owner Sarah Wiener realized she would like to keep the brides as customers *after* the wedding. (Sarah was a fancy window dresser in New York City in her former life.) Bridal shoes, which are around $65 per pair or less, include a complimentary redye after the wedding (meaning if you want to dye your scuffed white wedding shoes black after the ceremony and wear them to work, the store will dye them black—or another color—for free).

In the neighborhood: Head to the nearby Village Green shopping center, at Maple and Nutley, to pick up a slice of apple pie or get a homemade chicken pot pie for the family dinner from the **Pie Gourmet Ltd.**, 507 Maple Avenue West (www.piegourmet.com), (703) 281-7437. If pie isn't your thing, this wonderful place also sells frozen containers of lasagna, chicken cacciatore, and other dinner foods.

Also noteworthy:

IRRESISTIBLES
Wildwood Shopping Center
10301-B Old Georgetown Road
Bethesda, MD 20814
(301) 897-2574

Bethesda has the only metro location of this East Coast chain, which caters to women as young as twenty-five—often referred to as "the stroller brigade"—*their* mothers, and their grandmothers. With colorful, fun sweaters by Sigrid Olson, Christine Foley, Marisa Christina, and Canvasbacks, and jeans by French Dressing, it's no wonder that the original store in Marblehead, Massachusetts (near Boston), has expanded to eleven shops. Sizes range from 4 to 16, tops go from small to extra-large. Prices are competitive, especially during the big 40-percent-off sale.

In the neighborhood: In Bethesda's **Wildwood Shopping Center,** which has several nice women's boutiques and gift shops such as **XYZYX!** Be sure and stop in **The Red Orchard** to see the beautifully crafted decorations and home furnishings.

LEMON TWIST
4518 Lee Highway
Arlington, VA 22207
(703) 524-4680

This spacious women's clothing store in the Lee Heights Shopping Center in Arlington has a large selection of resort wear by Lily Pulitzer and Jade; festive sweaters by Icelandic, Sigrid Olson, Canvasbacks, and Michael Simon; and pants by such designers as Northern Isles. It also carries fancier couture, including tops fit for an evening out and elegant dresses by Maggie London and others. Accessories include scarves, jewelry, an extensive collection of Vera Bradley bags, and even some men's ties.

Other location: 8534 Connecticut Avenue, Chevy Chase, MD 20815, (301) 986-0044.

In the neighborhood: The Lee Heights Shopping Center is chock-full of inviting shops, including **Kinder Haus Toys** and a must-visit bakery, **Pastries by Randolph.**

PIRJO
1044 Wisconsin Avenue NW
Washington, DC 20007
(202) 337-1390

Pirjo features high-quality, versatile clothing, mostly imported from Germany and France, with designers not often found in the United States: Rundholz, Sarah Pacini, and many more. Prices range from tops that are a bit over $100 on up; some jewelry is less. Sizing is mostly European, and a lot of items are one-size-fits-all. Many of the styles can be worn for casual or elegant occasions.

Other location: 4821 Bethesda Avenue, Bethesda, MD 20814, (301) 986-1870.

In the neighborhood: Next to **The Shops at Georgetown Park** in Georgetown.

TEN FASHION-FORWARD BOUTIQUES

"Fashion-forward" means trendy (and sometimes it means expensive and super-thin), but the owners of the following boutiques seem to just *hate* that "trendy" term. Suffice it to say, they pore over the pages of *Vogue* and *Elle* and other fashion magazines—to bring you the latest styles by he hottest designers, the coolest jewels, and fun accessories.

> **ALL ABOUT JANE**
> 2438½ 18th Street NW
> Washington DC 20009
> (202) 797-9710
> www.allaboutjane.com

AN ADAMS Morgan boutique that carries designer labels such as Easel, Juicy Couture, Laundry, and Joie as well as jewelry, handbags and accessories, and high-end jeans.

Other Location: 2839 Clarendon Boulevard, Arlington, VA 22201, (703) 243-4424.

In the neighborhood: The 18th Street store is in the heart of Adams Morgan, a trendy and perpetually up-and-coming neighborhood with a slight urban edge. The Clarendon Store is across from **The Market Common** outdoor shopping center, which has **Pottery Barn**, **Williams Sonoma**, and **South Moon Under**.

JOËLLE SOLIMANO can make you look beautiful. The owner of this stylish Old Town boutique full of European and American designer clothing is also

> **AN AMERICAN IN PARIS**
> 1225 King Street
> Alexandria, VA 22314
> (703) 519-8234

a personal style consultant. Daughter of a French mother and Italian father, Joélle prides herself on being able to dress you in the best, in the belief that if you're trying to look good, why wouldn't you shop somewhere that can help? Or, in her words, "Why would you eat fish at McDonald's?" Whether it's jeans and a T-shirt or an elegant gown to wear to the White House, a prom, or graduation, she can help. Exuberant over her clothing lines, Joélle offers example after example of her high-quality merchandise: classic-cut business suits that never go out of style, high-fashion, pin-striped suited skirts, a very hip woman's tuxedo, silk and chiffon formal wraps, and stunning gowns by such designers as New York's Kathlin Argiro (a native of Alexandria). Sizes generally range from 0 to 14, but you can order up to a 20.

~~~~

FORMER CPAS Shiva Zargham, Sherri Hatam, and their mom, Betty Barati, opened this upscale contemporary sportswear shop in Bethesda in 2003. Geared toward women in their thirties to sixties, the store favors classic designs with an edge and not-too-trendy—very wearable—separates. The creations of over thirty designers, mostly American, include James Perse shirts, jeans by Serfontaine, Joe's Jeans, Blujeanious, and Rock & Republic (jeans all in the $110–$130 range). The shop's goal, says the fashionable Shiva—wearing an Essendi gray heather zipper-front sweater with geometric holes cut down the long sleeves—is to help customers buy one of pair of good jeans and three tops and be set for the season. The shop also has a few accessories, including handmade purses by local designer Lee G.

> **BELINA**
> 10215 Old Georgetown Road
> Bethesda, MD 20814
> (301) 897-2929

In the neighborhood: Accessories from the neighboring **Secrete Jewelry Store** or **Blanca Flor Ltd.** might be in order.

FIND THE cute pink and white striped awning on St. Elmo Street in Bethesda and you know you've arrived at this popular boutique that favors pastels and feminine separates. Designer labels include Paper Denim and AG Jeans, James Perse, Frankie B., Billy Blues, and many more. This particular store also has a good selection of shoes.

> **DAISY II**
> 4940 St. Elmo Avenue
> Bethesda, MD 20814
> (301) 656-2280

Other Location: 1814 Adams Mill Rd. NW, Washington, DC 20009, (202) 797 1777.

LOCATED IN the heart of the popular U Street area, this boutique has separates and dresses by Classic Girl (a sweatshop-free, Made in the USA label) and other good designers, Levi's jeans, bath products by Elizabeth W, and colorful handbags by Hobo. Prices are generally very affordable for cute, quality goods—less than $100 for most items—and there is a room full of vintage (mostly 1970s, we judged) plaid skirts and pretty formal dresses. Sizes generally run from 0 to 14, sometimes larger for vintage.

> **NANA**
> 1534 U Street NW
> Washington, DC 20009
> (202) 667-6955
> www.nanadc.com

In the neighborhood: In a vintage mood, are you? The legendary **Meeps** store is but a few doors down. Need any shoes to go with the dress? Head down the block to **Wild Women Wear Red**, 1512 U, for some "friendly, functional footwear for women." Since you're there, ditch that diet for a day so you can splurge at **Love Cafe**, 1501 U, the sit-down, across-the-street extension of **Cake Love**, Warren Brown's sumptuous bakery—serving the most talked-about cakes, cupcakes, and other delectable confections in D.C.

YOUNG STRANGERS we met on the streets of Georgetown told us they love to buy things for work and play at this small boutique near Capitol Hill. Jeans by Paper Denim and Citizens of Humanity, Bed Head sleepwear, clothing by Tocca and Trina Turk and the less well-known Filo, and vintage-style bags by Glenda Gies are just a few of the lines. Plaid also carries some items by local artists and organic-looking jewelry by Me&Ro, a Julia Roberts favorite.

> **PLAID**
> 715 8th Street, SE
> Washington, DC 20003
> (202) 675-6900
> www.plaidstore.com

In the neighborhood: New shops keep popping up on Eighth Street. Don't miss **Hoopla Traders**, an artsy gift shop made up of individual rooms leased by local artists whose wares include soap, candles, and brightly colored wooden mirrors.

LOCATED IN the same stretch of 14th Street as Home Rule, Go Mama Go, and Pulp, this hip but affordable boutique carries men's and women's lines, including Ben Sherman, Free People, Couture, and Penguins. Boys can try on Mod Fit blue plaid, short-sleeved shirts by the very British Ben Sherman or separates by Couture, while their female companions go for jeans by Dollhouse (usually under $50) and separates by To the Max and the Seattle-based Kaliwear. Pop has jewelry, including colorful necklaces by the very popular Kiln Enamel. Owner Sheila Sharma is yet another lawyer who abandoned the profession for something she loves.

POP
1803a 14th Street NW
Washington, DC 20009
(202) 332-3312
www.shoppop.com

In the neighborhood: On 14th Street (in the U Street area) above **Pulp**, a card and stationery store at 1803 14th Street, (202) 462-7857. See "In the Neighborhood" for Nana, above, for more detail.

BE SURE to check out the chairs and pillows in the back of this Wisconsin boutique in Georgetown. They are upholstered in a fabric that was once the owner's mother's tablecloth; the chairs themselves came from Grandmother "Sugar's" house, and the store logo was designed by sister Robin. But it's really contemporary clothing by Kingsley Greene and Melinda Looi, jeans by Japanese designer Oligo Tissew, Joie, and Yanuk denim that bring the Georgetown crowd and other trendsetters into this hot pink and fuchsia shop.

SUGAR
1633 Wisconsin Avenue NW
Washington, DC 20007
(202) 333-5331

In the neighborhood: Head directly to **Sassanova Shoes**, 1641 Wisconsin, which is almost next door.

SOUTH MOON UNDER
(See description under For Men and Women above.)

FASHION-CONSCIOUS Washingtonians were overjoyed when this boutique opened a couple of years ago in Pentagon Row. Husbands, boyfriends, and other parties who were dragged along weren't upset, either, when they learned they could watch Redskins games on a big flat-screen TV while

WHAT'S IN
1101 S. Joyce Street
Arlington, VA 22202
(703) 414-3353

their significant others shopped for clothing by hot designers such as Trina Turk, Maria Bianca Nero, Tocca, and Milly. Owner Michelle Stowers has made customer service a priority and has attracted a loyal clientele with her shop, which looks more like a Soho boutique than a shop in a prefab shopping center. Accessories include work by local jewelry designers Jade, Queen Bee Designs, and Kep.

THE SCOOP ON SHOES

When it comes to shoes, well—this isn't New York, but we are getting there. The popular shoe stores here are mostly chains: megastores such as DSW and Broadway, and the stores you find in every mall in America. However, a few independent little shoe boutiques are making names for themselves.

Slip on a pair of pricey heels with jeweled details or go for a pair by designer Stella McCartney (Paul's daughter, as if you didn't know) at **Sassanova,** 1641 Wisconsin Avenue NW, (202) 471-4400, in Georgetown. Try on some beach stripe heels (close to $300) or casually fancy leather sandals for about $75, while you take a load off your shopper-weary feet in this pretty little pink and chocolate brown shop, which always has nice touches like fresh flowers.

Dainty little heels not your thing? Try the funky, little New Yorkish **Wild Women Wear Red** shoe boutique on U Street. Pictures of Rosie the Riveter, Indira Gandhi, and 1960s activist Angela Davis empower you as you shop in the vibrant-colored boutique that carries boots, shoes, and accessories (jewelry, handbags, hats) by such designers as Lisa Nading, Bronx NY, and Faryl Robin. Most things are handmade, functional (you can actually walk in the shoes), and very eclectic—we saw highly fashionable purple boots and funky yellow mules.

The sight of boots hanging in a store window made us put stop in our tracks. Virginia residents will love the selection of Doc Martens, and other brands such as Goody Goody and Campers at **Shoe Fly,** 2618 Wilson Boulevard, Arlington, (703) 243-6490. It's just around the corner from **The Market Common** shopping area in Clarendon.

Some of the fashion-forward boutiques (see above) carry shoes in addition to clothing. Check the shoe selections at **Daisy II** (see above) and **Luna,** 7232 Woodmont Avenue, Bethesda, (301) 656-1111 (www.shopluna.com), a small chain out of South Carolina that carries contemporary clothing, sizes 0–12, jewelry, etc.

STRICTLY FOR CHILDREN

PARENTS WHO don't want their kids to look like Britney Spears but still like popular styles frequent this very delightful two-floor infants/kids boutique in Georgetown. Although it carries a lot of pricey European imports that you might not find outside of New York or Los Angeles, Piccolo Piggies also has highly affordable and adorable baby things. We loved the set of Zutano jungle overalls in the baby boys' area and were as pleasantly surprised at the $30 price tag as we were with the $51 brightly colored toddler dress by Lipstick.

> **PICCOLO PIGGIES**
> 1533 Wisconsin Avenue NW
> Washington, DC 20007
> (202) 333-0123

Those with a bigger budget can find beautiful, well-made outfits in the $100-plus range as well. Brands include Cakewalk, Archimede, Bonpoint, and Lily Pulitzer (of course!). And be sure to check the sale rack upstairs—some items might be as much as 50 percent off.

In the neighborhood: After you make the kids try on scratchy dresses and proper little suits, reward them with a chocolate cone at **Thomas Sweet** ice cream or buy them a cookie at **Marvelous Market,** both on Georgetown's Wisconsin Avenue hill. Don't miss **Beyond Comics** at 1419 Wisconsin. Besides comic books and action figures, its floor is covered in laminated comic books and posters.

THIS VERY popular store near the Torpedo Factory in Old Town Alexandria has two floors full of kid's clothing, toys, and accessories. On the first floor, you'll find moms shopping for the huge selection of cute outfits and accessories for infants. The kids themselves know to head upstairs, where the proprietors keep the art sets, stickers, and bigger toys and togs for the older set. As one of the shop owners down the street told us, "You *have* to write about that place. They have everything!"

> **WHY NOT**
> 200 King Street
> Alexandria, VA 22314
> (703) 548-4420

In the neighborhood: Why Not is on King Street in Old Town Alexandria near the **Torpedo Factory Art Center.** Other kid-friendly shops within easy walking distance include the **Discovery Channel Store,** 118 King

Street, (703) 549-1352. For a treat, try **Scoop Grill & Homemade Ice Cream**, 110 King Street, (703) 549-4527, or **Ben & Jerry's**, (around the corner at 103 S. Union Street, (703) 684-8866. **A Likely Story**, 1555 King Street, (703) 836-2498, is a great children's book shop that's a long walk or a short drive up King.

~~~~~

THIS FAMILY-OWNED East Coast chain store has such terrific prices on name-brand clothing that it's worth making a trip to Iverson Mall to stock up on Carter's, Rocawear, French Toast, Phat Farm Kids, and Guess?, to name a few. This huge store is also a great spot to buy school uniforms, super-cute baby gifts, underwear, socks, and everything else for the tiniest infant up to the preteen.

> **YOUNG WORLD**
> Iverson Mall
> 3723 Branch Avenue
> Temple Hills, MD 20748
> (301) 423-0883

In the neighborhood: Hunt for more bargains on kid's clothing at **Value City Department Store** or **Kids for Less**, also in Iverson Mall.

Also Noteworthy:

MADELEINE'S KIDS INC.
1521 King Street
Alexandria, VA 22314
(703) 836-9046
www.madeleineskids.com

Specializing in new and gently used clothing, this is a great store for well-priced, high-quality stuff for very young kids, size 0 to six years. Brands include Jacadi, Gap, Gymboree, Ralph Lauren, Tommy Hilfiger, and Nautica, and we spied at least one Lily Pulitzer dress. Madeleine's has boots and coats and all kinds of great things crammed into its two floors, and many items have actually never been worn.

In the neighborhood: Many local moms check Madeleine's stock weekly after story hour at **A Likely Story** children's book shop, 1555 King Street, (703) 836-2498. (See chapter 6, Books, for a full description.)

THE RED APPLE
2922 Chain Bridge Road
Oakton, VA 22124
(703) 281-1701

Our son was ever so happy the day he realized he had outgrown The Red Apple. Getting him something "decent" for school picture day (and no, we weren't trying to make him wear a suit and tie, although they certainly can be had at this store) was always a chore; skateboard gear was more his style. The Red Apple has nice but not nerdy clothing—a couple of steps above the faded Batman T-shirt. Girls can find all kinds of cute, coordinated separates, and the store is often jam-packed in the Spring with girls trying on white dresses for their First Communion.

In the neighborhood: Stop for toys at **Toy Corner**, (703) 255-3232, in the same strip shopping center as The Red Apple, or for school supplies at **Hammett's Learning World**, (703) 938-0047.

JEWELRY AND ACCESSORIES

THE SPIKEY, Koolaid green, purple, and periwinkle sandblasted glass necklace in the window literally screamed at us to check out the Arts Afire gallery in Old Town Alexandria. While most of the other artist-created jewelry turned out to be far more subdued (and wearable) than the vertebrae-like creation, all of it is beautiful and unique. There are pretty glass square-beaded necklaces, glimmering oval-stone bracelets, mixed media metal and glass earrings, and individual artist-created beads for those who make jewelry themselves. As the owner says, "You're not likely find these artists at craft shows."

> **ARTS AFIRE**
> 102 N. Fayette Street
> Alexandria, VA 22314
> (703) 838-9785

Prices range from the very affordable (blown glass earrings for $15 and up) to very expensive. The necklace described above, which would look fabulous on the right person, was just a tad shy of $2,000. Most things are priced in between.

Besides jewelry, Arts Afire has incredible kaleidoscopes of all kinds. Our favorite was the size of a small telescope and eye-level, because it was mounted on a tree-like structure. The store also has home accessories—plates and vases, and Judaica items such as menorahs. Occasionally, Arts

Afire sponsors jewelry-making classes, such as the Spiny-Knotted Bracelet session with artist Stephanie Sersich. Limited to ten students, this class always has a waiting list.

In the neighborhood: Check out the artist-made clothing at **Imagine Artwear** (see description above), then head down to **Artcraft**, one of our Top ten stores.

~~~

YOU WON'T find many jangly jester hats or goofy dunce caps at this hat store in Georgetown Park. Owner Anthony Gaskins sells real hats—the kind you wear on the subway during icy weather—at his shop.

> **THE HATTERY**
> The Shops at Georgetown Park
> 3222 M Street NW
> Washington, DC 20007
> (202) 364-HATS

How does a young man get into the business of peddling fedoras and bowler hats? Anthony's education began when he became a fixture at a (now-closed) store, called The Hattery, in Wheaton Plaza. The owner, John Harrison, mentored Anthony in the hat business, and later the two formed a partnership by opening the current Georgetown store. John is now deceased, but an artist's rendering of his head, complete with top hat, is painted on the shop's window.

Today Anthony is busy learning the lost art of hat cleaning, blocking, and refurbishing. Look behind the counter and you will see hundred-year old stretchers and hat blocks, and an old hat steamer stands by the checkout stand. This equipment, which is on loan to Anthony from his "teacher," retired dry cleaner Vince Corvelli, is a real standout in trendy Georgetown Park. The Smithsonian would love to get its hands on Corvelli's blocks (they are truly neat, and they look like heads), but Vince is leaving his equipment to Anthony, who will use it and help to preserve a dying profession.

When not refurbishing old hats or making new ones, Anthony is on the lookout for hats he doesn't already have. It's hard to believe he can find any, as he appears to have every winter and summer hat ever made: beaver hats, straw hats, and a ladies' custom-made, ostrich feather Kentucky Derby hat for $700. He even has a collapsible top hat that pops down into a small frisbee-like disk. These hats were originally made to fit on little shelves hidden under the seats in opera houses, and Anthony would love to find some of these old seats and install them in his store.

Famous customers have included Melanie Griffith, Harrison Ford, Dennis Quaid, and Laurence Fishburne. Vice President Dick Cheney bought a hat from Anthony, but sent his secretary to retrieve it so the shopping area wouldn't be disrupted by the Secret Service.

We even bought a hat—it was irresistible. We usually look dorky in headwear, but it was five degrees outside. We now own a green bucket-style with an upturned brim—$40—and we love it.

GEORGETOWN IS full of great stores, unique items, and unusual knickknacks, but this shop lets the customer have a hand in the creative process. At Fornash Designs, you pick the fabrics to create your own bag, be it a purse, cosmetic bag, or even a diaper bag for your friend's baby.

FORNASH DESIGNS
The Shops at Georgetown Park
3222 M Street NW, Suite W-025
Washington, DC 20007
(202) 338-0774

Fornash Designs was born after owner Stephanie Fornash took liberal leave from her computer job to bask in the tropical sunshine of St. Thomas. She loved the bold print purses with bamboo handles and began designing her own bags as a hobby. Of course, friends and relatives loved her creations and wanted one, too, and when she got laid off from her job, she turned her sideline into a business. Voila!

Walk into Fornash's shop in Georgetown Park and you see hanging fabric—lots of it—lining both sides of the store. Examples of finished products are displayed on shelves above, as are other items, such as grosgrain ribbon belts with sparkling buckles, scarves, jewelry, monogrammed underwear, and accessories (these are actually consignment work of other artists). Prices start as low as $27 for a mini makeup bag. A small custom handbag is $150; medium, $160; and large, $180. Custom-designed diaper bags are $225.

In the neighborhood: Fornash Designs is next door to **The Hattery** (see description above). Find a great ceramic sculpture or handcrafted jewelry made by an American artist at **The Magical Animal**, also in The Shops at Georgetown Park.

THE TINY Jewel Box touts itself as "A Washington treasure filled with treasures from around the world." Since the 1930s, this family business has

> **TINY JEWEL BOX**
> 1147 Connecticut Avenue NW
> Washington, DC 20036
> (202) 393-2747
> www.tinyjewelbox.com

been providing prominent and affluent Washingtonians with engagement rings, antique and estate jewelry, and contemporary designer pieces. Explore the five "intimate" (the shop's words) floors for high-end gifts, angora scarves, Baccarat crystal, silver baby cups, picture frames, and desk accessories fit for an executive or even a world leader. This shop is a well-known Washington institution.

In the neighborhood: The Tiny Jewel Box is next door to the **Mayflower Hotel**. Traditional men can pick up shirts and ties at the nearby **J Press** (1801 L Street, [202] 857-0120) or a new trench coat at **Burberry's Ltd.** (1155 Connecticut). Women can find designer goods at **Rizik Brothers** (1100 Connecticut) or contemporary fashions at **Betsy Fisher** (1224 Connecticut). Check out **Pampillonia Jewelers** (1213 Connecticut) for more traditional and contemporary jewelry.

CHAPTER 5

Music

You don't need a weatherman to tell you which way the wind blows, and you don't need a guidebook to tell you where to pick up the latest top-forty hits or chain store musical instruments. This section, therefore, is about specialty, especially used and hard-to-find CDs, records, and sheet music. It's also about musical instruments that will, as the saying goes, blow your mind.

We have eclectic and wide-ranging tastes, from Thelonious Monk to the Clash to Steve Earle to Johann Nepomuk Hummel. We've also earned money writing about and performing music (and learned a valuable lesson when foolishly trying to do both: Be careful when you write a critical review of a band whose bass player has a day job as the engineer in a recording studio, especially if you're about to record there—because now he controls *your* sound).

But enough with the bona fides. We let our tastes do the shopping, and if there was an area in which we needed help, we asked others, like Ken Lee, of Lee Studios of Music in Vienna, a preeminent clarinet teacher who has sent more than one student to just the right place to get hard-to-find sheet music. Here's what we got.

CDS AND RECORDS

ONE OF the most impressive CD stores in the metro area, CDepot made our Top Ten list of favorite things because of its awesome selection (see chapter 2). With hundreds of thousands of compact discs, roughly 60 percent of them new, you're likely to find almost anything you're looking for in rock, blues, and jazz. The shop, in a nondescript building on Baltimore Avenue, has more Miles Davis CDs than many competitors have jazz. "We like to be a complete store," says owner Sandy Williamson, in business since 1992. "Everybody thinks that since we're in College Park, we would cater to college kids. But we cater to all music lovers."

> **CDEPOT**
> 9039 Baltimore Avenue
> College Park, MD 20740
> (301) 982-3472
> www.cdepot.com

In the neighborhood: **Atomic Music,** a wonderful used guitar-and-amp bazaar, is next door, but otherwise you can't walk from CDepot to other shops. But **downtown College Park** and the **University of Maryland** are a short drive, as is **Ikea** in the opposite direction. **Barefeet Shoes,** 9300 Baltimore Avenue, just up the street, is worth a stop if you like stylish footware.

THOUGH CD Cellar was recommended to us by a couple of musicians, it didn't look all that impressive at first blush. We almost didn't include it in this book—and that would have been a shame, because we kept coming back and buying CDs, fueled by an almost always-satisfied craving: We were looking for used CDs, and CD Cellar had what we wanted.

> **CD CELLAR**
> 709 W. Broad Street
> Falls Church, VA 22046
> (703) 534-6318

On one recent trip we went in with an odd list, put together just to test the place: Gram Parsons, T. Rex, the Byrds, Shelby Lynn, Ryan Adams, and Pharoah Saunders. Of those, we found Parsons's *Return of the Grievous Angel,* all of Lynn's postcountry selections, and T. Rex's *Transformer* (for $7.99). Not bad at all.

Then we went into the store's second room, where discs with multiple copies or slight cosmetic blemishes sell at a fair discount; the discs play just fine, and you can try them out before buying. This room also houses the jazz, classical, and blues titles. Sax player Saunders was on our wish list, but no luck. We considered Charles Mingus's *Complete Town Hall Concert* CD for a long time. We wound up buying Tom Petty's *Full Moon Fever* instead. Though we bow before Mingus, sometimes you've gotta rock.

In the neighborhood: This store really is in a cellar, though an expansion has taken it upstairs, too. In the same building is **Caffeine**, a comfortably funky coffeehouse that feels like coffeehouses felt before a certain Seattle-based chain ruled the world. Falls Church has a number of other noteworthy shops and restaurants, including **Bangkok Blues**, 926 W. Broad Street—a popular Thai restaurant for dinner, with terrific live jazz and blues. (See chapter 7, Toys, Games, and Hobbies; and chapter 9, Electronics and Cameras, for other neighborhood highlights.)

WE COULD be mistaken, but we think we spotted the entirety of our long-lost record collection here. And our best friends' collections. And the entire collections of both of our college campuses. Store owner Joe Lee has been collecting and selling vinyl for more than thirty years, and his store hits you with a tidal wave of nostalgia and desire. We merely walked in the door and instantly spotted Led Zeppelin's untitled fourth album (the one with "Stairway to Heaven"), Paul McCartney's *Ram*, John Cougar's *American Fool* (recorded before he demanded his real name, Mellencamp, back), the Grateful Dead's *Wake of the Flood*, and the soundtrack to the counterculture musical, *Hair*.

> **JOE'S RECORD PARADISE**
> 1300 E. Gude Drive
> Rockville, MD 20850
> (301) 315-2235

The jazz selection is world-class—thirty Lester Young albums (!!!), Bill Watrous's *Manhattan Wildlife Refuge*, and Stanley Clarke's *I Wanna Play for You*—a never-opened copy, with the original label from Korvette's, for $9.98. Proprietor Lee, a raconteur and occasional producer and former band manager, travels far to find collections for sale, and he has equally far-flung tastes. In the 1970s, saxophonist Rahsaan Roland Kirk would hang out in his store; Lee would give him records, and Kirk would invite Lee to his D.C. shows.

If you really miss the days of *American Bandstand*, check out the selection of 45s—the Boxtops (quick, what was the B-side of "The Letter"?*),

---

*The B side of "The Letter" was "Happy Times."

Chubby Checker, Bobby Darin, Paul Anka.... Then there's a section with nothing but R & B and doo-wop LPs (the Platters, Shirelles, Drifters, Flamingos). Joe's has schmaltz like Ferrante & Teicher and Johnny Mathis and a very, very large rock section. We didn't even know Spooky Tooth released six albums—not that we ever expected to find them under one roof.

Even if you've given up the turntable, Joe's is worth a trip for the memories. The store sells new and used CDs, though nowhere near the number as vinyl records. If you have kids, bring them, because everyone should see what cover art looked like when it really was just that: art. It'll break your heart.

~~~~~

IF YOU'RE looking for opera, classical, and, especially, international, Melody (in business since 1977) is worth a trip. If you're looking strictly for pop, it's fine but not overly impressive. Consider the Talking Heads selection: a single CD on a recent trip. But in jazz, Melody had Miroslav Vitous—even displayed prominently. In other words, this is a store for the knowledgeable music lover who knows what he or she wants.

> **MELODY RECORD SHOP**
> 1623 Connecticut Avenue NW
> Washington, DC 20009
> (202) 232-4002
> www.melodyrecords.com

In the neighborhood: Melody is in **Dupont Circle**, home to no shortage of cool shops, ethnic restaurants, chess games in the park, and street life (see chapter 14, Getting to Great Shopping). Scour the side streets for hard-to-find parking.

~~~~~

IF YOU want to know where you can take your old records for cash, know this first: Rick Carlisle's Orpheus Records, in the Little Saigon section of Arlington's Clarendon neighborhood, really does not need a single more Billy Joel or Genesis record. Hey, *The Stranger* was good, but there is zippo market for it today.

> **ORPHEUS RECORDS**
> 3173 Wilson Boulevard
> Arlington, VA 22201
> (703) 294-6774

Not that Carlisle really needs many more records of any kind—though if you've got hard-to-find psychedelic rock albums like the Chocolate Watch Band, or jazz records on the Blue Note label, you'll definitely pique his interest. With an estimated 160,000 records on the racks, under the racks, in the back of the store, and behind the counter, it would take a new turntable fad and a dozen years before his stash would be depleted.

That's what makes Orpheus Records fun: you never know what you'll find. Check out Ozzy Osbourne's *Live Mr. Crowley* EP, with Ozzy's crazy-train face taking up the whole disc (a collector's item at $30). Take a trip back to the 1960s and 1970s with Steve Hackett, Herman's Hermits, the Manfred Mann Album featuring "Do Wah Diddy Diddy," or Bo Donaldson and the Heywoods (was "Billy, Don't Be a Hero" one of the worst songs ever written or what?).

Orpheus also sells classical, jazz, soundtracks, and country. The selection in these categories seems less comprehensive than in rock, but it's still worth browsing. Remember jazz guitarist Cal Collins? We hadn't, until we spotted two of his albums on the Concord label at Orpheus.

If you don't have a turntable, Carlisle will be glad to sell you one, used but in prime condition. We were surprised to learn that a lot of contemporary bands, from Ryan Adams to the Donnas, still put out music on vinyl. "For those who are willing to expend the effort, vinyl sounds better than CDs," Carlisle insists. "For those who don't care how it sounds, vinyl can be cheaper than CDs."

In the neighborhood: Several Vietnamese restaurants are in the area, and just a few blocks closer to D.C. are a number of recently opened shops. On a warm day, walk to **Lazy Sundae** at 2925 Wilson Boulevard, a popular homemade ice cream parlor. The specialty is apple crisp folded into cinnamon ice cream.

MUSICAL INSTRUMENTS

Megastores and chain stores that sell musical instruments abound, and many are competitive on price and selection. The stores listed here are local and stand out because they offer what the chains either cannot or do not, giving them a loyal following among area pros.

"WHEN ARE you going to be finished?" It's a question not of time, but of quantity of equipment—guitars, amplifiers, gizmos—that significant others tend to ask when they discover that their loved ones can't stop acquiring stuff. The best

ATOMIC MUSIC
9035 Baltimore Avenue
College Park, MD 20740
(301) 474-5752

way to answer is with another question: Would you ask Picasso when he was going to be done buying paint? Does Mrs. Yo-Yo Ma, ask Yo whether he really needs to try out another set of cello strings? Did Al Einstein's main squeeze complain when he came home with an extra slide rule?

Okay, so it's not nuclear physics, but it's rock 'n' roll, and we like it. (Well, one of us, anyway.) Besides, when the guy at Atomic Music said he'd let the used Sunn Concert Slave go for only $75, who could say no? (What's a slave do? In purely technical terms, it helps you go from "loud" to "really loud." Think of Nigel's amp in the mockumentary, *This Is Spinal Tap*; it took the volume all the way to 11, whereas ordinary amps stopped at 10. That's basically the idea.) There it was, a gem amid the densely packed mass of used gear.

It's that mass that makes Atomic a must for any electric guitarist or bassist—even those who can't play. Proof: a mohawk-sporting, black-studded-jacket-wearing dude trying out a Kustom amp, one of those padded, glittery models (the amp, not the jacket or the hair). Man, was he awful! But he had the look and the cash and now he has the Kustom. Long live rock!

If eBay had a store, it would look like Atomic. Turn a corner, enter another room, and you never know what you'll find, including used keyboards and pro-audio gear. But this is an electric guitarist's (regular or bass) dream store, where amid some junk is no shortage of high-quality used Fender Stratocasters (how about one in paisley pink or banana yellow?), Telecasters, Warwick basses (we counted twelve on one visit), and amps by Marshall, Fender, and Ampeg. A used Alembic bass that lists for more than $3,000 new was recently going for $849; it was gone the next time we returned. Luis Peraza, the store's co-owner, says Atomic generally stocks about seven hundred guitars at any given time.

"I spend a lot of money in this store," says Scott Decker, a veteran Maryland guitarist checking out amps. "It's dangerous for a weak person like me, who likes trying new stuff all the time." But the store will take back anything it sells, giving a partial refund—and providing an incentive to try out an instrument and then, if you get sick of it, try another.

"There's people that have owned ten guitars this year," says Peraza. "They figure the $60 they're going to lose [on the trade-in] is worth it for all the guitars they get to use."

In the neighborhood: See **CDepot** in the section above, CDs and Records.

If Atomic Music in College Park is like a giant flea market, Action Music in Arlington is like a boutique. In a basement corner of the Williamsburg Shopping Center, where a florist and bakery are more apropos in this residential neighborhood, Action offers a prime selection of quality used, reconditioned, and vintage guitars and amplifiers. Like Harley riders at a motorcycle shop or surfers at a board store, Action's clientele takes pleasure just being in the presence of its merchandise. If you don't play guitar, you might as well skip this entry. But if you do play, you either know about Action already or you're about to make plans to go.

> **ACTION MUSIC**
> Williamsburg Shopping Center
> 6501 N. 29th Street
> Arlington, VA 22213
> (703) 534-4801

Walk in and face a wall of Marshall amps—half-stacks (one cabinet), full stacks (two cabinets stacked, which brings back memories of roadies rushing to keep one of Hendrix's amps from toppling over as he bashed it with his Stratocaster . . . but we digress). About 85 percent of the gear is used, and Action owner Matt Baker—a guitarist and former Congressional assistant who decided that owning a music store is more fun—buys from local players and guitar shows. Still in the amplifier section, we've found as many as twelve Marshall heads on one visit, plus a stash of 1960s-era Fender Bandmasters, Bassmans, and some newer Super Reverbs, Deluxes, and Twins—not to mention a couple of old Vox amps. Behind glass cases are pedals with exotic effects: Carl Martin, Voodoo Lab, Xotic Effects, plus the standard MXR.

The guitars, though, are the primary draw. A Telecaster from the early '70s ($1,500), an acoustic Martin D-28 Brazilian from 1967 ($3,850). Lots of Strats, vintage and recent, and if you don't care if it's made in the United States, you can pick up one that plays like a dream for a few hundred dollars. Action also has a handful of cool Jazzmasters (think Elvis Costello), some gorgeous archtops from Gibson and Epiphone, an old Mosrite (remember the Ventures?), and a row of laptop steel guitars from National, Rickenbacker, and Gibson.

Everything sold here is inspected when it comes in, cleaned, set up, and sometimes reconditioned, so you know when you leave that it'll work. In the words of a former Action repair technician, if you want shiny and new, go to Guitar Center, whose Seven Corners store is only a five-minute drive away.

Action in fact gets repairs from that national chain and it doesn't begrudge the big chain's market and variety. Neither do we, as we've laid down our own share of cash and tried out plenty of guitars and amps at Guitar Center. But if you want vintage and cool, come to Action.

~~~

FOLK, TRADITIONAL, roots, ethnic—call it what you want, you're going to wind up at the House of Musical Traditions sooner or later if you play acoustic, nonclassical tunes. Befitting its Tacoma Park location—think "crunchy granola"—the store sells Tibetan singing bowls that are sometimes used in Unitarian services, African drums of all kind, "Ozark harps" (how's that for political correctness?), Irish drums known as bodrams, and lots of acoustic guitars. If Cajun, Tejano, or Polish music is more your style, check out the accordions; you'll get a free lesson with any accordion purchase.

> **HOUSE OF MUSICAL TRADITIONS**
> 7040 Carroll Avenue
> Takoma Park, MD 20912
> (301) 270-9090
> www.musicaltraditions.com

The House of Musical Traditions even sells sitars, washboards, Dobros, and zithers. On Friday nights, the upstairs becomes home to "Beatjam," an informal drum circle ($10 to participate, $5 for students). Bring your own drum or borrow one from the store.

In the neighborhood: Fineawares, a gallery of American handicrafts, is next store, and **Amano**, a clothing store for grown-up flower children, is just up the street at 7030 Carroll Avenue. Window-shopping is fun in this neighborhood and worthy of a Saturday afternoon.

~~~

WASHINGTON MUSIC Center is such a large and well-known landmark, many D.C. musicians simply refer to it as "Chuck's." Buying an instrument at Chuck's is not just a purchase, it's an experience. In fact, after our first visit to buy a clarinet for our then-middle-school-age daughter, we e-mailed the school music teacher and said just that: "That was quite an experience." It's all positive, but if you go ex-

> **CHUCK LEVIN'S WASHINGTON MUSIC CENTER**
> 11151 Viers Mill Road
> Wheaton, MD 20902
> (301) 946-8808
> www.wmcworld.com

pecting a sanitized room full of keyboards and drums you can play for kicks, think again.

The family that runs Chuck's is so successful, we don't think they'll offended when we say that their store is not pretty. It's actually a set of four warehouses, with separate repair facilities next door. As you walk into the main building, a greeter of sorts, or guard if you will, asks what you need. If you're there to buy a band or orchestra instrument, an escort will lead to a freight elevator. Once you've landed, head down a long hall piled with boxes until you arrive at the appropriate instrument room

It can all be a bit intimidating on the first visit, but we were old pros by the time we made our second trip up the freight elevator to buy a trumpet at the recommendation of our son's trumpet teacher, classical and jazz virtuoso Daniel Lee. Daniel went with us and knew the staff by name. Our son was instructed to turn his back to us and play five different trumpets while the teacher and Roger, the store's trumpet expert, analyzed the sound. To be honest, we couldn't hear that much of a difference, but the trumpet masters did, and we picked a Bach—but not before heading over to the next room to try out a couple of double basses, just for sport.

The selection and prices at Chuck's are as good as you'll find anywhere. Before we bought either instrument, we carefully checked the Internet, and Chuck's was cheaper. It can afford to sell cheap because it has tons of inventory—including a showroom for guitars, amplifiers, and drums—and sells a high volume. In addition, there is a state-of-the-art pro sound room and home keyboard showroom in a building adjacent to the main store.

In the neighborhood: Washington Music Center is in Wheaton, among an abundance of eateries and fun stores bounded by the Viers Mill, University Boulevard, and Georgia Avenue triangle. See chapter 3, Food and Drink; chapter 7, Toys, Games, and Hobbies; and chapter 14, Getting to Great Shopping, for more Wheaton details.

TOM PETTY, John Mayer, Eric Clapton, and George Harrison have done business with Southworth Guitars, one of the most amazing used guitar stores this side of New York's West 48th Street. You can shop at Southworth, too, if you have spare dollars to invest (and these guitars *are*

SOUTHWORTH GUITARS
7845 Old Georgetown Road
Bethesda, MD 20814
(301) 718-1667
www.southworthguitars.com

investments) and possess a keen appreciation for the finer things in life—such as one of Gibson's prototypes for its Les Paul model. Electric guitarists are in awe of this shop and rightly so. It's one of our Top Ten favorite businesses in the area (see chapter 2). Check out Gil Southworth's Fender amplifier collection, all vintage blond and tweed.

(Six degrees of separation time: Gil Southworth collects and sells vintage guitars to players, collectors, and rock stars. So does Gary Dick, of Garys Classic Guitars—www.garysguitars.com—based in Cincinnati, Ohio. Gil and Gary know one another and have done business together, because theirs is a small universe. Gil even knows what kind of guitar Gary played in high school [1964 sunburst Fender Stratocaster]. What Gil didn't know was the kind of guitar Gary subsequently played: a Mosrite that played like a dream. We know this firsthand; we were in junior high, and Gary was our guitar teacher—well, Steve's teacher, anyway.)

In the neighborhood: Southworth is in downtown Bethesda, with lots of window-shopping and restaurant-hopping options. Stop by **Hinata**, a nifty Japanese grocer with a first-rate sushi bar at 4947 St. Elmo Avenue, for lunch or just to pick up some seaweed-wrapped crackers or the Japanese candy, Pocky.

SHEET MUSIC

SINCE 1949, the Burchuk family has owned and operated this outstanding resource for music educators, students, and professional musicians. After you see the files, drawers, and rooms filled with the music books and sheet music Dale has in stock, you'll understand why the store is known throughout the world. Dale has some fun stuff, too—musical tote bags, neckties, pencils with little notes on them—but this truly is, as the store calls itself, "The Musicians' Music Store." Dale Music also sells and rents musical instruments and offers studio music lessons.

> **DALE MUSIC CO.**
> 8240 Georgia Avenue
> Silver Spring, MD 20910
> (301) 589-1459
> www.dalemusic.com

In the neighborhood: Parking can be a little tricky on a busy Saturday in Silver Spring; search the side streets for metered parking. If you need some strength before that flute lesson, head to nearby **Tropical Ice Cream**, 9324 Georgia Avenue, for a scoop of papaya-, passion fruit-, or even Guinness- (yes, the beer) flavored ice cream, some of the most unusual in Greater D.C. If you're really hungry, go hog wild with a "Reggae Sundae": two scoops of tropical ice cream, half a banana, strawberry and pineapple topping, and nuts.

HAVING TWO kids in high school band, we've become intimately familiar with Foxes Music Co. Other music stores are fine for a quick hit of valve oil or a new clarinet spit swab, but when you need sheet music for a competition or festival, the music teacher sends you directly to Foxes. Not that that's a bad thing. Its great selection of instructive books and sheet music has made the store a Virginia landmark for half a century. Students can thumb through the file drawers full of trumpet solos or order extra-thick blank $3^1/_2$ clarinet reeds, while their parents peruse the pop collections, standards, Broadway scores, rock, jazz, and blues books. Foxes has tons of music in stock and can order anything that isn't. Foxes also sells and rents instruments and gives music lessons.

> **FOXES MUSIC CO.**
> 416 S. Washington Street
> Falls Church, VA 22046
> (703) 533-7793 or
> (800) 446-4414
> www.foxesmusic.com

In the neighborhood: Head slightly south to the **German Gourmet**, 7185 Lee Highway, for a wonderful selection of German chocolates (see chapter 2, Food and Drink). Or go slightly north to downtown Falls Church, where you can find doll furniture at **Miniatures from the Attic**, 111 Park Avenue (see chapter 7, Toys, Games, and Hobbies), among other area finds.

CHAPTER 6

Bookstores

THE BEST IN A CITY FULL OF GREATS

Maybe it's because they're smart or because they have long subway and bus commutes and prefer not to stare at strangers or talk to seatmates. Regardless, Washingtonians always tend to have a book by their sides, on their bed stands, and in their briefcases. Is it any wonder that so many good book stores dot the landscape?

The biggest of them, with music sections and, in many cases, coffee bars and pastry selections, are impressive for their breadth: homegrown Olsson's, with its bookwise staff and record section workers who can be counted on to make good recommendations, and national chains Borders and Barnes & Noble. Their prices are competitive, especially on best sellers, and their sale books are hard to resist—as our own cookbook collection demonstrates. So how is it that, despite this kind of competition, several single-location bookstores manage to survive and, once in a while, even thrive?

One word: depth. They specialize, and they do their specialties especially well. That's where the bookstores in this chapter come in. Whether it's books on art, poetry, literature, first editions, acre upon acre of used volumes, they're tops in their fields. They're not megastores dominating the market—and they're not even trying to be.

IT'S ONLY appropriate that a store specializing in first and rare editions and Americana would be housed on the second floor of an old brick building, in a throwback to pre-chain store Georgetown. This is how a collector's store should look: nicely cluttered (but not junky), with wood floors and floor-to-ceiling windows that let in plenty of natural light and ward off a "grandma's attic" feeling. And although more than a century ago this happened to be the coffin display floor of the funeral home that occupied the building, there is nothing funereal about Bartleby's.

> **BARTLEBY'S BOOKS**
> 3034 M Street NW
> Washington, DC 20007
> (202) 298-0486
> www.bartlebysbooks.com

But collectors go for the books, not the building, so let's get started. Looking for a twenty-three-volume collection of the works of Friedrich Nietzsche, published in 1922? That was a good year for publishing—and for Bartleby's, which on one recent visit had not only the Nietzsche, but a 1922 first edition of Jane Austen's *Love & Friendship* as well.

More fascinating for the casual browser are the journals, guides, and catalogues: *Upland Game Shooting in America*, a 1930 Derrydale Press first edition—one of only seventy-five copies. In 1776, E & C Dilly of London published Lionel Chalmers's two-volume *An Account of the Weather and Diseases of South-Carolina*. Chalmers lived in what was then known as "Charles-Town, South-Carolina," where the weather and diseases were apparently dreadful.

In 1806, Thomas Asche published his *Travel in the South*, a two-volume account of his explorations on the Allegheny, Monongahela, Ohio, and Mississippi rivers. He was not kind; one reviewer wrote, according to the card in a Bartleby's display case: "An unmeasured hatred of America pervades the whole of Mr. Asche's narrative."

Antiquarian books aren't cheap—Dr. Chalmers's inventory of Carolinian weather and disease will set you back $4,500, while the Jane Austen novel is $350. But Bartleby's has less expensive collectibles, such as a set of instructions from A.C. Spalding and Brothers on "How to Inflate Foot Balls Properly," or the photographs of Richard Nixon or Lady Bird Johnson at the White House. "If you want to understand a period, in addition to reading the books, you go back to the pamphlets that were published at the time," says Karen Griffin, who with her husband, book buyer John Thomson, owns Bartleby's. "Like an 1804 pamphlet complaining about Thomas Jefferson."

Bartleby's has a decent selection of contemporary but used books, such as Nicholas Lemann's acclaimed but fairly recent account of black migration from the South to America's industrial cities, *The Promised Land*. Why? The shop's specialty may be American history, but that doesn't have to mean every volume is old.

In the neighborhood: Georgetown is a shopping, browsing, and dining mecca, a mandatory stop for every recreational shopper and tourist. For fun in the area near Barleby's, check out **Movie Madness**, in the basement at 1083 Thomas Jefferson Street NW, just off M Street. It features a good selection of movie posters, from Marilyn Monroe to recent hits, and the music posters range from jazz greats to the Beatles and Pink Floyd to contemporary pop groups. **Georgetown Frame Shoppe**, 2902$^1/_2$ M Street NW, has a delightful collection of animation art, including hard-to-find cels from movies, and limited edition prints from Chagall and Miró. **Grafix**, 2904 M Street NW, offers magazine covers as art, from vintage copies of *Esquire* to *New Yorker*.

A FRIEND first told us about Bridge Street Books' outstanding poetry selection, but what struck us on our first visit to this small shop on Georgetown's eastern edge was the choice selection in every other genre. Almost immediately, we spied not only a Miles Davis biography we'd been seeking (and promptly bought) but also a title about a certain former member of George W. Bush's cabinet. Never mind that this book was said, in that very day's *Washington Post*, to be unavailable for several days, and speculation and hype were building about what this cabinet secretary had to say (it wasn't kind). We walked into Bridge Street Books and voilà, it was on the shelves. (So as not to land Bridge Street proprietor Phil Levy in hot water for displaying the book early—hey, he didn't know—our lips are sealed on the title, subject, author, and author's previous employment at a certain newspaper based in lower Manhattan. Even Wen Ho Lee's attorney couldn't pry it out of us.)

BRIDGE STREET BOOKS
2814 Pennsylvania Avenue NW
Washington, DC 20007
(202) 965-5200

But poetry, not politics, is what has built Bridge Street's reputation. Rod Smith, the avant-garde poet, works here, and his book picks—and readings by guests on Sunday nights in the spring and fall—have made a mark. Of about twenty-two thousand titles in the two-story shop, roughly two thousand seven hundred are books of poetry, including poetics and anthologies. "He's the one responsible," Levy says of Smith. A lifelong Washingtonian who grew up two blocks from his shop, Levy brags about his poetry selection like a proud father: "We are as strong as any bookstore in the country. It's a very small niche, but we do it really well."

Bridge Street also does drama and literature well, and it fills a number of the other niches in this neighborhood of college students, professors, and influential Washingtonians. Never mind that Bridge Street is mere blocks from a very good Barnes & Noble superstore. "I would say that 50 percent of our books, they don't have there," Levy says. Such as? "We certainly don't have the biggest film selection in town, but we're very focused, and it's the most serious."

To learn about upcoming poetry readings, go to www.dcpoetry.com.

In the neighborhood: See Bartleby's, above.

～～～

CALL IT confidence or call it guts. In 2003 Terri Merz and Steve Moyer steered a course that few small business owners would dare try. After eighteen years in other locations, they moved their bookstore, Chapters, smack dab into the shadow of the giant Barnes & Noble on E Street NW. And they did it with their eyes wide open. Asked how they could possibly compete, Merz, a literature lover since childhood, said matter-of-factly over the soft strains of a recorded Vivaldi cello concerto: "Because we're Chapters Literary Bookstore. We're a specialty bookstore, and I think people realize it."

> **CHAPTERS A LITERARY BOOKSTORE**
> 445 11th Street NW
> Washington DC 20004
> (202) 737-5553
> www.chaptersliterary.com

What's so special? The selection. Serious readers of literature, poetry, history, biography, and political nonfiction know they'll find something great to read, much of it contemporary, and that the proprietors—who seem to work here around the clock—are delighted to offer suggestions. In fact, they have a rack with their own recommendations, like Charles Baxter's *Saul and Patsy*.

Says a handwritten card: "One always wonders how a favorite author can follow up a perfect book, i.e., Charles Baxter and his *Feast of Love*. No fear; his newest novel, *Saul and Patsy*, is again replete with his editorial magic, and his loving eye."

Chapters counts on its proximity to Pennsylvania Avenue law firms and the National Endowment for the Arts and National Endowment for the Humanities to attract a smart, well-read crowd. Provocative titles like Azar Nafisi's *Reading Lolita in Tehran* and Deborah Larsen's *The White* line the rack of new paperbacks. You won't find Stephen King novels here—something King would probably find an injustice, though Chapters does stock his book on writing. You will find Alan Furst, John le Carré, Walter Mosley, and Josephine Tey mysteries.

Making a bold statement, Merz and Moyer have stationed a rack of new poetry releases in an alcove near the front door. Chapters claims to have the biggest poetry selection in town, which Bridge Street Books in Georgetown might challenge; we're not about to settle this one because, regardless, it's pretty amazing that a city could support two such stores.

Authors Günter Grass, Richard Ford, Anthony Hecht, and many more have given readings at Chapters, and lunchtime literary events help to attract the nearby office crowd. The great book picks by Merz and Moyer keep people coming back. Our own weakness is for travel literature; with Chapters' array of titles, including Paul Theroux's *Dark Star Safari*, Ben Nimmo's *In Forkbeard's Wake: Coasting Around Scandinavia*, and Brian Bouldrey's *Traveling Souls: Contemporary Pilgrimage Stories*, we could travel the globe from our living room for a long, long time.

In the neighborhood: The Penn Quarter area has been up and coming in recent years, and building renovators and retail and residential pioneers are striving to create a district of urban chic. Check out **Teaism**, an Asian-inspired tea house/hangout at the corner of 8th Street and D streets NW; **Landmark's E Street Cinema**, an arts and indy-oriented movie house at 555 11th Street NW (at E Street); **Barnes & Noble**, 555 12th Street NW; and **Penn Camera**, 840 E Street NW. (Note to out-of-towners: you'll find the **Old Post Office**, the **FBI**, and **Ford's Theatre** nearby, and the **International Spy Museum** and **Chinatown** are within easy walking distance. On-street parking is hard to find, but the Metro Center Metro stop is nearby.)

WHEN A store impresses us, we often ask the owner or manager to tell us about his or her favorite retail finds. Franz Bader has the honor of being the store most recommended by other shop owners, and the reasons are always the same: excellent customer service and a huge selection in its niche market. Sandwiched in an indistinct maze of buildings between the White House and George Washington University, Franz Bader carries only books about the visual arts (as opposed to the performing arts): graphics, design, architecture, photos, ceramics, and textiles.

> **FRANZ BADER BOOKSTORE**
> 19111 Eye Street NW
> Washington, DC 20006
> (202) 337-5440

Such titles as *Minimalist Houses* and *Firecrackers: The Art and History* (a book about the design of firecracker wrappers) line the shelves, along with those on Indian embroidery, tall buildings, and beautiful libraries. We're natives of Cincinnati, Ohio, so a book on Cincinnati Art–Carved Furniture and Interiors, published by the Cincinnati Art Museum, caught our eye—not exactly something you would come upon in a bookstore every day.

Franz Bader caters to art students in the area and the wealth of architects with offices in the surrounding neighborhood. Decorator calendars imported from Germany are themselves real works of art and make wonderful gifts, though they really are too gorgeous to waste by marking up with reminders of dentist appointments and back-to-school nights. Though it offers some designer wrapping paper and a few washable tattoos for the younger set, Franz Bader pretty much sticks to its core mission: selling terrific art books for those who appreciate the subject. Don't think you can't afford anything—there's a large shelf of sale books as well.

~~~

WASHINGTON, D.C.'s oldest independent book and music store, Olsson's was mentioned as a favorite by many when we polled people about booksellers. Its willingness to special order, its frequent author signings and even live musical performances, and its smart staff (whose taste in music has led us to discover a CD or two) keep Washingtonians fiercely loyal. Olsson's branches are mostly in urban areas where people walk to stores

> **OLSSON'S**
> 1307 19th Street NW
> Washington, DC 20036
> Books: (202) 785-1333
> Music: (202) 785-2662
> www.Olssons.com

(Reagan National Airport is an exception). Olsson's offers a free "frequent buyers card" entitling the recipient to discounts.

Other locations: Reagan National Airport/Terminal C; **Arlington-Rosslyn** (next to Starbucks, across the street from the Roslyn Metro), 1735 N. Lynn Street; **Arlington-Courthouse**, 2111 Wilson Boulevard; **Bethesda**, 7647 Old Georgetown Road.; **The Lansburgh at Penn Quarter**, 418 Seventh Street NW (between D & E streets NW). Washington DC; and **Old Town Alexandria** (a half-block from King Street near the river), 106 S. Union Street.

WHAT WAS former Secretary of State Madeline Albright doing in a place like this? Why, signing books, of course, and with little hullabaloo, just as some other author—often a literary or political heavyweight—is almost every day. Politics and Prose is one of the most popular booksellers in metro D.C., especially among readers of history, politics, public affairs, and literature. If you can't come to a signing, order the book in advance and Politics and Prose will have it autographed and, if you can't pick it up, shipped.

> **POLITICS AND PROSE**
> 5015 Connecticut Avenue NW
> Washington, DC 20008
> (202) 364-1919 or
> (800) 722-0790

We are writing this, incidentally, in the dimly lit downstairs coffee bar, our notebooks spread out on a large oak table. There's a mishmash of couches and chairs haphazardly arranged, and light fixtures are covered with lampshades that look like white-lined notebooks. Several moms carrying infants in hanging slings and clutching toddlers are wandering out from the 10:30 Monday morning story time. Besides housing the coffee bar/café, which serves sandwiches and desserts, the downstairs features a well-stocked section of children's books.

The store's main feature is grown-up books, of course, and an extra-large section on politics and history is featured near the front door. A special area is reserved for books currently reviewed by the *New York Times* and *Washington Post*, but Politics and Prose also tracks its own best sellers. On one visit, books about Benjamin Franklin and by Noam Chomsky were in the top ten. That, as well as the table with anti-Bush and pro-Kucinich activists out front one day during the early 2004 presidential campaign (not that they had anything to do with the proprietors), says something about the neighborhood. You're not in Fairfax County anymore, Dorothy.

In the neighborhood: The parking lot in the back is often full, but street parking is available on nearby 36th Street. This strip of stores also includes a **Marvelous Market** bakery and take-out eatery, **Besta Pizza**, which sells by the slice, **Bucks Fishing and Camping** restaurant, and **Sheffield Wine and Liquor.**

~~~

STUDENTS AT George Washington, Georgetown, and Howard know Reiter's and its "sister store," Washington Law (see below), are must-visits for anyone looking for professional books in law, medicine, business, computers, and mathematics. Reiter's, in operation since the mid-1930s, houses huge selections on computer, mathematics, engineering, and almost every branch of the sciences. We've counted several hundred on cryptography alone. Other specialty selections include business and economics, the history of science, and engineering. Need a deck of pathology flashcards? Medical books are the big specialty and rate a room of their own. While medical books generally are not discounted, frequent shoppers may want to join the free Cranium Club, a frequent buyer program that allows you to receive discounts and participate in special sales.

> **REITER'S SCIENTIFIC AND PROFESSIONAL BOOKS**
> 2021 K Street NW
> Washington, DC 20006
> (202) 223-3327
> www.reiters.com

In addition to drawing the college crowd, Reiter's attracts World Bank employees and lawyers who need to bone up on a specialty, such as chemistry, for a current case. Reiter's also has a fair selection of fun stuff appealing to its market: science-oriented toys and puzzles and posters ranging from anatomical drawings of the female reproductive system to one of jazz musician Charlie Parker.

There's smart-guy humor, too: T-shirts with slogans like, "Hey! This IS Rocket Science," and a "little thinker doll"—a wind-up likeness of Sigmund Freud, playing the tune "The Way We Were." (We'll help you out with this one. Think of Freud. Now think of the song's first line: "Memories . . .")

~~~

BIGGER THAN some library branches, the Rockville location of this store made our Top Ten favorites list (see chapter 2) because it's a must for anyone who likes books—art books, literature, sports, history of all periods, religion, military, biography, science (from anatomy to zoology) . . . well, just about every subject imaginable. Owner Allan Stypeck has put the store on the map not only because of selection but also because he hosts a public radio show on books. Second Story also carries a selection of old phonograph records.

> **SECOND STORY BOOKS**
> 12160 Parklawn Drive
> Rockville, MD 20852
> (301) 770-0477
> www.secondstorybooks.com

Other location: Dupont Circle, 2000 P Street NW, (202) 659-8884.

LAW STUDENTS at any of the area schools should check out Washington Law and Professional Books before they buy from theie college store. Sometimes Washington Law has lower prices. Better yet, the selection is unbeatable in this slightly messy, well-stocked shop crammed with legal textbooks, hornbooks, and study aids. Specializing in legal books, forms, and industry-specific aids for practitioners and students, the store also serves employees of the World Bank, located directly across the street (in fact, Washington Law is a tenant of one of the World Bank's buildings) and the Organization of American States.

> **WASHINGTON LAW AND PROFESSIONAL BOOKS**
> 1900 G Street NW
> Washington, DC 20006
> (202) 223-5543
> www.washingtonlawbooks.com

> **Tip**
> If you're looking for a specialty used bookstore, The Washington Antiquarian Booksellers Association produces a free annual directory, *Used, Collectible, & Antiquarian Booksellers of the Greater Washington DC Area*. Available at most used bookstores and on the Web (www.wababooks.com), the directory provides store locations and hours and lists them by "open" and "by appointment only" status.

Also Noteworthy:

BONIFANT BOOKS
11240 Georgia Avenue
Wheaton, MD 20902
(301) 946-1526
www.abebooks.com/home/bonifant

In the heart of Wheaton, Bonifant stocks forty-five thousand volumes with an emphasis on history, African-American culture, mystery, science fiction, and literature.

IDLE TIME BOOKS
2467 18th Street NW
Washington, DC 20009
(202) 232-4774
www.idletime.com

This popular Adams Morgan used bookstore is a great place to browse after you've been to the local coffeehouses and ethnic eateries in the neighborhood.

KARIBU
Prince George's Plaza
3500 East-West Highway
Hyattsville, MD 20782
(301) 559-1140
www.karibubooks.com

This local specialty chain of five stores has books by and about people of African descent. It carries everything from cookbooks (*African Cookbook: Tastes of a Continent*; *Al Roker's Big Bad Book of Barbecue*) to books on revolution, African studies, and art (*African Style: Down to the Details*). We checked to see if the store happened to have any books illustrated by Jerry Pinkney, a children's author/illustrator who gave a presentation at our daughter's school when she was in kindergarten, and found an astounding twenty-five titles.

Other locations: Bowie Town Center, 15624 Emerald Way, Bowie, MD; Iverson Mall, 3817 Branch Avenue, Hillcrest Heights, MD; Forest Village Park Mall, 3289 B Donnell Drive, Forestville, MD; Pentagon City, 1100 S. Hayes Street, Arlington, VA.

KRAMERBOOKS AND AFTERWORDS CAFÉ AND GRILL
1517 Connecticut Avenue NW
Washington, DC 20036
(202) 387-1400
www.kramers.com

"Serving Latte to the Literati since 1976," the always-packed Kramerbooks is a Dupont Circle landmark. Where else can you have your morning coffee and newspaper break, then return to hear live music at night? The café is a full restaurant—not just a place to grab a muffin and cappuccino. Serving breakfast, lunch, dinner, and late supper, as well as brunch on weekends, Afterwords café has real meals: French-cut hanging tenderloin of beef ($15.25), pasta dishes, sandwiches, and desserts. Kramerbooks has a full liquor license, with eighteen beers on tap and a small wine list. Desserts include pie, cake, and ice cream. Oh, yeah, and Kramer's has books, too.

TALKING BOOK WORLD
Sugarland Crossing
47010 Community Plaza (Route 7)
Sterling, VA 20164
(703) 433-2400
www.talkingbookworld.com

Those popular motivational speakers charge a mint for audiotapes, but you can listen for a fraction of the cost by renting them from Talking Book World. The store, with locations in Sterling and Rockville, also offers tapes for sale, but most customers are commuters who join a "plan" that allows them to rent all the mysteries, thrillers, and self-help tapes they can stand to listen to on the way to work.

Other location: 11431A Rockville Pike, Rockville, MD.

TEMPO BOOKSTORE
4905 Wisconsin Avenue NW
Washington, DC 20016
(202) 363-6683

ESL (English as a Second Language) teachers drive from all over the metro area to pick up materials at this store, which calls itself, "The Languages Resource Center." But teachers aren't the only customers of this foreign-language specialty store that carries Harry Potter books in French, cassette courses on colloquial Arabic, "teach yourself Finnish," and bilingual baby language videos for children whose parents also speak Dutch, Swedish, Spanish, Hebrew, etc.

A NOTE ON NEWSSTANDS

One would expect to see terrific newsstands on every corner in a city where news rules, but Washington doesn't have any of the "mind-blowing" stands we've seen in other cities. One of its best is **The Newsroom,** 1803 Connecticut Avenue NW, in Dupont Circle, (202) 332-1489, which carries a large selection of magazines and newspapers in twenty-five languages. In Alexandria, **Old Town News,** 721 King Street, (703) 739-9024, is your best bet.

STRICTLY FOR CHILDREN

MARILYN DUGAN'S youngest child was nine when she opened her children's bookstore in 1984. Although her son is now an adult, Marilyn is still in touch with the smaller set as she recommends books for kids of all ages. Toddler story hour was in full force when we arrived one day, and we practically teared up as we heard the kids in the special story room chanting, "Wishy washy, wishy washy"—a line from the first book our son, who's now a young teen, learned to "read."

> **A LIKELY STORY**
> 1555 King Street
> Alexandria, VA 22314
> (703) 836-2498
> www.alikelystory.com

After we asked an employee to recommend a book for a thirteen-year-old boy who would rather play video games than read, she produced two: *The Ender's Game* by Orson Scott Card and *Point Blank* by Anthony Horowitz. And, indeed, both were hits. The commitment of the staff really shows. During the December holiday season, the store holds "A Season of Sharing" drive where customers donate books to children living in various shelters in the area.

A Likely Story has three story times a week, each for a different age group. Newer moms will be thrilled to learn that the Tuesday story times are designed for children from six months to two years old and feature lots of hand rhymes and songs. Wednesdays are for kids two and up and Saturdays age three and up.

Costume character readings and other special events take place frequently, such as the *Where the Wild Things Are* costume event in which Maurice Sendak's classic is read, and a costumed "wild thing" is on hand to meet and greet fans. The store also allows customers to preorder autographed copies if a special author is doing a signing.

A Likely Story also has a few games and a great selection of book-oriented birthday cards, featuring readily recognizable characters such as Madeline, Arthur, and Thomas the Tank Engine.

In the neighborhood: This store is on King Street in Old Town right near the Metro exit. Infant/toddler moms can trek right on over to Madeleine's Kids (used and gently worn), a children's clothing store, to find bargains on high-end baby and toddler dresses and such.

Also noteworthy:

ALADDIN'S LAMP BOOKS
Lee Harrison Shopping Center
2499 N. Harrison Street, Lower Level, Suite 10
Arlington, VA 22207
(703) 241-8281

Don't get lost looking for this large children's bookstore. You have to go down some stairs in the middle of this strip shopping center (the one with Harris Teeter and H&R Block in Arlington) to find a basement full of shops. This one has twenty thousand titles for children of all ages as well as some dolls, puppets, puzzles, and more.

IMAGINATION STATION
4524 Lee Highway
Arlington VA 22201
(703) 522-2047
www.kinderhaus.com

Affiliated with the **Kinder Haus Toys**, Imagination Station has children's books and music. The store takes particular pride in its knowledgeable staff and its large selection of foreign-language books for children.

CHAPTER 7

Toys, Games, and Hobbies

For the younger set, big-box discount stores and chains such as Toys "R" Us are fine for everything from Barbie dolls to video games, but you aren't likely to get suggestions from an informed staff about what to buy your eight-year-old niece, or from a wise old hobbyist on the best train set for your money. We picked the toy, game, and hobby stores in this chapter because they impress us with their selection, their customer service, or their unique niche, whether it's magic, costumes, hobbies, or just old-fashioned toys like they sold when we were kids.

Sadly, one of our favorite picks, **Nostalgic Plastic**, a highly specialized shop in Silver Spring carrying new and vintage model aircraft and ships, has closed. The good news, however, is that the owners still have a Web-based business, www.nostalgicplastic.com. That's the reality of today's marketplace: It's hard for the mom-and-pop shops to compete. It's also the obligation we share: patronize the great locals—and this region has lots of great ones—so we can ensure they'll live on.

TOY AND GAME STORES, MAGIC SHOPS, HOBBY STORES

METRO WASHINGTON has so many upscale toy stores filled with Breyer horses, Playmobile sets, and other high-quality toys that you sometimes wonder whether it's possible to find a great-but-basic all-around toy store: not too fancy, not too expensive, and not *that* basic. Anglo Dutch Pool and Toys is a large, unpretentious store that lacks fancy decorations like hanging dragons and cutesy painted walls. Instead, it's jammed with model kits, marionettes, LEGOs, art supplies, games, sports equipment, Radio Flyer wagons, and, yes, Breyer horses and Playmobile sets.

> **ANGLO DUTCH POOL AND TOYS**
> 5460 Westbard Avenue
> Bethesda, MD 20816
> (301) 951-0636

This is the perfect place to buy an inexpensive novelty toy, such as a potato gun or a Tickle Bee game, a set of jacks or a hand buzzer. A huge wall is devoted to the small toys such as jack sets, paddle balls, "Barrel Full O' Monkeys," and inexpensive card games—old-fashioned, fun toys worthy of a child's allowance. Another large section is devoted to sporting goods. A back room of the already large store is stuffed with swimming pool chemicals and supplies, swimsuits for kids, and pool toys. If you can't find something fun and affordable at Anglo Dutch, you probably can't find it anywhere.

In the neighborhood: In the Westwood shopping center in Bethesda, try **China Café** for a quick lunch, then throw a few spares at **Strike Bethesda** bowling alley, 5353 Westbard Avenue, across the street.

~~~

FAMOUS ACTORS, dancers, and playwrights have been spotted at this costume/makeup/theatrical bookstore located midway down Eighth Street near Capitol Hill. Need to rent or buy a seriously great Halloween costume? Want to humiliate your teenage children? It's easy if you try on huge Afro wigs and dance around the store. That Backstage also multitasks as a bookstore—the only theatrical bookstore in the area, with some scripts signed

> **BACKSTAGE INC**
> 545 Eighth Street SE
> Washington, DC 20003
> (202) 544-5744
> www.backstagebooks.com

by authors—ensured it a position as one of our Top Ten favorite stores (see chapter 2 for the full story).

In the neighborhood: Near the Navy Yard, Backstage is not far from the **Eastern Market.** The Eighth Street area also has a variety of interesting little stores and restaurants.

~~~

SO A guy walks into a magic shop. The owner starts telling him about how he used to hold magic shows upstairs, and how he hopes to open a hot new show soon. He pulls out a calling card advertising the old show, and as soon as he starts to hand it over, poof! The card's on fire.

How could you not love a shop like this?

Barry's Magic Shop is popular among local magicians, so don't be surprised if you walk in on a Saturday to find a group of them sitting around a card table, chatting, eating, and checking out the latest tricks that Barry Taylor and his wife, Susan Kang, just got in. If you're real lucky, you'll see a jam—a group of magicians trying out tricks and gags on one another. Professional magician Eric Henning comes in every week or two. "Partly it's to say hi to the guys, but also because these magic shops are like community centers for the magic world," he says.

BARRY'S MAGIC SHOP
11234 Georgia Avenue
Wheaton, MD 20902
(301) 933-0373
www.barrysmagicshop.com

The store, in a strip of shops that existed before "strip" shopping centers lost their allure, is loaded with instructional DVDs and thousands of tricks: cards, coins, ropes, mind reading, sleight of hand. The finger guillotine is especially appealing.

Hundreds, maybe thousands, of Washingtonians have learned magic from Barry's since it opened in 1974. "The majority of our customers are walk-ins," says Susan. But some of the old walk-ins are now coming by with their children, even grandchildren. Some of the oldsters get so excited, they can't wait to get home to learn their just-acquired tricks—so they try them at every red light on the way. Barry and Susan have gotten used to the phone calls that follow: "I figured it out!" "Everybody who comes in here," says Susan, "is nothing but a big kid."

In the neighborhood: Bonifant Books, 11240 Georgia Avenue, Wheaton, (301) 946-1526, in the same strip as Barry's Magic Shop, has a big selection of used books, a solid reputation, and a knowledgeable staff. Some CDs, too. The surrounding area of Wheaton is a mecca for specialty store and ethnic food shopping (see chapter 14, Getting to Great Shopping). Park in the back, load up a meter (pay attention to the time, as these lots are patrolled), and go exploring.

~~~

IT'S SATURDAY morning in Chevy Chase and the conversations start like this: "Six-year-old boy." "Eight-year-old-girl." That could mean only one thing: you're in line at Child's Play and you need a birthday present. The staff, largely teens who could fill you in on the latest punk fashions, is so knowledgeable about this store's impressive inventory that clerks merely need to know a child's gender and age—and your price range—and they instantly make a handful of suggestions. It's no wonder that in parts of Northwest Washington and its Maryland suburbs, half the kids show up at parties with presents wrapped in Child's Play trademark colorful fish-pattern gift wrap.

> **CHILD'S PLAY**
> 5536 Connecticut Avenue NW
> Washington, DC 20015
> (202) 244-3602

The selection is impressive and complete, from LEGOs to Brio trains to Schleich plastic animals and Roller Blade inline skates. The book selection is big, and you can find just about everything you need to give to a child or to attend a child's party, from invitations to thank-you notes. But it's the staff that draws raves throughout the area.

"It's a wonderful store because the staff is extremely knowledgeable," says Richard Ashford, a school librarian shopping with his eleven-year-old son, David, one recent Sunday. "You know the movie, *Big*?" he asks. That's the movie (starring Tom Hanks) about a toy company that relies on big kids to know what other kids want. "You kind of get a feeling like everybody who works here would fit into that corporation."

In the neighborhood: Child's Play is in the same strip as **Chevy Chase Liquors** (301) 986-4372; the **American City Diner**, (202) 244-1949; and the Chevy Chase location of **Potomac Video**—a store that practically makes us weep. From the outside, it looks like an ordinary, garden-variety, so-so video store. But go in and head down the stairs and you'll find a selection unrivaled in this region: fifty-five thousand titles, including whole sections of Hitchcock, documentaries, British drama, foreign directors,

Australian, opera and ballet.... Why would we weep? Because we live too far from Potomac Video to use it regularly.

ROBERT WEIGEND opened his first game store in Chantilly, not to sell games but to provide a clubhouse of sorts for members of the Washington Gamers Association to meet and play the games they loved. Selling games merely helped the former trade association lobbyist pay the rent. More than a decade later, Weigend is the owner of two of the most successful gaming establishments in the United States. The original Chantilly store has expanded to five thousand square feet; the Woodbridge facility is a whopping seven thousand.

> **GAME PARLOR**
> 14400 Smoketown Road
> Woodbridge, VA 22192
> (703) 551-4200
> www.gameparlor.com

Walk into either store and you're likely to find adults and some teens hunkered over rows of wooden tables, provided free of charge. Some might be setting up military or fantasy miniatures and props (grass, mountains, trees—you name it) for a battle game. Others are paired up at smaller tables, playing Magic cards, chess, or board games, while fans of role-playing games such as "Dungeons and Dragons" might be found in the windowed room in the back of the store. Video game lovers gravitate toward the computers loaded with high-tech games, such as "Rogue Spear" and "Starcraft," which may be rented for $5 an hour, or less if you buy multiple hours at a time.

Open from 10 a.m. to 10 p.m. every day except Christmas, the stores have played host to gamers even on Thanksgiving Day and New Year's Eve. Weigend has attended the weddings of more than one couple who met at the Chantilly location. Candy, soda, and chips are sold practically at cost, because the idea is not to gouge patrons but to provide a space for like-minded players—and if they happen to buy a game or game pieces, great. Each store has a calendar of meetings and special events, such as a "Lord of the Rings Gaming Session" or a gathering of the Prince William County Chess Club.

Other location: Sully Place Shopping Center, 13936 Metrotech Drive, Chantilly, VA, (703) 803-3114.

In the neighborhood: Both locations are in strip shopping centers. The Woodbridge store is across from the Potomac Mills outlet mall. After a gaming session at the Chantilly store, head over to **Milwaukee Frozen**

Custard, 13934 Lee Jackson Memorial Highway, (703) 263-1920, www.milwaukeefrozencustard.com, to try one of the best frozen custards around.

≈≈≈

WE'D SEEN the woman who worked behind the counter somewhere before. Ah, yes—a couple of years ago, she'd enchanted us at our neighborhood bookstore by creating one of several rooms from a Harry Potter book. After Crown Books went out of business, Cheryl Miller parlayed her hobby into a job at Miniatures from the Attic and was delighted to show us her favorite store's incredible array of dollhouses and dollhouse kits, small furniture, little people, and items such as teeny rolls of toilet paper and loaves of Wonder Bread. It is a small world, after all, and this is a place where dollhouse mansions sit in the window and a sign says, "If you dream it, we can do it."

> **MINIATURES FROM THE ATTIC**
> 111 Park Avenue
> Falls Church, VA 22046
> (703) 237-0066
> www.minis4u.com

Miniatures from the Attic does just that by building custom structures in a woodshop in the back. It isn't uncommon for someone to bring a photo of her grandfather's house and commission a miniature version. Store manager Gary LaPorta once showed us a photo feature of actor Sidney Portier's poolhouse in *Veranda* magazine (April 2003). A customer wanted his dollhouse to look like that. The folks at Miniatures had a contact in England hand-paint a set of ceramic plates and ginger jars to look just like Sidney's dining room china. Such houses can be pricey, of course. Most expensive was the display house in the window, $13,500 with custom parquet floors and a hand-laid chimney made of three thousand real miniature bricks.

Miniatures also carries accessories and supplies for any miniature project, including building components, electrification (a way to put electricity in a dollhouse), decorating, and landscaping. A "builder" can chose from over fifty types of windows. Restoration of old houses is also an option. "How to" classes and workshops are offered regularly, and dollhouse artists come for special events.

In the neighborhood: Miniatures is in heart of old Falls Church near **Brown's Hardware**, 100 W. Broad Street, (703) 532-1168. **New to You**, 125 N. Washington Street, (703) 533-1251, is a high-end consignment boutique.

IF YOU'RE a fan of teddy bears, this little store in Leesburg is quite a find. Sure, you can buy your grandchild a Beanie Baby here, but bears are the animals that rule at My Friends and Me. Be forewarned: designer bears don't come cheap. Take the new arrival we spotted on one visit: a little guy just a few inches tall, wearing a green suit and costing more than $900. And we thought $40 had been a lot to pay for our daughter's "Muffy" bear a few years ago! But then the salesclerk explained that Muffy is mass-produced and not made lovingly by hand. Who knew we'd been shortchanging our kid.

> **MY FRIENDS AND ME**
> 118 South Street SE
> Leesburg, VA 20175
> (703) 777-8222
> www.myfriendsandme.com

You don't have to buy one of the expensive handmade designer bears to enjoy this charming shop. The store carries adorable creatures from the Bearington Collection, selectively chosen based on quality and price. We once nervously eyed the price tag of a cute Scotsman (bear) replete with an outfit and golf clubs, only to be pleasantly surprised: he was under $25, and his counterpart, a smaller girl bear also dressed in an outfit, was only $12. My Friends and Me once sold twenty different Bearington bears to a woman who was having a holiday celebration—she chose an appropriate Bearington bear for each member of her family.

The store also has Madame Alexander collectable dolls, and a few non-bear animals (we've spied a couple of dogs, a giraffe, and a frog). My Friends and Me does a large mail order business because it's the only place in the United States where you can get bears designed by certain artists—some of whom come from as far as Germany, Australia, and the Netherlands for signings.

In the neighborhood: My Friends and Me is in Leesburg's **Market Square Shopping Center,** which is made up of original log buildings and a mill—home of **Tuscarora Mill** restaurant (www.tuskies.com). For a quick lunch, try **Scoopers Deli and Bar.**

THIS IS a model train store, and there's nothing "cute" about trains. They're fun, some of them are intricate, and most of them remind us of our childhood. So, despite its name, and despite the outside appearance—a

Toys, Games, and Hobbies

> **PEACH CREEK SHOPS**
> 201 Main Street
> Laurel, MD 20707
> (301) 498-9071
> www.peachcreekshops.com

pink and turquoise house—let's get one thing straight: Peach Creek Shops is not cute.

It's merely neater than all get-out.

It has trains for everyone, from the serious collector to kids just getting started. On the first floor is one of the most remarkable selections of engines anywhere, ranging from Bachmans for under $100 to shining brass collectibles costing thousands. The owner, John Glaab, travels to Germany to get a lot of his trains, and he sells some used collections on consignment. Glaab, a hobbyist turned proprietor, is author of *The Brown Book*, a collector's guide for evaluating brass model trains.

The shop's upstairs is crammed full of kits for building the landscapes, towns, and factories that trains typically run by, including an electric power plant and an amusement park. Walls and windows are also sold separately so you can construct your own custom buildings. Among the structures on display is an entire Rust Belt–era steel plant complete with smoke and a lighted, fiery coke furnace.

The staff is enthusiastic, the shop repairs engines, and Peach Creek discounts almost everything over $10 by 25 percent. What could be better than that? Well, there's the cute Peach Creek building—built as a home in 1906 and used since as a gift shop, jewelry store, boarding house, and model train store, among other things. "There's some evidence," says Glaab, "that it may even have been a house of ill repute."

In the neighborhood: Historic Laurel is nearby, with its authentic old downtown home to small shops and businesses. Pick up some handmade chocolates from **L and L Gift and Gourmet**, 512 Main Street, (301) 725-7539, www.llgiftsgourmet.com, or stop for a lunch of barbecue at **Red, Hot and Blue**, 677 Main Street, (301) 953-1943.

≈

> **POTOMAC TRADING COLLECTIBLES**
> 3610 University Boulevard West
> Kensington, MD 20895
> (301) 949-5656

THE FACT that this region can support two great train stores, not to mention several hobby shops with good collections, speaks volumes about the number of tinkerers and gizmo junkies in greater D.C. It'd be hard to say which is better, the aforementioned Peach Creek Shops in Laurel or Potomac Trading

Collectibles in Kensington. The biggest difference may be this: Potomac Trading sells antique and collectible guns and military relics downstairs. Even nonenthusiasts admire the Revolutionary War swords for $450; the real Civil War bullets for $2; the World War II rifles, carbines, and small arms from Europe; and—okay, we'll admit it—the heavy ordnance.

But upstairs, the train selection is nothing short of extraordinary, and so are some of the model planes hanging from the ceiling. Bill Printz and his staff know their stuff when it comes to trains of bygone days—the makes, models, transformers, tracks, and replacement parts—and chances are they can replicate whatever gauge train you're seeking to replace. Lionel is king in this huge collection, but the store stocks other brands as well. Pick your gauge, even if it's no longer made, and Bill and crew will set you up. In fact, during one visit we saw a guy bring in a gleaming silver engine that his father received as a gift in 1932 or '33. He put it on the test track, and off it went.

With great trains come cool accessories, and Potomac Trading has a demo area to try out those that move, light up, or make sounds. Kids and adults amuse themselves by pushing buttons to make a streetlamp light up, a man pop out of a door, or a pumping station pump. Our favorite is a little plastic conductor who goes up and down stairs.

In the neighborhood: There isn't much right next to Potomac Trading, but drive just up the street to **Savannahs**, 10700 Connecticut Avenue, (301) 946-7917, for burgers, pizza, appetizers, subs, and dessert. Then head to the Howard Avenue antique shops and check out the political memorabilia at **banning+Low**, 3730 Howard Avenue, (301) 933-0700.

WE JUST about guarantee you'll be wowed by the sea of bright blue, spike-hair robots, green Mister Peanut figures, Matchbox cars, used video games, electric trains, and all the X-Men, Star Wars, and Ninja Turtle action figures you can dream of in this vintage- and new-toy paradise in Wheaton. Even the ceiling is covered with brightly packaged toys, helping make this one of our Top Ten favorite stores in the entire metro area. (A full description of The Toy Exchange is found in chapter 2.)

THE TOY EXCHANGE
11265 Triangle Lane
Wheaton, Maryland 20902
(301) 929-0690
http://montgomerycountymd
.com/shopping/toyexchange.htm

In the neighborhood: Other fun stores in the area include **Barry's Magic Shop** (street entrance on Georgia Avenue) and **Barbarian Comics**, on the lower-level behind Barry's, 11242 Triangle Lane, (301) 946-4184.

~~~

CALLING ALL NASCAR fans. If you don't already own any Budweiser red to show your support for Dale Earnhardt Jr., a visit to Trakside in Woodbridge is in order. Father-son owners John and Jeff Fisher will sell you all the NASCAR hats and shirts you could ever need. For collectors, they also have a large assortment of die-cast cars priced in the $55–$75 range. Even if you need a glossary (we did) to find out what "dirty air" and "happy hour" mean in NASCAR lingo, you're likely to find this store way cool. So cheer for Mark Martin with a new Viagra hat—hey, if this dude isn't ashamed to emblazon it on his car, you shouldn't be, either—or just buy the hat for your friend who's getting up there in years.

> **TRAKSIDE**
> 14457 Potomac Mills Road
> Woodbridge, VA 22192
> (703) 497-8725

In the neighborhood: Before you hit I-95 for Richmond International Raceway, have a plate of cinnamon-enhanced Cincinnati-style chili at the **Hard Times Café** in the same shopping center as Trakside.

Also Noteworthy:

ANIME PAVILION
7395-B Lee Highway
Falls Church, VA 22042
(703) 204-1844
www.animepavilion.com

A must-visit for anime (Japanese animation) fans, Anime Pavillion has one of the largest selections of imported anime CDs, DVDs, and books in the area.

GRANDDAD'S HOBBY SHOP
5260-A Port Royal Road
Springfield, VA 22151
(703) 426-0700
www.granddadshobbyshop.com

Boasting more than seventeen hundred colors and twenty-five brands of model paint alone, Granddad's has something to fill almost every hobby need, including a large selection of airbrushes (parts and equipment), electric trains, books, craft kits, rocket kits, ship models, and military miniatures.

KINDER HAUS TOYS
4510 Lee Highway
Arlington, VA 22207
(703) 527-5929
www.kinderhaus.com

A solid, high-quality toy store in the Lee Heights shopping area of Arlington.

SULLIVAN'S TOY STORE
3412 Wisconsin Avenue NW
Washington, DC 20016
(202) 362-1343

If can't find a great party gift at this good old-fashioned toy store, head next door to Sullivan's Art Supplies.

TREE TOP TOYS & BOOKS
3301 New Mexico Avenue NW
Washington, DC 20016
(202) 244-3500
www.treetopkids.com

With locations in Foxhall Square in Washington and Langley Shopping Center in McLean, (703) 356-1400, this store has everything for infants on up, including a good costume selection.

VIDEO GAMES

For video and computer games, it's hard to beat the big chains. One of our favorites is **EB Games (Electronics Boutique)**. Another, **Gamestop**, is owned by Barnes & Noble and also operates under the names **Funcoland**, **Babbages**, and **Software, etc**. Both stores carry new and used video games and consoles—Nintendo, PlayStation, Xbox, and Dreamcast—and have locations all over the metro area. **CD Game Exchange** also has been expanding in the area; our son is a fan of this chain because of its bargain prices.

Note: See chapter 3, Potpourri, for listings of other hobby-related stores (woodworking, art supplies).

CHAPTER 8

Home and Garden

In a perfect world, every apartment and house would come ready-made with knockout European designer furniture; exotic rugs from Africa; artisan-crafted ceramic vases in reds, yellows, and blues; and craftsman-carved mantlepieces. All lawns would be seeded and weeded just so; towels would be thick and fluffy and sheets luxurious; floors would never scuff; and paint would never peel—but, of course.

Then again, perhaps that's a poor model for nirvana, because some of the finest stores in greater Washington would close, and shopping would be dreary. Fortunately, necessity *is* the mother of invention, and the shops in this chapter offer the mother lode for all your household needs. And for most of your wants, too.

BASIC GOODS: HARDWARE, FIREPLACE, AND PATIO

TIME TO 'fess up: We live in the 'burbs, where construction is new enough that the walls are hollow; the glass windows, unrippled; and the bathroom fixtures; off-the-shelf. So what's a nice family like ours doing in a place like The Brass Knob?

THE BRASS KNOB
2311 18th Street NW
Washington, DC 20009
(202) 332-3370
www.thebrassknob.com

Reminiscing and dreaming, that's what. We've lived in enough old houses to gush over architectural antiques, brass doorknobs, tear-shaped, cut-glass chandeliers, carved wood mantles, and other high-quality knick-knacks and hardware that make an older house a home.

The Brass Knob, in a Victorian row house on 18th Street in Adams Morgan, gets two kinds of customers—browsers like us who go for the memories; and buyers who own or are renovating older homes and might actually ring up a sale, whether a heavy brass hinge pin to replace a broken one, a doorknob spindle, or an antique floor lamp. Owners Ron Allan and Donetta George and their staff scour for remnants of those beautiful old buildings you hate to see torn down and make sure their parts live on—perhaps in your home. This merchandise is made to last.

A block away is the store's counterpart, the nine thousand-square-foot Back Doors Warehouse. This is where you'll find claw-foot bathtubs, pedestal sinks, dozens of solid wood doors, leaded glass doors, wood and marble pillars, medicine cabinets from old bathrooms, and indoor and outdoor window shutters. A bright yellow toilet reminded us of our friend Joann's impossible quest to replace a pink one in her 1940s home.

Whether at the main store or the warehouse, it's hard not to find something to admire, from a gorgeous chandelier for the dining room to a pair of wooden pillars for the front porch. Who knew that looking at doorknobs could be so fun!

Other locations: The **Back Doors Warehouse**, where you'll find the "big stuff" (bathtubs, doors, fountains), is at 2329 Champlain Street, near the Adams Morgan parking garage off 18th Street.

In the neighborhood: Shop for cool new furniture to go in your revamped house at **Skynear & Co.**, 2122 18th Street NW, (202) 797-7160.

THEY DON'T build hardware stores like Fischer's anymore, as any customer of this fifty-year-old family-owned institution will tell you. From the wrought iron patio furniture outside to the extensive housewares inventory inside, you'll find nearly anything and everything here to maintain or fix your home, paint and then cook in your kitchen, seed and then water your lawn, wax your car and then take out the trash. The selection of wind chimes alone exceeds that of most gift stores, and the hand tools, like miniature needle-nose pliers, cry out to be taken home and used.

Fischer's is one of two amazing hardware stores in the metro area (the other is Strosnider's, also in this chapter), and we have been known to wander through its merchandise-packed twenty thousand square feet of space with wonder and glee. You can buy garden seed by the ounce and grass seed in bulk, which attracts customers from as far as Maryland. More than three dozen bird feeders are on display. The hardware for drawers and cabinets—knobs, pulls, handles—is extensive. Hoses, sprinklers, scissors, toggle switches, lawn mower parts, playing cards, axes and a big array of axe handles, paints and stains of every color and shade, glassware, door sweeps, gas grill parts, bathroom scales, plumbing supplies, garbage disposals, insulated cups and mugs—even lanyards for your government security passes—are available here.

> **FISCHER'S HARDWARE**
> Concord Center Plaza
> 6129 Backlick Road
> Springfield, VA 22150
> (703) 451-3700

But all the merchandise in the world won't help if you can't figure out how to use it. Fischer's stands out in that department, too, with about fifty employees glad to help you match a single bolt, cut a sheet of glass, thread a pipe, and tell you the part you need to repair your faucet. We've never been in Fischer's without being approached at least a half-dozen times by employees asking if they can help. "It's service-oriented," says manager James Bowe, a statement we can absolutely confirm.

In the neighborhood: Fischer's is in the Concord Shopping Center, home to **Woodcraft**, a wonderful shop that sells woodworking tools and designs (see chapter 13, Potpourri).

THE GARDEN patio of this secret garden of a shop would be the perfect place for Peter Rabbit to hide from the fictional Mrs. McGregor. It's hidden on the side of a strip center, but the lower-level patio comes alive with flowers and plants during the spring.

This shop was recommended to us as a "must include" by a few people who love owner (and former tax lawyer) Nancy Schuhmann's personal taste

> **MRS. MCGREGOR'S GARDEN SHOP**
> 4801 First Street North
> Arlington, VA 22203
> (703) 528-8773

in garden urns, flats of annuals, plants, and gifts. At Christmas, the live plants are gone, but the shop comes alive with ornaments and decorations.

Mrs. McGregor, of course, was the farmer's wife in Beatrix Potter's *The Tale of Peter Rabbit*. Sadly, when Nancy chose the clever name for her shop, she didn't remember that Mrs. McGregor had made a pie out of Peter's father.

In the neighborhood: In the Arlington Forest Shopping Center next to **Country Curtains**. An **Outback Steakhouse** is also in the center.

~~~

'TWAS JUST before Christmas and all through the house, the children were wondering: *What's he building down there?* The answer was hidden behind the do-not-open basement door: a Ping-Pong table—store-bought, assembly required. Predictably, we were missing one hex bolt, one lock nut, and two washers. What to do? If we'd lived near Bethesda, we'd have gone to Strosnider's, that's what.

> **STROSNIDER'S**
> 6930 Arlington Road
> Bethesda, MD 20814
> (301) 654-5688
> www.strosniders.com

There are ordinary hardware stores, there are big-box stores (Lowe's and Home Depot), and there's Strosniders. The difference between the last two can be appreciated by anyone who's needed a single screw or bolt in a specific size, only to find that you have to buy a plastic bag with screws half a size up, or down, or improvise altogether, if you go the Home Depot route (as we did with the Ping-Pong table). Not to denigrate the big orange store too much; it's come in handy many times in our years of homeownership. But that's largely because there's not a Strosnider's anywhere near our home. Not a Fischer's, either (see entry in this chapter).

Strosnider's is the place to go when you need a plastic shelf support—just one—for your faux Scandinavian bookcase left over from your newlywed days. It's where you'll find Baldwin doorknobs, door knockers, and doorbells. Need kitchen utensils? Strosnider's sells a line of heat-resistant spatulas by Cuispro that more than rival anything put out by Cuisinart. Holiday decorations? Check. Tools—power and manual? Check. Plumbing supplies? You bet. Paint, varnish, stain . . . and fireplace accessories, shelf paper, cleaning supplies. One reason why Strosnider's has such good variety is because it's an

Ace hardware store *and* a True Value store. It's been around so long (since 1953) that it's retained purchasing power from both of these co-ops.

In less cosmopolitan cities, a shop like Strosnider's would be standard fare, but locally owned hardware stores have had a tough time competing with the giant home improvement chains in Washington. And a giant hardware store like this, well, that's a real find.

Other locations: 10110 River Road, Potomac, MD, (301) 299-6333; 815 Wayne Avenue, Silver Spring, MD (301) 565-9150.

In the neighborhood: In the Bradley Shopping Center, right next to the impressive **Bruce Variety Store**. You might have to wait to get a parking space, but it'll be worth it.

IT'S A frigid cold day and you're cranky. You almost don't make it through the maddening intersection at traffic-clogged Seven Corners, and then, when you park, the wind practically knocks everything out of your hands. But, as you enter this unassuming-looking store plunked on an access road off Route 50, you start feeling much, much better. Come on in—the air smells of pine and cinnamon, and you can warm your hands by one of the many crackling fireplaces.

WOODBURNERS TWO
6600 Arlington Boulevard
Falls Church, VA 22042
(703) 241-1400
www.woodburnerstwo.com

This is Woodburners Two, which began as a small store during the energy crisis in 1979, when people were buying wood stoves so they didn't have to rely on fossil fuel. Now it's the place to furnish your new home with a state-of-the-art and very efficient direct-vent gas fireplace.

Partners Margaret Laurenson and Judy Miller have moved three times to expand and accommodate their large selection of everything fireplace-related. Freestanding wood stoves are still part of their inventory, but gas fireplaces, and gas inserts for existing fireplaces, are the more popular items. You see, unlike wood-burning fireplaces, which tend to suck the heat right up your chimney, gas ones heat the home and work during power outages. The store also stocks some electric fireplaces, which are more decorative than utilitarian, although some have built-in heaters.

Of course, the store still has all the tools for fans of wood-burning stoves, including fire-tending sets with pokers and shovels, decorative containers to hold fire starters, and sacks of Magical Color Cones to make your fire change color. Mantles—either the one-piece shelf type that you install on the wall, or the full-size, fireplace-framing jobs—are also for sale. We priced a pretty oak finished wall mantle for $410—plus $175 for installation—but you can install it yourself if you have the right tools.

Woodburners Two also sells weathervanes for your roof and garden, nifty house numbers and plaques, and incense that smells like burning logs.

Also Noteworthy:

PARK PLACE
2251 Wisconsin Avenue NW
Washington, DC 20007
(202) 342-6294

The park benches outside and plants in the window will lure you into this enchanting store full of planters, sundials, birdbaths, and everything else for the garden and patio. Park in the free lot in the rear.

RESTORATION HARDWARE
1222 Wisconsin Avenue NW
Washington, DC 20007
(202) 625-2771
www.restorationhardware.com

Don't expect much actual hardware from this national chain store, which sells Mission-style furniture, garden goods, cleaning products, and a few paint colors. The selection of drawer handles and hinges is great. We love the Precision Pop-Up Tool Set, and the screwdriver with six interchangeable heads has been our favorite since we bought it here several years ago. But to call this a "hardware" store is pushing it.

Other Locations: 614 King Street, Alexandria, (703) 299-6220, and Tyson's Corner Center, (703) 821-9655.

SMITH & HAWKEN
1209 31st Street NW
Washington, DC 20007
(202) 965-2680
www.smithandhawken.com

National chain selling everything for the garden from plants to patio tables and chairs. The prices are on the high side, but so is the quality. We asked local garden/home shop owners where they prefer to buy tools for their personal gardens, and they all named Smith & Hawken.

Other Locations: 8551 Connecticut Avenue, Chevy Chase, (301) 215-5960; 6705 Whittier Avenue, McLean, (703) 506-0065.

HOME FURNISHINGS AND ACCESSORIES

HAND-CARVED wooden furniture from Ghana, Kenya, and Nigeria, huge African drums, and handwoven kente cloths are just a few of the imports from Africa at this large, beautifully decorated store in Prince George's Plaza. But it was the African clothing, made of brightly colored, woven fabrics, that really drew us in as we navigated the jean and T-shirt stores that surround it.

It was that clothing that inspired owners Robert and Agnes Duker to begin selling imported goods from Africa. Friends in the United States admired the bold prints and beautiful embroidered clothing the Dukers brought back from Africa (they are from Ghana), so the delightful couple began selling them on a small scale. Eventually Robert began supplying small local shops with goods from African nations, and the next logical step was to open a store. Named after two of the Dukers' four children, Starmanda and Georgina, the African Stargina Collections store was born in 1988.

> **AFRICAN STARGINA COLLECTIONS**
> Prince George's Plaza
> 3500 East-West Highway
> Hyattsville, MD 20782
> (301) 559-8418

Many items might not be familiar to Americans, so the Dukers sell several decorative charts explaining African symbols or how a kente cloth is woven. Besides the hand-carved furniture, there are soapstone sculptures from Kenya, wooden animal pieces, handwoven silk thread pictures for the walls, leather goods, and handmade baskets. Among our favorites are the hand-crafted veneer-framed art pieces—wooden pictures made of different-colored pieces and shapes of wood inlaid to form a picture of an animal, house, or landscape.

The variety and uniqueness of these pieces has helped African Stargina Collections count among its clients professors from Howard and Temple universities. University of Maryland students might recognize furnishings from the store in the Nyumburu Cultural Center on campus.

In the neighborhood: Located in Prince George's Plaza, across from **Karibu Books** and many great clothing stores.

TWO CHIHUAHUAS, a cat, and a cockatiel are often on hand to greet visitors to this impeccably arranged, fun shop on Capitol Hill's Eighth Street. Specializing in Mexican folk art, the store also has handpicked furniture from more than ten different countries, jewelry (some unisex), leather accessories, and a unique selection of Day of the Dead figurines. They range from Freddy, a life-size one ($700), to smaller figures, including feathered yellow and red decorative roosters—a symbol of wealth and prosperity in Mexico.

> ALVEAR STUDIO DESIGN
> AND IMPORTS
> 705 Eighth Street SE
> Washington, DC 20003
> (202) 546-8434
> www.alvearstudio.com

Alvear was open even before D.C. invested $8 million in the Eighth Street renovation project. Its owners, designers Chris Alvear and Francisco Pliego, take such pride in the neighborhood that they host a margarita party every second Saturday from 6:30 to 10 p.m.

In the neighborhood: Walk the length of Eighth Street to find boutiques, gifts, bikes, restaurants, and **Backstage Inc.**, which is one of our Top Ten.

IF YOU think Georgetown has become nothing but a maze of chain stores, head to the part that starts at Pennsylvania and M and you'll find a bunch of terrific and unique local shops, among them, American Studio. Focusing on American contemporary design, American Studio has lots of colorful and contemporary ceramics and glassware: vases, bowls, glasses, and pitchers.

> AMERICAN STUDIO
> 2906 M Street NW
> Washington DC 20007
> (202) 965-3273

But it also has some unique furniture that blends style and art, including, on one visit, a Frank Gehry corrugated cardboard rocker reissue from the 1980s priced at $650 and a Hermon Futrell twig chair. Other nonvessel items included an AEJ lamp, the shade depicting a scene of New York City, and trendy UFO lamps by Pennsylvania artist Daniel Sadler.

In the neighborhood: Frank Milwee Antiques and Fine Art, 2912 M Street, carries a fabulous collection of antique corkscrews that you don't want to miss. **Grafix,** 2904 M Street, is fun if you like art deco posters and magazine covers from the '20s onward.

~~~~~

SHARYN AND Jay Winer turned their hobby of visiting unique American art galleries during family vacations into a family business when they opened the first Artcraft store in historic Savage Mill, Maryland, in 1992. The result is an enticing spectacle of colorful armoires, whimsical accessories, high-quality wood cutting boards, and small cabinets painted and cut in the shapes of famous people such as Mark Twain. This store made our Top Ten list (see chapter 2).

> **ARTCRAFT COLLECTION**
> 132 King Street
> Alexandria, VA 22314
> (703) 299-6816
> www.artcraftcollection.com

Other locations: 8600 Foundry Street, Savage Mill, MD 20763, (410) 880-4863; Reston Town Center, 11960 Market Street, Reston, VA 20190, (703) 964-0145.

~~~~~

JUST AS we were starting to think of shopping as a tedious activity, we happened upon the artfully arranged Chinoiserie. Our first impression was, "modern," but as we progressed through the store's three small rooms, we thought, "Asian." After puzzling a bit, we broke down and talked to Peter Zia, a former architect and the owner of this pristine store. Turns out, according to *Merriam-Webster,* Chinoiserie means "a style in art (as in decoration) reflecting Chinese qualities or motifs; also an object or decoration in this style."

> **CHINOISERIE**
> 1024 King Street
> Alexandria, VA 22314
> (703) 838-0520

Zia grew up in Taiwan but moved to the United States in time to attend high school in Baltimore. "He has great taste," another store owner said of Zia. It's obvious he is particular about what he carries; every item is displayed so carefully you feel you could be in a gallery. Large white cubicles contain one item each—a decorative vase, a modern lampshade by Mibo, a set of colorful tumblers. Black, red, and white lacquered wrapping paper

($4.50 per sheet) becomes a work of art hanging from wooden dowels, and greeting cards, displayed in see-through cubicles, become wall art.

The centerpiece is a table set with Asian tableware—boat-shaped serving dishes and whimsical children's cups containing "training chopsticks." A colorful mobile ($90) hangs in the corner.

Good design, quality, and price are the three factors Zia considers when he chooses his merchandise. The few pieces of furniture he carries are vintage, although most look brand new because of their high quality—and new would be prohibitively expensive for his market. Chinoiserie also carries personal accessories such as watches.

In the neighborhood: There's the historic and tidy section of King Street in Old Town (see **Artcraft** and the **Torpedo Factory**), closer to the Potomac, and there's the formerly funky but increasingly stylish part as you get west of Washington Street. **Chinoiserie** is in the latter section. Both sections are worthy of exploration, window-shopping, and lunch, though you might want to break up your outing into two separate days.

TORPEDO FACTORY ART CENTER
105 N. Union Street
Alexandria, VA 22314
(703) 838-4565
www.torpedofactory.org

The Torpedo Factory, on the Potomac River in Old Town Alexandria, is one of the most successful visual arts centers in the United States, attracting approximately 800,000 visitors annually. Originally a working torpedo factory operational after World War I and during World War II, the building was used as a government storage facility until the City of Alexandria and its citizens took over and renovated it. More than 165 artists in eighty-four studios create pottery, jewelry, paintings, sculpture, and other visual art, often working while the public browses.

Besides the three levels of galleries, stalls, and studios, two torpedos on display attract visitors as well. The torpedo in the main hall was actually made at the factory in 1945; it was painted bright green so the Navy could find it in the water during testing, and a logbook in the exhibit case lists the submarines it was on. The other torpedo, this one silver, was not produced at the Alexandria facility.

> Open daily from 10 a.m. to 5 p.m. except Christmas, New Year's Day, Easter, Independence Day, and Thanksgiving.
>
> *Parking Note*: While street parking is available in most areas of Alexandria, it can be tough to find and is restricted to two or three hours. Metered parking is limited to two hours. A free twenty-four-hour parking pass, valid at two-hour meters only (not two-hour signs), is available at the Ramsay House Visitor's Center (open daily from 9–5) at 221 King Street. It can be renewed once.

~~~~

THE NAME of this ultrafun gift and home store alone makes it darn near impossible to resist. Plus, it's in the popular U Street area (though this shop is on 14th Street). Go Mama Go is full of Asian dinnerware, chopsticks, red and yellow decorative chickens, and floor-lamp-high candleholders.

> **GO MAMA GO**
> 1809 14th Street NW
> Washington, DC 20009
> (202) 299-0850

In the neighborhood: The 14th Street area is a great place to begin an afternoon of fun in the U Street corridor—a neighborhood once known as the "Black Broadway" before the 1968 riots and now undergoing a renaissance. The New York–style **Home Rule** is next door to Go Mama Go. **Love Café**, the sit-down arm of lawyer-baker Warren Brown's renowned **CakeLove** bakery (across the street from the café), is a block up at 1506 U Street. Head the other way on U to try a half-smoke or chili at **Ben's Chili Bowl**, 1213 U Street, where you may run into anyone from Mayor Anthony Williams (he'd be the guy in the bow tie) to Bill Cosby.

~~~~

CHECK OUT the "Swinging London Batchelor Pad": an Eames orange chair coupled with a '60s "Tulip" cocktail table by Knoll and a '40s modern orange and black floor lamp. Pick up a set of vintage tiki glasses, a walking robot waiter, or just the paper napkins and calendars by artist Shag. Good Eye is *the* place for hip, retro, and colorful furniture/home accessories from the era of Maxwell Smart. The inventory changes rapidly, so visit the Website to see what's new (see chapter 2, Top Ten Stores).

> **GOOD EYE**
> 4918 Wisconsin Avenue NW
> Washington, DC 20016
> (202) 244-8516
> www.goodeyeonline.com

Home and Garden

A BARGAIN hunter's paradise, Old Luckett's Store has three large stories full of wares from more than twenty dealers who sell their antiques, tableware, soaps, and whatnots at rock-bottom prices. We've never been big fans of antiques, yet we have personally bought framed pictures, a marble cutting board, some vintage china, and countless other things at this fun store chock-full of finds. Hordes of people line up "all the way back to the shed" to get in during the once-a-year Groundhog Day sale (see full description in chapter 2, Top Ten Stores).

> **OLD LUCKETT'S STORE**
> 42350 Lucketts Road
> (Route 15)
> Leesburg, VA 20176
> (703) 779-0268
> www.luckettstore.com

In the neighborhood: If you're coming from Virginia, you'll pass through **Leesburg**, so stop in the historic downtown for some antiquing.

IT WAS done with lamps and classical music. How else could a big old paint store with a tin ceiling become this cozy-feeling gift shop, perfect for those seeking something old or new or different? Owner Ann Donahue has been going to auctions and other sources since Reunions opened in 1988, and she has a knack for finding the perfect blend of unique new jewelry, ribbons, lamps, and antique furniture and china.

> **REUNIONS**
> 1709 Centre Plaza
> Alexandria, VA 22302
> (703) 931-8161

Reunions doesn't have a central theme—Ann relies on her personal taste when looking for high-quality items and good lines. Although the store, in Alexandria's Fairlington neighborhood, has a Virginia address, it is deceptively close to DC via I-395. It stocks items in virtually any price range, so those desperate for a gift know they can always find something: baked bean-shape earrings for $13.95, a colorful necklace by a local artist for a bit over $100, and a set of old Abbey Limoges china for $1,150.

Vera Bradley bags and bolts of ribbon make for an attractive display, while formally packaged graphite objects shaped like feathers make good novelty gifts. Nineteenth-century, high-end sterling silver serving pieces and mahogany and walnut furniture top off the order. Reunions attracts both older women and younger ones looking for inspiration.

In the neighborhood: Reunions is in Alexandria's Fairlington neighborhood, off Quaker Lane. If you enjoy cracking crabs with a wooden mallet while seated at paper-lined tables—you're not a Washingtonian if you haven't tried it—check out **Ernie's Crab House**, just around the corner. If you don't want to go to that much trouble, get your seafood at **Simply Fish** or **Ramparts**.

~~~

BEAUTIFUL GALLERY/GIFt shop filled with high-end imported treasures, mostly from Africa. After you take in the masks, African currency, cloths, and brightly colored caftans, be sure to check out the fascinating selection of African-American documents hanging on the wall. We were impressed with a framed and mounted postcard signed by poet Langston Hughes, who lived in the area briefly in 1925. Too good to pass up (so we bought it): a framed 1940s-era photo of a very young Miles Davis.

> **ZAWADI**
> 1524 U Street NW
> Washington DC 20009
> (202) 232-2214

In the neighborhood: There is a wealth of great stores in the U Street around 14th (see the "In the neighborhood" for Go Mama Go, above, for the rest). If you're in the market for clothing, check out the selection of vintage duds at **Meeps**, the shoes at **Wild Women Wear Red**, and the attire and accessories at **Nana**. Cross the street for beautiful clothing and conversation at **Trade Secrets** and books at **Sisterspace**, upstairs.

Also Noteworthy:

FRENCH COUNTRY LIVING
10135 Colvin Run Road
Great Falls, VA 22066
(703) 759-2245
www.frenchcountry.com

The owners of this large, freestanding store make semiannual trips to Paris and the provinces to bring you the best selection of French Country furnishings and accessories. French Country Living has a national reputation (and a great catalog) and is worth an excursion to Great Falls, even if you don't live in the immediate area. You can get anything from a dining room set to table linens, rugs ceramics, and the wooden, animal-shaped Christmas ornaments we bought last year.

BACK DOOR
Lee Harrison Shopping Center
2499 N. Harrison Street
Arlington, VA 22207
(703) 237-6117
www.thebackdoorinc.com

This unusual consignment shop sells mostly new merchandise from designers and decorators at substantial savings. Items are still pricey, but if you're there at the right time, you can get a real deal, especially on expensive fabric.

In the neighborhood: On the bottom floor of the Lee Harrison Shopping Center in Arlington; enter in the middle of the center and head down the stairs. Check out some vintage and designer clothes at **Boutique Unique** across the hall, and if you have young ones, go to **Aladdin's Lamp Bookstore**.

SIXTEEN FIFTY-NINE
1659 Wisconsin Avenue NW
Washington, DC 20007
(202) 333-1480

Fans of mid-century modern furniture will love this Georgetown shop full of neutral high-end and mid-price pieces. Before you buy that brand-new, $3,000 end table, scope out this store. We saw a 1950s Baker piece for $575 and some terrific accessories for $20 on up. Owner Mike Johnson scours the Midwest (that is, Illinois and Iowa) for most of his vintage pieces

UPSCALE RESALE
8100 Lee Highway
Falls Church, VA 22042
(703) 698-8100
www.upscale-resale.com

Stop by this twenty-eight-thousand-square-foot consignment furniture store often to look for bargains. Some inventory changes every two or three weeks, with everything from dining room sets to upholstered chairs, tables, and lamps.

POTTERY, GLASSWARE, AND CHINA

WE WERE poor newlyweds in 1980, when we treated ourselves to a hand-painted Italian chicken water pitcher from the Williams-Sonoma catalog. (This was before Williams-Sonoma popped up in every mall in America.) We've seen a lot of chicken pitchers since then but never as many as we found at A Mano on upper Wisconsin Avenue in Georgetown. "A mano" means "handmade," and every item in this nest of cozy rooms is just that. Never have we seen so many brightly colored, hand-painted Italian and French ceramic dishes, lamps, and table linens. Frequent buying trips to Europe yield the best Italian and French bistro-style ceramic tabletops, garden urns, and glassware available in Washington.

> **A MANO**
> 1677 Wisconsin Avenue NW
> Washington, DC 20007
> (202) 298-7200

During the warm months, plants grow and fountains splash in an outdoor garden area. Indoors, the exposed beams of the upstairs ceiling, chocolate brown walls, and gurgling sound from an inside fountain create the perfect mood for viewing folding French wine-tasting tables from the eighteenth century, nineteenth-century French mirrors, and twenty-first-century French farm chairs.

In addition to the intricately painted Quimper plates and Deruto French pottery, A Mano has other hand blown glassware, including some stunning pastel handblown glasses that we would be afraid to use but loved looking at. A Mano is also one of very few stores to carry William Yeoward bone china and crystal.

Pieces from the Palio tablewear collection are big sellers here. Each piece bears a "mascot" representing one of the seventeen *contrade* (districts) in Sienna: giraffes, dragons, panthers, and fourteen other creatures.

A Mano is also a source for handmade lamps and other glassware by Vermont glassmaker Simon Pearce. Yes, they slipped an American in there.

In the neighborhood: A Mano is up the Wisconsin Avenue hill (at Reservoir) in Georgetown. Nearby shops include **Sugar** boutique and **Sherman Pickey** preppie clothing and antique shops such as **Gore Dean**.

SEVERAL PEOPLE told us they head straight for the small gray house adorned with decorative ceramic plates on Wilson Boulevand just west of

Home and Garden 109

Ballston when they want a wedding present, a gift for a special occasion, or a personal treat. Since 1979, a four-partner team of women has been creating hand-thrown ceramic cups, plates, bowls, lamps, and much more at Grey House Potters.

> **GREY HOUSE POTTERS**
> 5509 Wilson Boulevard North
> Arlington, VA 22205
> (703) 522-7738

Actually, eight potters have their wares on display. The four partners (the members have changed just a little bit over the past twenty-odd years) rotate jobs every month—bookkeeping, mailings, housekeeping, and public relations—and four others rent space from the partners.

Prices here are very reasonable: a beautiful green leaf cheese plate or ten-inch-wide bowl for $40, decorative baby and wedding plates—custom-printed with names and dates—from $35 to $55, and a handmade ceramic lamp for $155.

In the neighborhood: That Grey House stands alone, amongst other houses along Wilson, is very much part of its charm. The Ballston shopping district is just a few driving blocks up the street.

Also Noteworthy:

MY PLACE IN TUSCANY
1127 King Street
Alexandria, VA 22314
(703) 683-8882
www.myplaceintuscany.com

This charming shop carries beautiful hand-molded, hand-painted Italian ceramics, ranging from dinnerware to large urns and garden fountains. It also has some original Italian paintings.

In the neighborhood: This little area of Old Town is chock-full of international delights for the home. Head up the block for hand-painted French ceramics from **Quimper Faïence**, 1121 King Street, (703) 519-8339, and imported French sheets from **Yves Delorme**.

LINENS AND FABRICS

WHAT DOES a University of Maryland poly-sci major from a small town outside of Cincinnati do when she gets tired of her job at the State Department? She opens a high-end linen shop in Georgetown, of course! She sells a carved wooden canopy bed to Oprah Winfrey, who (while visiting D.C.) stops by the store to thank her personally. She buys her own building in Georgetown. She adopts a stray dog and is featured in a book about dog rescue. Could the Nobel Prize be next for Lisa Mullins Thompson, proprietor of Baldaquin, a shop specializing in bed and bath linens and tableware?

> **BALDAQUIN**
> 1413 Wisconsin Avenue NW
> Washington, DC 20007
> (202) 625-1600
> www.baldaquin.com

It truly was her job at the State Department that inspired Thompson to open the store. Her travels abroad exposed her to beautiful linens made in Europe. In 1996, after researching the market, she took out a loan and opened a tiny shop specializing in high-end, unique European linens in Georgetown. Within two years, she moved her store to its current, substantially larger location on Wisconsin Avenue.

Besides selling bedding (sheets, duvet covers, bed skirts, etc.) with a thread count that goes up to 1020—prices range from about $120 to about $700 per sheet—Baldaquin has high-end towels; table linens and bathrobes by D. Porthault, Palais Royal, Anichini, and Sferra Bros.; formal china and flatware; silver; and bath fragrances and toiletries from D.R. Harris & Co., Bigelow Chemists Ltd., Acca Kappa, and L'Authentique.

McCoy, the aforementioned stray dog, a nine-year-old yellow lab, can often be found by the cash register when not on his mid-day trek (with a walker) through Georgetown. Like Thompson, he has achieved a degree of recognition. Check him out in a book about rescue dogs, called *Second Chances*, by Elise Lufkin and Diana Walker.

≈≈≈

WHEN WE asked the bearded salesman in the Orioles cap if he was the owner of Kugler's Home Fashions, he simply said, "I work here." And work he does, carefully choosing the twenty-five-thousand-plus linens, housewares, and pillows stuffed into this jam-packed alternative to Bed Bath & Beyond. Sam Kugler—warming to us after he realized that not only weren't we a pair of wackos with a scam, but that we were customers, too—offers a New York–style mix of higher-end bedroom furnishings sold at full retail price, interspersed with terrific bargains.

> **KUGLER'S HOME FASHIONS**
> 20 University Boulevard East
> Silver Spring, MD 20902
> (301) 593-8805
> www.kuglers.com

Take the six-hundred-thread count, 100 percent cotton sateen, queen-size sheets we got for $49 a set—"the best bargain in here," Kugler assured us. A week later, we were shopping at a bargain store closer to home and saw those same sheets for 69.99, which was still a bargain for the luxuriant fabric—but not as good as Kugler's.

The store's narrow aisles—a friend tell us it reminds her of shops in her native Brooklyn—are filled with a terrific selection of gift items and picture frames, loads of cooking gadgets, and every kind of linen and accessory you could ever want for your bathroom. A preferred dealer for Hunter Douglas blinds, Kugler's discounts them from 30 to 74 percent, depending on the blind.

Kugler's also sells some paper products for 99 cents a pack—impressive, because the seasonal goods are actually sold during the correct season. Sam has massive sales the day after Thanksgiving and during the months of July and August.

Important note: Kugler's is not open on Saturdays.

WHEN AN out-of-town guest wanted to see if she could find some quilt fabric that wasn't available at home, we immediately knew a trip to G Street Fabrics was in order. So, after doing the tourist thing at the Museum of Natural History (great mammal exhibit), a group of us headed for Potomac Mills, thinking there'd be plenty of time for fabric shopping, outlet mall shopping, and maybe even Ikea shopping across the street.

> **G STREET FABRICS**
> Potomac Mills
> 2700 Potomac Mills Circle
> Woodbridge, VA 22192
> (703) 494-5900
> www.gstreetfabrics.com

Fat chance. We spent over an hour in the cotton print section alone, marveling at the patterns. They're grouped by color, with different hues of yellow merging into yellow prints and so on. Bolder cottons occupy side aisles. Our home decorator friend spent the majority of her time in the upholstery remnant area, purchasing one large remnant for a floorcloth and another for a tablecloth. (We just received a report that the floorcloth has transformed her dreary third-floor finished attic into a place of beauty.)

The pattern area fascinated us next. Sitting next to the drawers of Simplicity, Vogue, and McCalls were patterns by tiny companies, usually a specialty outfit reflecting a certain era. For example, Past Patterns features authentic reproductions of patterns of ladies' fashions at the turn of the century, while Folkwear makes patterns for folk outfits. Patterns for tunics and other non-western clothing are abundant.

Just when we thought it was safe to hit the rest of the mall, we discovered the bargain area. An employee was so helpful that, even when it was time for her to go, she hunted us down in the back of the store to let us know she was leaving—but that our fabric was cut and waiting at the front register. Two and a half hours after entering, we left. It was dark outside, and the outlet mall was forgotten.

Other locations: 6250 Seven Corners Center, Falls Church, VA, (703) 241-1700; 5077 Westfields Boulevard, Centerville VA, (703) 818-8090; 11854 Rockville Pike, Rockville, MD, (301) 231-8998.

In the neighborhood: G Street Fabrics' Potomac Mills store is in the **Potomac Mills** outlet mall.

Also Noteworthy:

LA CASA BELLA
1213 King Street
Alexandria, VA 22314
(703) 684-1213

Drop by Carmie Giuliano's Old Town shop for embroidered guest towels and sheets as well as other unusual, beautiful, and comfortable soft goods for the bed, bath, and kitchen—fine Italian linens by Sferra Bros. and Dea of Italy, printed tablecloths and placemats by Karen Ballard, and sleepwear by Simple Pleasures, to name a few.

COUNTRY CURTAINS
4805 N. First Street
Arlington, VA 22203
(703) 522-7111
www.countrycurtains.com

This shop version of the popular catalog store has high-quality curtains (and curtain hardware), bedding, and home accessories.

WATERWORKS
3314 M Street NW
Washington, DC 20007
(202) 333-7180

High-end bath store ("bath" as in tubs, fixtures, sinks, tile) carries its own line of very high-quality towels, robes, etc. Beautiful, well-made items and price tags to reflect that.

YVES DELORME
1125 King Street
Alexandria, VA 22314
(703) 549-6660
www.yvesdelorme.com

International chain sells French linens for the bed, bath, and kitchen as well as china, soap, silver, and more.

Other locations: McLean Square Shopping Center, 6651A Old Dominion Drive, McLean, VA, (703) 356-3085.

CHAPTER 9

Electronics and Cameras

CAMERAS AND PHOTO GEAR

We've been lucky enough to work alongside some world-class photographers over the years, and we've done our own stints involving photo research, picture editing, even shooting a cover for a newspaper's Sunday magazine. What we've learned: a camera in the wrong hands can be mighty dangerous. With that in mind, we turned for shopping tips to some terrific Washington professionals who earn their living behind the lens. They know they sometimes get only one chance to get the picture; screw it up with the wrong equipment, and there goes the next assignment—not to mention the front-page or cover picture. They offered advice; we followed up with our own investigative shopping. Here's the close-up.

BIG STORES can offer big discounts, but professional and skilled amateur photographers have gone to Dominion Camera since 1969 for its service and staff expertise—and, yes, its prices. "One of the reasons you need stores like this, whether a hardware store or a small music store or a small

> **DOMINION CAMERA**
> 112 W. Broad Street
> Falls Church, VA 22046
> (703) 532-6700
> www.dominioncamera.com

camera shop, is that if you need a three-eighths-to-one-quarter tripod adapter, they're going to know what the heck you're talking about," says Gary Padgett, Dominion sales manager.

Tripods, adapters, lights, umbrellas and stands, and darkroom supplies fill the space, and a photo lab is in the back. But what's likely to keep you coming back to Dominion is the gear behind the display cases. New cameras, both digital and film, are offered with the array of brands you'd expect, including Nikon, Canon, Minolta, and Pentax. Now that digital single-lens reflex cameras have come down under $1,000, photo hobbyists with high-quality SLRs from the days of film will be able to afford the convenience of digital without giving up the precision of their old SLR lenses. And that could mean another reason to head to Dominion: to check out additional lenses.

The store sells an impressive range of used lenses and has some great deals on used but perfectly good camera bodies. We spotted a 1976 Nikon F2 body in excellent condition for $525 at Dominion. "And it's built like a brick outhouse," said Padgett. "If you're going to be marching through the desert shooting pictures, this is the only camera you'll need." The fifty-something sales manager has been shooting since he was seventeen, but then, everyone working here has been shooting for some time, most at the professional level. That matters when you need advice or when you need a repair, which for many brands and models is done in-house.

If you have a student who needs a good 35mm camera with lens, Dominion can set you up with good used equipment for about $150. On the other hand, if you're an architect looking for a Mamiya large-format camera, we scoped out an awfully nice used one for $958 at Dominion.

In the neighborhood: Dominion is next door to **Brown's Hardware**, a good old-fashioned hardware store that does your heart good just to visit. **Miniatures from the Attic** is around the back; **CD Cellar**, 709 W. Broad Street, is six blocks away. Check out **Crisp & Juicy**, 913 W. Broad Street, for our favorite Peruvian chicken. Pass up the fries and order fried yucca instead—but get extra sauce, preferably mild, so you can dip the yucca as well as the tender, charcoal-cooked chicken.

PENN CAMERA, started in 1953 by Washington's Zweig family, has grown into a six-store operation and is arguably the best-known photography store in the metro area. It is also, photography sources say, one of the best. Part of the reason is inventory: Nikon, Cannon, Minolta, Pentax, Mamiya, even Hasselblad, the Rolls Royce of the large-format photo world. Prices are competitive not only with other stores but with Internet outlets as well, an advantage that comes with size. Film, whether in rolls or sheets, is kept refrigerated. Penn sells lights, tripods, umbrellas, darkroom accessories, everything a photographer could ever need, and its film processing and printing regularly wins prizes for quality.

PENN CAMERA
840 E Street NW
Washington, DC 20004
(202) 347-5777
www.penncamera.com

But what sets Penn apart from others is its extra features. For one, it rents equipment, offering partial refunds if you wind up buying. For traveling photographers, being able to rent lighting saves a lot of time and hassle, especially at the airport.

Second, Penn's staff knows its stuff—because you don't get hired at Penn if you haven't worked in photography, and you're going to be quizzed to prove it. In turn, customers rely on Penn to learn how to use bounce flash and filters, and how to get rid of whatever problem is preventing them from shooting that Pulitzer Prize-winning photo. "It's real personal," says Jim Barr of Arlington, a serious amateur who's taken pictures around the world and estimates he has spent $10,000 at Penn over the last dozen years. "Most of the people have been working here for years."

Finally, but perhaps most significant: Penn, like Dominion, also sells used gear. For high-end photography, whether film or digital, secondhand can mean saving lots of money, especially as you start adding second and third lenses.

"The secret for saving money and getting good stuff is to go for secondhand," advises Jake McGuire, a professional Washington photographer. You've probably seen his photos—the White House, the monuments, Marine One (the presidential helicopter) flying down the National Mall. "Doctors, dentists, lawyers, people with high disposable incomes get this stuff and don't use it, so they turn it back in," he explains. Even McGuire, who knows his stuff, doesn't buy new if he needs an extra lens or camera. "I buy one at half-price that some oncologist never used."

Other locations: 1015 18th Street NW, Washington DC; 8357-E Leesburg Pike, Vienna, VA; 6699-D Frontier Drive, Springfield, VA; 352 Domer Avenue, Laurel, MD; 12266-F Rockville Pike, Rockville, MD.

In the neighborhood: Chapters A Literary Bookstore is two blocks away (see chapter 6, Books) on 11th Street, as is the **E Street Cinema** on E Street. The FBI is half a block away, and the **International Spy Museum** is nearby as well.

≈≈≈

WALK IN Pro Photo and you'll know right away that the name doesn't lie. An array of heavy-duty camera cases and crates lies near the entrance, along with tripods and monopods. There's a rack of tan Domke Photogs vests—the kind with multiple pockets and pouches for lenses and film—and in a corner are stepladders, which serious shooters use to rise above the crowd and capture the action. Half the stuff sitting around the back of the White House press briefing room must have come from here. Photographers from the *New York Times*, *Washington Post*, *Time*, and *Newsweek* make Pro Photo their personal Washington supplier. Pulitzer Prize winner David Hume Kennerly was among those who told us they sing Pro's praises.

> **PRO PHOTO**
> 1902 Eye Street NW
> Washington, DC 20006
> (202) 223-1292
> www.prophotodc.com

What makes Pro Photo unique is not the gear, however, but the owners, brothers Dick and Sebouh Baghdassarian. Their maternal grandfather used to shoot photos in Ethiopia, and when his daughter married, her husband, Varouge, got involved in the photo business. One day someone needed a camera repaired, so he put his mind to it and figured out how to do it. "He was probably the first one fixing cameras in Ethiopia," Sebouh says of his late father.

Sebouh's brother, Dick, came to the United States some thirty years ago and worked as a repair technician in a camera shop. Sebouh followed, and the two have been in business since 1980—in the same Eye Street building, in fact, though their shop used to be off the lobby rather than street-side.

The guys sell the usual camera brands, including Nikon and Canon, and the German brand, Leica, but it's the fact that they can fix practically anything that makes them popular among professionals and high-end amateurs. Paul Kent, from Chantilly, bought a Canon A1 here in 1981 and it started acting up not long ago. "He put it back together for me," Kent says, referring to Sebouh, "and I expect it to last another twenty years. If he tells me it works, I know it works."

Dennis Brack, a highly regarded pro whose photos grace many a magazine cover—*Time, Newsweek, U.S. News and World Report, Stern, Paris Match*—agrees. "When I have something that needs immediate attention, I give it to Dick or Sebouh and they go to it." They've been "a great help over many years," Brack says.

The shop has an excellent array of used lenses and cameras—we counted twelve Nikons on one visit—displayed with price and descriptive stickers to make it easy to find what you want. While not junky, Pro Photo has the comfortable feel, and the gear, of a store you definitely won't find in a mall. "Our thing is the repeat customer," says Sebouh. "We don't count on just one-time deals."

Preserving Valuable Photos

In a block of century-old row houses populated by law firms and advocacy groups, just beyond the Eastern Market on Capitol Hill, is a gem of a place for anyone with heirloom photos or important pictures worth preserving. **Asman Custom Photo,** 924 Pennsylvania Avenue SE (202) 547-7713, was founded in 1961 by former *Life* magazine photographer George Asman, who saw the need for a processor and printer for photographers and picture owners who care deeply about their photos. It's a premier place to take valuable black and white family pictures, or new portraits, and have them remade on fiber-based paper—which can last one hundred-plus years. Unlike the resin-coated paper on which most prints are made, fiber-based paper is resistant to age and pollutants, says Barry Asman, George's son. Restoration work is done by hand in an old-fashioned darkroom, with dodging, burning, and cropping to bring out details and, if necessary, to hide flaws in the original. What you'll get is top-of-the-line, archival quality—the same kind that the Library of Congress, one of Asman's main clients, counts on. Asman is not open on weekends.

STEREOS AND TELEVISIONS

Audio-video is a tough category because, frankly, the big chains serve 99 percent of the market well. Stores such as Best Buy, Circuit City, or locally, Belmont TV, have competitive prices and selections that suit most tastes and budgets. And for those who can afford home theaters, high-end chains like Myer-Emco and Tweeter do fine. They're so good, in fact, that it's tough for small, home-grown retailers to compete. Yet several very good ones do. Here's how.

IF THE world were your oyster and great choices abounded—and they do—why would you possibly wind up at DéjaVu, a little shop in McLean that purposely limits its inventory and whose display space looks like an apartment living room? Tubes, that's why. This little gem of a shop sells only amplifiers powered by vacuum tubes, those old-fashioned (though thoroughly state-of-the-art), glass-encased, glowing components that audio purists swear by. You won't find a transistor in any amp on the premises.

> **DÉJA VU AUDIO LTD.**
> 1401 Chain Bridge Road,
> Suite 203
> McLean, VA 22101
> (703) 734-9391
> www.dejavuaudio.com

DéjaVu sells high-end CD players, very cool turntables, and speakers, too, but owner Vu Hoang won't sell you those unless you have a very good amp. You wouldn't buy racing tires if your engine couldn't deliver the performance, would you?

It'll cost you at least $1,000 for the amp alone—a simple but wonderful-sounding Italian model—and can cost you multiples of that if you want. Hoang—a University of Maryland-trained medical doctor whose postgraduate love of tubes changed his life and livelihood—has been known to turn unworthy customers away, no matter how deep their pockets.

He wants you to love the sound. He'll have you sit and listen, and if you're not knocked out, well, you don't deserve to buy here anyway. Don't act all audiophile-like, either; one guy buying a pair of speakers wanted to know how many watts they put out. Audio lesson #1: Speakers don't deliver watts; their output is measured in decibels. Besides, a good pair will put out more than your ears can stand anyway. (As will a great tube amp with as little as a few watts of power; tell *that* to your friends bragging about their 300-watt stereos.)

Anyway, Hoang told the customer to leave, and he wasn't joking. The fine speakers would have been lost on this guy, who left the store utterly confused—and speakerless.

In the neighborhood: Moorenko's Ice Cream Café, 1359 Chain Bridge Road, is next door to DéjaVu and serves super-premium flavors made on the premises. Practically across the street is **Langley Shopping Center,** worthy of a side trip to visit **Tree Top Toys, The Artisans** gift shop, and, if you like vinegar-flavored Carolina barbecue, **Three Pigs Restaurant.** Make sure you check out the wonderful candy wrappers at the **Russian Gourmet,** also in this shopping center.

JOE STROMICK makes no bones about it. Many of his customers want the best because they've earned it, and—hey, why make excuses—they can afford it. Some people buy a Honda, some a Lexus, and some the biggest, baddest truck, he says, giving an analogy. J S is where you go if you're that leather-seat Lexus or big-ass truck guy. Not that they don't appreciate the difference between a woofer, tweeter, crossover, preamp, or any of the components they take home from J S; to the contrary, this is a stereo lover's store, and a certain National Public Radio host is among J S's patrons.

> **J S AUDIO**
> 4919 Saint Elmo Avenue
> Bethesda, MD 20814
> (301) 656-7020
> www.jsaudio.com

Stereo systems start at $5,000, but if you need just a single component, you can save a grand or two, even more if the component was previously owned and the customer traded up. (Don't say "used." Mercedes and Lexus don't, and neither does J S.) But you also could spend $100,000 on a stereo; a killer set of Dynaudio speakers alone can set you back $30,000, and a top-of-the-line home theater comes in at $150,000. (It's fun for us to throw around these figures; hey, it's not our money you're spending.)

Like several other high-end electronic boutiques, J S showcases home theater and stereo setups in different rooms. That way, you can experience the sound and feel of watching or listing in your den. If your den has rustic but impeccably crafted wood furniture and rugs—Stromick is big on cherry—so much the better, because J S does. He's attracted customers from all over the country and followed up by going to some of their homes to install their new toys. "We know their kids, their dogs, and their cats," he says.

You can spend a lot less and get a terrific system at any number of local or chain stores. As Stromick himself says, the Honda's a perfectly good car. (We agree, and own one; we're also serious music listeners and have gotten by fine without shopping at this kind of audio boutique, though we are developing a serious case of audio envy.) And J S certainly has no monopoly on high-end gear, like McIntosh amplifiers, Sony plasma screen televisions, and JVC video.

But J S won us over because its equipment and selection are awfully fine, and Stromick makes it kind of fun. Unlike a nearby store that we entered while a sale was taking place and were ignored—as was another customer who might have had serious cash in his pocket—we walked into J S unannounced, as we always do, and said we were just looking. We were promptly invited to look around and, if we had any questions, to ask. Service and attitude matter.

In the Neighborhood: Southworth Guitars (see chapter 5, Music); **Hinata**, a small but very good Japanese grocery and sushi bar at 4947 St. Elmo Avenue, and **Francevision**, 4930 St. Elmo Avenue—a unique video/DVD rental store that specializes in French films and music. It bills itself as the largest source for French videos and music in the United States.

~~~

> **SOUND IMAGES**
> 6541 Arlington Boulevard
> Falls Church, VA 22042
> (703) 534-1733
> www.soundimagesusa.com

SOMETHING TELLS us that Sound Images would prefer that we focus on its new audio products, its home theater systems, and its installation and service. Yeah, yeah, yeah, we'll get to that. But we weren't born yesterday, so we have a keen appreciation for stereo components that weren't made today. If you grew up in an age when a Marantz receiver was the standard, a pair of cream-grill-cloth Advent speakers meant something special, and an old Crown tube amp stirred your soul, Sound Images is for you, too.

The used gear, also sold through eBay, is kept on shelves toward the back of this store on Route 50, west of Seven Corners. You'll find old two-track reel-to-reel tape recorders; collectibles like a KLH model Eleven turntable with speeds of 78, 45, 33, and 16; and even, depending on your timing, a 1928 Victorola with a supply of extra needles. (One needle only lasts for about twenty plays.) There's also some contemporary equipment obtained in trade, like a pair of JM Labs speakers for $600.

Now on to the new stuff: brands including harman/kardon, TAGMcLaren Audio, NAD, Musical Fidelity, Legacy, and Cambridge Audio. Home theaters. Six listening/viewing rooms, plus three more theater setups in the open areas. JM Lab Berrilyium speakers that list for $20,000 a pair, though a salesman lets on that you can probably snag them for $16,000. Gadgets and gizmos that let you run video in one room, watch stereo in another, and practically brew your coffee in a third.

Don't believe it? Well, just listen to this: "The crystal DSP along with AMK Sigma-Delta high resolution analog-to-digital and digital-to-analog converters are evidence of the superior ingredients used to complete the package." We got that from a piece of sales literature that customers at Sound

Images read, and while we think it means "this sounds really, really good," the Sound Images staff will be glad to give you a more precise definition.

Though the sky's the limit, Sound Images can get you into a home theater setup for about $5,000 to start. But like its competition, this store (which also has a location in Bethesda, but that one didn't impress) also uses the car analogy. Except that sales associate Geoffrey Davis didn't mention Lexus, Mercedes, or Honda. He cited Volvo versus Chevrolet, although to his credit he spoke of used—oops, we mean preowned—vehicles. We get the point: Sound Images is the Volvo of the audio/stereo world. For the record, our other car is a Nissan.

In the neighborhood: This is a driving-only destination, as you must pull off and on busy Arlington Blvd.—Route 50—to get anywhere else. **Loehmann's**, 7241 Arlington Boulevard, (703) 573-1510, is nearby if you're in the mood for clothes shopping, and it's a quick drive to an assortment of destinations in Falls Church.

COMPUTERS

You use computers, we use computers, and among the bunch of us we all know how and where to get a great deal. (Just ask the Dell dude.) Nevertheless, we had some great recommendations for independent computer stores—only trouble is they all went out of business. As one of our sources, a technician at a McIntosh repair facility, told us, name-brand PCs are so inexpensive today, single-owner stores can't make them any cheaper or better.

Still, we can recommend a few favorite computer retailers.

NEED AN extra computer for your kids? Want a computer but don't have the money? Have we got a deal for you. You *can* afford something at the Computer Warehouse, a used-computer store specializing in business-class computers and related equipment. This store usually sells computers cheaper than the best deals on eBay. Prices are low because the owner of Computer Warehouse recovers computers in bulk from companies that have gone out of business or are upgrading. A team of people then removes everything but the operating

COMPUTER WAREHOUSE
Tysons Station Shopping Center
7516 Leesburg Pike
Falls Church, VA 22043
(703) 821-1800
www.pcretro.com/webstore

system (that is, Windows), tests them thoroughly, and sells them to you at bargain prices.

The Dell we are writing this book on is a used model; we bought it at Computer Warehouse a couple of years ago. We do have a brand new, state-of-the-art Dell downstairs, too, and an old HP Pavilion in the other room, but with two kids, and two parents who are writers, we just plain can't have enough computers. (We also have blue wires strung about the house because we can't figure out how to use a wireless networking device with all this disparate hardware, but don't tell that to the computer experts.)

We're reluctant to give you exact prices from Computer Warehouse because they fluctuate daily. Even in the world of new computers, things change so fast that by the time this book is published, the prices will be different. But suffice it to say that today's $99 special is a Dell GX1 Pentium 2 (400 Mhz) loaded with Windows 98 and including a seventeen-inch CRT (monitor), keyboard, mouse, with 128mb RAM and a 4.0-6.0GB hard drive, CD-ROM, etc. Of course, for a bit more, you can get a larger hard drive and add more RAM, but for an extra home computer used mostly to surf the WEB, you can't beat that price.

Computer Warehouse carries computers of all kinds: Macs, IBMs, HPs, Dells, whatever the owner is able to buy. It has big bargains on high-end PCs, too, and notebook computers, which seem to be the hottest item. The store is always filled with customers, some of whom seem to show up weekly to check for the latest bargains. Most computers are warranted for ninety days after purchase.

In the neighborhood: Pick up a container of healthy frozen enchiladas, a bottle of wine, and some chocolate-covered toffee at **Trader Joe's** next door, so you don't have to cook while you're setting up the "new" computer. The shopping center is also the home of **Metro Run & Walk**, a good source of shoes and clothing for runners.

MICRO CENTER
Pan Am Plaza
3089 Nutley Street
Fairfax, VA 22031
(703) 204-8400
www.microcenter.com

COMPUTER EQUIPMENT has become so commonplace, we can pick up an inkjet for the printer or some blank CDs at the supermarket. But if we want anything else, we usually go to this Ohio-based computer megastore; the Fairfax location is one of only twenty in the chain.

Micro Center is always crowded—a melting pot of computer geeks, computer neophytes, and everyone in between. Not only does it sell entire computer systems (PCs and Macs), printers, and the like, but also digital cameras, speakers, scanners, PDAs, and, of course, a very good selection of software.

Bargains at Micro Center are almost legendary. We have a friend who prides himself on getting stuff practically free after rebates, especially blank CDs, if he shops wisely, and our son has gotten many dirt-cheap computer games from the store's Bargain Bin. Although they aren't sold at the same bargain prices, Micro Center has been expanding to carry video games for game consoles—Nintendo, PS2, and Xbox.

Personally, we shop at this store frequently, not for computers, but for hard drives, extra memory, wires, and software. Customer service is not always what we would like it to be—particularly for "big ticket" items—but we nevertheless consider it the best computer store around. It also has a large selection of computer books and magazines and in-store repair service.

In the neighborhood: Micro Center is in the Pan Am Shopping Center at the corner of Nutley Street and Lee Highway, close to the Vienna Metro (but not really within comfortable walking distance if you're carrying computer boxes). Have a fish taco loaded with guacamole and pico de gallo at **Baja Fresh** Mexican restaurant at the other end of the shopping center or buy some craft supplies at **Michael's** next door or oil paints at **Plaza Artist Materials**.

PC RETRO, specializing in recovered equipment from dot-coms, office closures, upgrades and relocations, charges rock-bottom prices. (Same ownership as Computer Warehouse, above, different name and location.)

PC RETRO
5031 Garrett Avenue
Beltsville, MD 20705
(301) 931-6630
www.pcretro.com/webstore

HIGH-VOLUME COMPUTER DEALERS

These stores are parts of chains with multiple locations and sell the brands you already know. At any given time they might have a sale. Most are good for peripherals, too, and CompUSA keeps a nice assortment of software.

APPLE STORE
Market Common at Clarendon
2700 Clarendon Boulevard
Arlington, VA 22201
(703) 875-9880

Tysons Corner
1961 Chain Bridge Road
McLean, VA 22102
(703) 893-5055

Westfield Shoppingtown Montgomery
7101 Democracy Boulevard
Bethesda, MD 20817
(301) 299-0723
www.apple.com/retail

COMP USA
5901 Stevenson Avenue
Alexandria, VA 22304
(703) 212-6610

Fair Lakes Promenade
12189 Fair Lakes Parkway
Fairfax, VA 22033
(703) 359-1401

500 Perry Parkway
Gaithersburg, MD 20877
(301) 947-0001

1776 E. Jefferson Street, #203
Rockville, MD 20852
(301) 816-8963

8357 Leesburg Pike
Vienna, VA 22180
(703) 821-7700

14427 Potomac Mills Road
Woodbridge, VA 22192
(703) 492-6262
www.compusa.com

CHAPTER 10

Health and Beauty

COSMETICS, PERFUMES, AND BEAUTY SUPPLIES

This chapter gave us fits. There's a reason the big chain stores are so successful—they're good at what they do. You almost can't beat Nordstrom's cosmetics department or the selection of high-end makeup at Neiman-Marcus. And Washington has all the specialty chains, too, from glitzy **Sephora** (our favorite), to discount **Sally Beauty Supply**. Check the malls for stores such as **L'Occitane, Crabtree & Evelyn, Caswell-Massey,** and other national/international chains. But first, check out the following stores, some for hard-to-find, high-end products, others for price. You'll feel good *and* look good.

STOP BY this elegant boutique specializing in high-end bath, body, skin care, hair care, and cosmetic lines if you have some beauty or skin care problems or concerns. Owners Kim Putens and Angela Sitilides and their employees promise to do their best to help you, and to tell you the truth if they can't.

BELLACARA
924 King Street
Alexandria, VA 22314
(703) 299-9652
www.bellacara.com

Sitilides, a former attorney, and Putens, a former lobbyist, opened their shop in March 2000 to bring to Northern Virginia the hottest lines in beauty and skin care products, and knowing their customers is the main priority. Bellacara carries some brands that are hard to find outside this area, such as bath and body products by Kai, lip gloss products by la Balmba, and more accessible brands such as Tocca and Bumble and bumble. Children will love Oinkment moisturizer or Hog Wash body wash by Little Piggy, and there are even some grooming products for men—assuming can get your man to use them.

THIS CLINICAL-LOOKING shop in Georgetown carries high-end skin products by companies such as Kiehl's and Dermalogica, hair care by Phytotherathrie and Bumble and bumble, bath and body products, fragrances, makeup, and scented candles. Makeup divas will want to be on the alert for special events, such as expert lessons for using Paula Dorf, NARS, or Laura Mercier products. Bluemercury also has a full spa offering facials, microdermabrasion treatments, and hot rock massages.

BLUEMERCURY
3059 M Street NW
Washington, DC 20007
(202) 965-1300
www.bluemercury.com

Other location: 1745 Connecticut Avenue NW (Dupont Circle), Washington DC, (202) 462-1300.

In the neighborhood: The area surrounding the Georgetown store is a beauty product bonanza. **MAC** and **Sephora** are in the same block, and **Lush** (see below) is across the street. If you need a purse, buy the real thing at **Kate Spade**, next door.

THE SOAPS, shampoos, and bath and body products at Lush are so organic, or at least so "natural," you aren't sure whether to put them on your body or eat them for lunch. Well, that might be stretching it, but this shop actually has a salad barlike area—instead of lettuce and cucumbers, the bowls are filled with "Volcano Foot Mask" and "More than Mortal" body

LUSH
3066 M Street NW
Washington DC 20007
(202) 333-6950
www.lush.com

scrub ready for you to dish up and buy by the container. Or follow the lead of Jennifer Love Hewitt and Victoria Wood and try some "Strawberry Boat," a skin cream made of water, ground rice, almond oil, fresh strawberries, sea salt, fresh ginger root, and a few other things.

Lush is an international chain that recently entered the U.S. market with a handful of stores. The Georgetown one seems to be perpetually jam-packed with folks buying soap cut from large chunks or specially shaped facial cleansers like Sweet Japanese Girl facial massage bar, in the shape of a girl's head. Most impressive are the solid shampoos cut in little bars that you rub on your head and the huge balls of colorful bath soap, just cuz they were pretty.

In the neighborhood: See entry for Bluemercury, above.

NATIONAL CHAIN featuring a wide selection of fragrances and beauty products for men and women at discount prices. Located in several malls:

PERFUMANIA
www.perfumania.com

FASHION CENTRE AT PENTAGON CITY
1100 S. Hayes Street
Arlington VA 22202
(703) 418-0877

POTOMAC MILLS
2700 Potomac Mills Circle, Suite #134
Prince William, VA 22192
(703) 497-4773

WHAT EXACTLY is Rodman's? A discount drugstore with gourmet food? A "variety" store with everything? A real Washington institution, the area's "original discounter of nationally branded products" (Rodman's words) has been family-owned and -operated since 1955.

Rodman's sells toothpaste and contact lens solution, vitamins, and nutritional supplements, right along with high-end European soap and body care products.

RODMAN'S
5100 Wisconsin Avenue NW
Washington, DC 20016
(202) 363-3466
www.rodmans.com

Oddly enough, the D.C. store also has fresh produce, mops, lightbulbs, sponges, wine, and small appliances as well as a pharmacy. We like Rodman's not only for the health and beauty products, but also for the deeply discounted gourmet food items. We've found Lindt chocolate bars (one of our weaknesses) on sale here for the best price we've ever seen.

Other locations: 4301 Randolph Road, Silver Spring, MD, (301) 946-3100; 5148 Nicholson Lane, Rockville, MD, (301) 881-6253.

≈≈

> **UNIVERSAL BEAUTY SUPPLY**
> 1055 W. Broad Street
> Falls Church, VA 22046
> (703) 534-8882

THIS SMALL shop in Falls Church sells fragrances from 10 to 50 percent off retail prices, depending on the brand. For more than fifteen years, it has sold and discounted cosmetics; professional-level electrical products such as straighteners; brushes; and salon-style shampoos such as Bedhead, Paul Mitchell, and Matrix.

Stabler-Leadbetter Apothecary Shop Museum Store

105–107 S. Fairfax Street
Alexandria, VA 22314
(703) 836-3713

Health care professionals and history buffs will love a gift from this museum shop that sells pharmacy and medical-related antiques. It once was a pharmacy that dispensed medicine to James Monroe and Robert E Lee. Now it sells pharmacy antiques: old medicine and poison bottles from the 1800s, for $5 on up, and antique surgeon's knives that can cost as much as $2,000. Books include old editions full of "recipes" for medicines and potions of the past. The museum store also has some new items; for the right person, "infectious wearables" boxer shorts and ties might make hilarious gifts.

VITAMINS, NUTRITIONAL SUPPLEMENTS, AND ORGANIC PRODUCE

BETHESDA CO-OP
6500 Seven Locks Road
Bethesda, MD 20818
(301) 320-2530

Anyone can shop here, but members get a discount. Membership is $50 per year, or you can work at the store, instead.

CO-OP SUPERMARKET
121 Centerway
Greenbelt, MD 20770
(301) 474-0522

Good for all your health food needs. Join for a one-time fee of $10.

EVERLASTING LIFE
Hampton Mall
9185 Central Avenue
Capitol Heights, MD 20743
(301) 324-6900

2928 Georgia Avenue NW
Washington, DC 20001
(202) 232-1700
www.everlastinglife.net

Both locations have healthy vegetarian food products and "The Juice Bar" restaurants. The facility in Capitol Heights is bigger, and is said to be the only African-American owned health food complex in the Washington, D.C., area. It includes a supermarket, restaurant, banquet hall, entertainment center, and bakery, and offers cooking and exercise (yoga, belly dancing) classes, and much more.

GENERAL NUTRITION CENTERS
www.gnc.com

An international health food/vitamin megachain with over five thousand outlets in the United States and twenty-nine foreign markets, GNC started in 1935 as a little shop in Pittsburgh, called Lackzoom, which sold an unusual product: yogurt.

MY ORGANIC MARKET
3831 Mount Vernon Avenue
Alexandria, VA 22305
(703) 535-5980

9827 Rhode Island Avenue
College Park, MD 20740
(301) 220-1100

11711 Parklawn Drive
Rockville, MD 20852
(301) 816-4944

Specializes in organic produce and other natural food products.

NATURALLY YOURS
2029 P Street NW
Washington, DC 20036
(202) 429-1718

Vitamin and health food store in the Dupont Circle neighborhood. Stop by Second Story Books while you're in the area.

SECRETS OF NATURE
3923 S. Capitol Street SW
Washington, DC 20032
(202) 562-0041

Sells vitamins, minerals, herbs, and healthy food items and has a restaurant on the premises.

TAKOMA PARK-SILVER SPRING FOOD CO-OP
201 Ethan Allen Avenue
Takoma Park, MD 20912
(301) 891-2667

8309 Grubb Road
Silver Spring, MD 20910
(240) 247-2667
www.tpss.org

Offers a large selection of groceries, fresh produce, cheeses, coffee, homeopathic and herbal remedies, and natural health and beauty aids. You don't have to join to shop, but a $100 refundable member fee entitles you to discounts.

THE VITAMIN SHOPPE
www.thevitaminshoppe.com

What started in 1977 as a single store in New York is now a national chain of more than two hundred stores offering over twenty-five thousand items from more than three hundred brand names—at discount prices. Besides its own Vitamin Shoppe brand, it carries common brands such as Country Life, Gary Null, Solgar, and Atkins, and hard-to-find ones, such as Nutricology, AMNI, Cardiovascular Research, and American Biologics. Check the Web site or yellow pages for local locations.

WHEATON HEALTH FOODS INC
2656 University Boulevard West
Wheaton, MD 20902
(301) 933-3066

First to introduce health food to the D.C. area, this store has been around for almost forty years. It has all your health food needs, including over four hundred low-carb products.

WHOLE FOODS MARKET
www.wholefoods.com

This is a national chain with a great selection of organic produce, herbs, vitamin and nutritional products, and natural cosmetics. See the Web site or check the yellow pages for locations nearest you.

YES! NATURAL GOURMET
1825 Columbia Road NW
Washington, DC 20009
(202) 462-5150

YES! ORGANIC MARKET
3425 Connecticut Avenue NW
Washington, DC 20008
(202) 363-1559

Yes, it's been popular in the area for a long time and has a deli and juice bar, too.

CHAPTER 11

Bargains

DISCOUNTS, CLOSEOUTS, AND OFF-PRICE STORES

WE'D BEEN wanting to try babka, a coffee cake-like creation, ever since episode seventy-seven of Seinfeld. You remember, don't you? Jerry and Elaine are forced to buy a cinnamon babka for their dinner party hosts because the last chocolate one was sold to a customer who was in front of them in line—in front of them, that is, only because they neglected to take a number. Amazing Savings doesn't sell babka, but if you visit this closeout store, you can pick one up at the kosher bakery nearby (which is partly why this is a "find"; the adventure is part of the trip).

AMAZING SAVINGS
4816 Boiling Brook Parkway
Rockville, MD 20852
(301) 770-9022

Located in a funky old shopping center hidden behind a short row of furniture stores, Amazing Savings offers great bargains on cookware and stemware, toys, cosmetics, and paper products, including party goods and gift wrap. Unlike many discount stores, Amazing Savings is relatively clean and well-organized—at least, on most of our visits. Nice giftware, such as cake plates and pretty glass containers, was in abundance on our most recent visit, but we opted for a seven-piece knife set, a bottle of name-brand foundation makeup and concealer, a pack of thumbtacks, and a set of marking pens—all for less than $10. Then we faced a dilemma: chocolate or cinnamon babka?

In the neighborhood: If you don't live in the Rockville area, it's fun to make a pilgrimage to this neighborhood. The Randolph Hills Center, home to Amazing Savings, also holds a resale shop; an Israeli gift store; Bolivian, Indian, and glatt kosher Chinese restaurants (yes, kosher Chinese); and **Kosher Mart/Katz's**, a large kosher grocery store and deli (the babka is in the bakery). **White Flint Mall** is close by, as is Loehmann's on Randolph Road. If you haven't filled up on babka yet, don't miss **eatZi's**, an incredible market where gourmet and prepared entrées, salads, pastas, sandwiches, and baked goods can be consumed on premises or taken home (see chapter 2, Top Ten Stores). Also noteworthy is **Rodman's**, at 5148 Nicholson Lane in the White Flint Plaza.

~~~

LIKE FINDING hidden treasure, this discount luggage store was one of those surprises we happened upon after striking out at a discount video store—because the videos turned out to be mostly of the "adult" variety. Maybe that's why The Complement seemed like such a wholesome discovery.

> **THE COMPLEMENT**
> 656 S. Pickett Street
> Alexandria, VA 22304
> (703) 751-5600

The Complement is a family-run business specializing in deeply discounted luggage, handbags, briefcases, and other travel goods. The Alexandria store has a large variety of brands, including Samsonite, Kenneth Cole, Targus, and Geoffrey Bean, many at 60 to 70 percent off retail. The Complement also carries backpacks, purses by leather companies such as Frye (impressive for their quality), wallets, cosmetics cases, computer cases, trunks, carts, and car-top luggage carriers.

Other Locations: 888 17th Street. & I N.W, Washington, DC, (202) 785-9111; White Flint Plaza, 5148 Nicholson Lane, Rockville, MD, (301) 770-2700.

In the neighborhood: The Alexandria store is in a small industrial area close to **Landmark Mall**, and there are plenty of restaurants nearby.

~~~

A SMALL chain with stores mostly in Manhattan, Daffy's motto is "Clothing Bargains for Millionaires." If you're a bargain hunter looking for very fashionable merchandise, Daffy's is a must.

Daffy's offers deep, deep discounts on high-end designer apparel and accessories for men, women, and children. Sometimes Daffy's fashions are a bit too trendy for the ordinary shopper, which may explain its claim that its prices are up to 80 percent off regular retail. It's a claim we can confirm, as the female member of our team bought one of her very favorite dresses here, a traditional, black velveteen spandex number, for $25.

> **DAFFY'S**
> 2700 Potomac Mills Circle
> Woodbridge, VA 22192
> (703) 494-3636
> www.daffys.com

Daffy's usually has some nonclothing items—we got a French country-style butter dish for $6.50 and wish we had bought more of that discontinued collection. Too late now.

In the neighborhood: Daffy's is in the **Potomac Mills** outlet mall.

~~~

SUITS AND formal wear aren't the only big bargains at K & G. This warehouse-like, no-frills store offers one of the best selections of discounted quality men's clothing in the metro area. Some of the lapels and patterns did not appeal to our conservative tastes, but a navy Chaps worsted designer suit originally priced at $400 certainly did—especially since it was going for $159.

Don't need a suit? How about a leather briefcase for $35, or a day planner, or a portfolio? We've bought attractive casual sweaters here for as low as $8.95, and shoes, dress shirts, ties, coats, and winter clothing are also heavily discounted, especially toward the end of the season. The staff is helpful but not overbearing—no one hovers.

> **K & G MENS MART**
> Bailey's Crossroads
> Shopping Center
> 5832 Columbia Pike
> Falls Church, VA 22041
> (703) 931-1124
> www.kgmens.com

Other Location: 4955 Nicholson Court, Rockville, MD, (301) 231-8140.

In the neighborhood: The Falls Church store is in Bailey's Crossroads Shopping Center, near a **Trader Joe's** supermarket, **Petco** pet store, and **Pier One Imports**.

~~~

WE HATE to write about mall stores, but Nordstrom Rack is a true treasure trove. The Rack boasts that it sells "quality basics to designer fashions." While we've personally not had much luck in the women's and children's clothing departments, the Rack's shirts and ties rule, if your tastes run to pinpoint cotton and colorful Italian.

> **NORDSTROM RACK**
> Potomac Mills
> 2700 Potomac Mills Circle
> Woodbridge, VA 22192
> (703) 490-1440

This also is a great place to buy purses, costume jewelry, and bath items. Discounts on name-brand cosmetics such as Neutrogena or Caboodles are super, and the store offers a wide and heavily discounted selection of makeup brushes and travel bags, bath salts, and candles. And the Rack gets the leftovers from the retail stores' near-legendary shoe department.

Other location: 15760 Shady Grove Road, Gaithersburg, MD, (301) 527-1133.

~~~

ONE OF us has been a fan of Value City, an Ohio chain, since 1975, when we had to buy a new wardrobe on a college student's budget. The other one got hooked more recently, when he received a luxuriously heavy black Pierre Cardin leather jacket—a gift purchased at one of the store's legendary closeout sales for $59.

> **VALUE CITY**
> Iverson Mall
> 3701 Branch Avenue
> Hillcrest Heights, MD 20748
> (301) 899-5101
> www.valuecity.com

The store has brand-name shoes, clothing, items for the home, and toys, usually at rock-bottom prices. It attracts a melting pot of shoppers; people of every race, religion, social, and economic class flock to Value City during its killer sales. We ran into a prominent judge's wife sheepishly shopping for area rugs at a Value City once, and a friend bought her Laura Ashley bedroom set there for a fraction of what she would have paid even at an outlet store.

Of course, like any closeout store, Value City can be hit or miss, so you've got to be willing to take a chance—and if you miss, to come back again. But watching the newspaper ads for notice of a recent bankruptcy buyout can really pay off. We recently bought our son two hockey shirts for $25 apiece and saw the same items in a sports store a few days later for $75. And one of us is still wearing the shoes she bought there in 1980.

Other Location: 6252 Greenbelt Road, Greenbelt, MD, (301) 441-9588.

In the neighborhood: The Value City in Hillcrest Heights is in **Iverson Mall**, which has many clothing and shoe stores, including **Young World**, a good place to buy school uniforms and name-brand clothing for infants and children at great prices.

CONSIGNMENT BOUTIQUES

We have it on good authority that prominent Washington women flock to certain consignment shops before the annual White House Correspondents Association Dinner and other big affairs. That's not surprising, since it's not uncommon to find a Chanel dress, Hermès scarf, or little Gucci bag on consignment somewhere in the metro area. We once found a designer-label wool wrap that had never been worn because the owner realized too late that she was too short to wear it well. Even "used" designer items are not "cheap," but you can get some real finds at these stores if you know what to look for and luck out. Happy hunting!

ENCORE
110 S. Union Street
Alexandria, VA 22314
(703) 683-1756

ENCORE RESALE DRESS SHOP
3715 Macomb Street NW
Washington, DC 20016
(202) 966-8122

INGA'S ONCE IS NOT ENOUGH
4830 MacArthur Boulevard NW
Washington, DC 20007
(202) 337-3072

NEW TO YOU
125 N. Washington Street
Falls Church, VA 22046
(703) 533-1251
www.newtoyou.net

THE RITZ BOUTIQUE
5014 Nicholson Lane
Rockville, MD 20852
(301) 230-2167
www.ritzconsignment.com

SECOND CHANCE
7702 Woodmont Avenue, #205
Bethesda, MD 20814
(301) 652-6606

SECONDI INC.
1702 Connecticut Avenue NW
Washington, DC 20009
(202) 667-1122

Also Noteworthy:

Metro D.C. is full of the large, off-price clothing stores. **Filene's Basement** (www.filenesbasement.com), **Loehmann's** (www.loehmanns.com), **Marshalls** (www.marshallsonline.com), **T.J. Maxx** (www.tjmaxx.com), **Burlington Coat Factory** (www.coat.com), **Ross** (www.rossstores.com), **Syms** (www.syms.com), and **Steinmart** (www.steinmart.com) all have stores in the area. **A.J. Wright**, owned by the same company that owns T.J. Maxx and Marshalls, is located in Woodbridge.

If you're looking for bargains other than clothing, check out **National Wholesale Liquidators** (www.nationalwholesaleliquidators.com), a cavernous discount department store packed full of furniture, appliances, candy, food, pictures, and clothing, with several locations in D.C. and Maryland. **Big Lots** (www.biglots.com), a national closeout chain, has both name-brand and off-brand merchandise.

On the upscale end, the national chain, **Tuesday Morning** (www.tuesdaymorning.com), offers deep discounts on high-end, name-brand fine crystal, china, decorative accessories, and toys and has stores throughout the region.

CHAPTER 12

Sporting Goods

Washingtonians are a fit bunch. If you need proof, check out the joggers on the National Mall most weekdays at noon, the crowds flocking to health clubs throughout the city and suburbs most evenings, and the bikers, runners, and skaters on the paths in Northern Virginia and Rock Creek Park on most warm weekends. Retailers more than adequately meet their equipment and clothing needs, and many good ones are listed at the end of this chapter. But first, we want to let you in on some of the best niche sporting goods shops around. They happen to be based in the Washington area, but most draw customers from around the world.

A FEW years back, a member of our family bought in-line skates at the Alpine Ski Shop's former Oakton location. They might have been cheaper at one of the sporting goods chains, but no chain store would have taken the care in fitting that we got at this store. The real selling point was Alpine's free in-line lessons in the parking lot on warm weekends. They proved to be an invaluable

> **ALPINE SKI SHOP**
> 45573 Church Road
> Sterling, VA 20164
> (703) 444-7844
> www.alpineskishop.com

part of the skating experience, especially since a forty-something man was learning to use them.

Of course, the store, open since 1971, also carries everything for skiing: skis, ski clothing, hats, sunglasses, you name it. It also has a good selection for in-line hockey players. The snowboard assortment is great, with all the usual brands and accessories by highly rated clothing manufacturers such as 686 and Orage. Summertime enthusiasts can find water skis and wake boards.

Maintenance is a big part of Alpine's service. We bought a pair of used aggressive skates for our son from another store and wanted to replace the wheels and bearings. No problem. Alpine installated the new wheels we bought there and gave us tips for maintaining the skates.

General manager Chris Bunch, whose family owns the store, says customer service is the key to Alpine's three-plus decades of success. Kids in high school who know about skiing get part-time jobs and stay for years, coming back during college breaks. Perhaps that's why people from as far away as Richmond drive to Northern Virginia just to go to Alpine Ski Shop.

Don't forget to check out the store's neat Adirondack chair. Actually made of old skis, it was donated by a customer.

~~~

A GOLFER'S dream shop, Golfdom has everything from basic and high-end clubs to framed poster-size aerial photos of famous golf courses such as Pebble Beach. Even novice golfers (that would be us) are awed by this store. It has an indoor putting green so you can try out the putters and an indoor driving range of sorts to try out drivers.

> **GOLFDOM**
> 8203 Watson Street
> McLean, VA 22102
> (703) 790-8844
> www.golfdom.com

The "Science Center" is designed to help players choose the right club and ball. For a fee (call for details), you get a forty-five-minute "lesson" as a high-tech monitoring device measures the speed of your swing, launch angle, spin rate, ball speed, trajectory, face angle, swing path, tempo, etc. These are toys for the serious golfer—not a free driving range for the kids.

Even nongolfers will admire the large selection sportswear by Tommy Bahama and Tommy Hilfiger. Goldom has such a good selection of both, it's actually worth going there just for clothing, and sometimes there are sales. Join the VIG (Very Important Golfers) membership program ($25 to join, $10 annual renewal fee) and receive a yearly patronage refund (credit of 8 to 10 percent, depending on amount of purchases).

One word of warning: If you don't play golf, you'll want to after you see this place.

In the neighborhood: Golfdom is located in the heart of **Tysons Corner,** an area so congested we try to avoid it at all costs. But this store is so good, it's worth fighting the traffic.

~~~~~

SOME OF the best bargains we've gotten over the years have come from Play It Again Sports, a shop that sells used and new sporting equipment. The used gear is the big draw; people who have outgrown or lost interest in an athletic pursuit bring in their equipment and offer it on consignment. Our son did that when he outgrew a pair of still-good Solomon ST-One aggressive in-line skates, which we bought new for $200. Play It Again Sports sold them for $60, and gave our son 60 percent of the proceeds.

> **PLAY IT AGAIN SPORTS**
> 5750 Union Mill Road
> Clifton, VA 20124
> (703) 266-8677
> www.playitagainsports.com

Meantime, we figured we'd have to spring for a new pair of expensive skates to replace the Solomons. To our eternal gratification, we spotted a barely used pair of Solomons, this time the Aaron Feinberg model, which sold new for up to $300. We bought them for a steal at Play It Again and, even with the cost of replacing the wheels and bearings a short time later, we got a good deal. Our son was elated, too, because these were such good skates, great for rails, grinds, *and* vert. (Hey, you gotta know the lingo.)

There's another terrific deal from Play It Again Sports in our family room: a mint condition Nordic Trak Pro-model skier. This is our second cross country ski trainer, and it's a better model than the first Nordic Trak we bought—which we took back and put on consignment after we spotted and quickly nabbed the second. We didn't pay more than $60 for either one. Play It Again Sports has stopped taking Nordic Traks—the fad apparently has faded—but it still deals in treadmills, exercise bikes, weights and weight-lifting equipment, golf clubs, baseball bats, tennis racquets, hockey gear, and skateboards. We're fairly certain that something will grab our interest again.

Though franchised nationally, each Play It Again Sports location is individually owned.

Other locations: 167 G Jennifer Road, Annapolis, MD, (410) 224-6180; 9150-3 Baltimore National Pike, Ellicott City, MD, (410) 419-9371.

IT'S HARD to know which makes Replay Sports—which has been toying with changing its name to Sport Pros—more appealing: its amazing prices or the truly nice guy, Bob Coffman, who with sons Andy and Chris owns this store in the Bailey's Crossroads neighborhood. Bob says with certainty, "We have the best prices of anybody in the country on tennis racquets." That appears to be true. How about a Wilson Hammer 2 H2, which retails for $240 but was going for $149.87? Or a Head I Prestige, listing at $225 but selling here for $126.87?

> **REPLAY SPORTS**
> Leesburg Pike Plaza
> 3537 S. Jefferson Street
> Falls Church, VA 22041
> (703) 998-4231
> www.tennisracketpros.com

How can an independent store do it? The Coffmans buy in mass—they have four hundred to five hundred racquets at a time, packed five and six deep and lining the walls throughout the store. And they do a ton of business with racquet maker Wilson—so much that they are among the top four Wilson dealers among independent stores in the United States. They get orders from Australia, Germany, England, and Poland and have four custom stringing machines to meet customers' individual needs.

Replay/Sport Pros impresses in a number of other ways, too. It sells new and used golf gear at more-than-competitive prices, with sets of clubs and individual drivers and putters for any age, skill level, and price range. During a sale, our son picked up a used Dunlop titanium-reinforced driver for $5, and because the Coffmans were remodeling and moving out merchandise, they threw in a used 9-iron.

They also sell tennis shoes, footballs, hockey sticks, and baseball gloves—new and used. Hard to believe, isn't it, that anyone would get rid of a good, supple ball glove with a pocket just made to catch? But that person's loss can be your gain.

In the neighborhood: This shop is in the heart of Bailey's Crossroads, in the Leesburg Pike Plaza off Route 7, just east of Columbia Pike. Stop by **Funcoland,** also in the Leesburg Pike Plaza, for video games. The popular Thai restaurants, **Duangrat's** and **Rabieng,** are in the 5800 block of Leesburg Pike.

DON'T MISS this small, freestanding structure dwarfed by towering buildings near Tysons Corner. Just look for the place with a black awning and a parking lot full of SUVs bearing ski racks and "SNO" stickers. Check out the American flag in the window; it's actually made of skis.

> **SKI CHALET**
> 8338 Leesburg Pike
> Tysons Corner, VA 22182
> (703) 761-3040
> www.skichalet.com

Founded in Arlington in 1969, The Ski Chalet is still a locally owned, family business, although now it's actually part of a five-store chain (one of the stores is in Richmond). The first floor of the Tysons location is filled with about thirty brands of ski apparel for men and women. Kids' clothes are in a room of their own. The selection of kids' coats is so good, you could easily make it your coat-buying destination, whether your kid skis or not.

The real heart of the store—the equipment—is in another room up some stairs. Sit in a director's chair for a boot fitting or check out the snowboards in yet another area. In addition to downhill skis, ski boots, bindings, and poles, Ski Chalet carries cross-country equipment and snowshoes. It also rents skis and has a full-service repair shop. During the warmer months, Ski Chalet changes gear, promoting its in-line skate and kayak lines.

Other locations: 2704 Columbia Pike, Arlington, VA, (703) 521-1700; 14130 Sullyfield Circle, Chantilly, VA, (703) 631-7880; 203 Muddy Branch Road, Gaithersburg, MD, (301) 948-5200.

In the neighborhood: Neighboring shops include fly fisherman's paradise **Orvis** (in the center next door; you don't even need to move your car). **Golfdom** (see above) is a short driving distance up Route 7; go east past Route 123/Chain Bridge Road and look on your left.

STOP BY Spokes if you need a break when biking along the W & OD Trail. The store offers clean restrooms, drinking water, air for your tires, and the companionship of others who love cycling. If you don't have a bike, Spokes will rent you one. If yours is broken, Spokes' repair shop can fix it.

> **SPOKES ETC.**
> 224 Maple Avenue East
> Vienna, VA 22180
> (703) 281-2004
> www.spokesetc.com

Spokes has bikes ranging from tricycles to little bikes with training wheels and the best racing bikes available, with brands including Trek, Specialized, Seven, Raleigh, Cannondale, Klein, Lightspeed, Bianchi, and Serotta. The store also has tandems and can arrange for custom-made bicycles for the cyclist looking for the ultimate fit.

Owners Bob Fadel and Jim Strang pride themselves on hiring well-trained people and offering terrific customer service. Several staff members are certified in bicycle fitting, and some of the mechanics have worked on pro cycling teams. Spokes also has clothing, bike racks, helmets, and nutritional supplements such as an energy gel that looks mighty unappetizing; we're assured that it's pretty good. Maybe after you've been riding for a few miles.

Other locations: 1545 N. Quaker Lane, Alexandria, VA, (703) 820-2200; 1506 Belle View Boulevard, Alexandria, VA, (703) 765-8005.

In the neighborhood: If you're done cycling for the day, stop by the **Vienna Inn**, 123 Maple Avenue East, for a beer and chili dog. If it's a night ride, cross Maple to **Jammin Java** for "open mic night" or a café au lait.

~~~

NEVER MIND that it looks like you're entering a warehouse development when you pull into the drive to Springriver. All that space means there are plenty of kayaks, canoes, and exercise equipment. Springriver is a unique and very neat store.

SPRINGRIVER CORP.
5606 Randolph Road
Rockville, MD 20852
(301) 881-5694
www.springriver.com

Started in 1973 during the trampoline craze (the "spring" part of the name), Springriver later abandoned the jumping sport but kept the "river" aspect and managed to stay in business through the winter months by selling exercise bikes, home gyms, rowing machines, treadmills, and other things to keep Washingtonians in shape.

This is one of those stores you can enter without any intention of ever setting foot in a kayak, but by the time you leave you're dying to try it. That's because Bradley Reardon, the owner, hires experienced paddlers—and exercise pros—rather than just anyone who turns in an application. Their appreciation for their sport is infectious. "Kayaking is very specialized, and it takes a lot of knowledge to be able to help somebody get the equipment they should consider," says Don Emery, a Rockville hobbyist who at age fifty-six has proved it's never too late to paddle. "I've had real fine relations with the people who work here."

Whitewater kayaking and canoeing takes skill, and some parts of the Potomac are strictly off-limits to novices, but you can get out on a lake or bay fairly easily—and stay relatively dry. To see if you like it, head to Sandy Point State Park, on the Chesapeake Bay near Annapolis, on the Friday or Saturday of Mother's Day weekend; Springriver lays out its kayaks then for its Sea Kayak Festival and lets you try them. The Annapolis store also has a dock on Spa Creek, ideal for a test paddle.

The Rockville store, with an adjacent canoe and kayak warehouse, the Annapolis store, and the Falls Church store rent canoes and kayaks, though the staff will quiz you first to make sure you have the requisite skill and aren't putting yourself in danger. Part of the rental fee is refunded if you buy. Kayaking is a relatively affordable sport; you can get into it for as little as a few hundred bucks. "We can listen to your needs and get you in a boat that's suited for you pretty well," says Steve Corbett, an avid paddler and Springriver employee.

Other locations: 2757 Summerfield Road, Falls Church, VA, (703) 241-2818; 311 Third Street, Annapolis, MD, (410)263-2303.

In the neighborhood: Close to Rockville Pike, which has practically every chain store known to mankind, and near **Second Story Books** (see chapter 6, Bookstores), the best used book store in the region.

DON'T BE deceived by the name of this full-service tennis store in Arlington. It is not a huge warehouse full of discount tennis racquets and closeout shoes. It *is* a first-rate store that draws local pros and their students to buy racquets, shoes, apparel, and everything tennis—and it has squash, racquetball, and badminton gear to boot.

Wind your way through a maze of boxes (the staff is always unpacking new gear), and you'll find the best selection of racquets (all brands are carried), apparel (fifty manufacturers, many high-end designers), socks, shoes, and even little kids' tennis dresses decorated with butterflies or other embellishments, size four and up.

> **TENNIS FACTORY**
> 2500 Wilson Boulevard,
> Suite 100
> Arlington, VA 22201
> (703) 522-2700
> www.tennisfactory.com

You'll also find employees who can fit you with everything you'll need, from racquets to socks.

We ran into local tennis pro Jason Wnuk at the Tennis Factory. Well, to be honest we accosted him—did he like the store, etc.? Yes, he did, so much that he was willing to give his full endorsement. He loves the store for its variety, accessibility, and fast turnaround on restringing. He sends his students to be fitted for the best racquets, because he trusts the staff. He bought five or six racquets before he left.

Having pounded the pavement for months working on this book (and having a hard-to-fit foot), we were in the market for comfortable shoes. Because we heard that shoe fittings at this store are taken very seriously, we challenged an employee to fit us. What an experience!

Refusing to use a measuring device, she looked at our feet from every angle, made us walk about in our socks while she watched, and came back with three pairs. We ended up with Reeboks ($79), which were the best for us but not the most expensive shoes in the store. The employees at the Tennis Factory want you to know that the customer comes first, and they will sell you the best item—not necessarily the one with the highest price tag.

We could tell you about more things, such as the letter from Singapore written by a customer who makes the Tennis Factory a destination whenever she's in the D.C. area, or that one of the store's founders, Gene Born, is a USRSA Certified Racquet Technician, or that the store was instrumental in bringing the Babolat (now number one) racquet to the United States. Instead, we recommend that if you are into tennis at all, wind your way through the boxes and get the best tennis equipment for the best value.

In the neighborhood: The Tennis Factory is just around the corner from **The Market Commons** outdoor shopping area in Clarendon (see chapter 14, Getting to Great Shopping). Stay on Wilson Boulevard one block and you'll find other small shops, including **Shoe Fly** shoe store.

WASHINGTON GOLF CENTER
2625 S. Shirlington Road
Arlington, VA 22206
(703) 979-7888

DIGNITARIES FROM around the globe, including the Sultan of Brunei, make this Arlington store a destination when they come to the United States. Hillary Rodham Clinton ordered clubs here for Bill when he was president. Open since 1978, Washington Golf is an institution among local golfers, too. While the thirty-thousand-square-foot Arlington location is the most awe-inspiring, all five locations are golf superstores offering brand-name equipment, excellent customer service, and good prices.

It goes without saying that a store of this magnitude is going to have all the brands of clubs, bags, balls, and gear you could ever want. The selection of apparel by Ashworth, Callaway, Tommy Hilfiger, Tommy Bahama, and others alone is enough to fill one store, and the Arlington facility actually contains a "Ladies' Club House," a store by itself.

Frankly, we wondered about the personal attention one could receive in a store this large. But we found a staff of well-trained golf enthusiasts who pride themselves on being the best club fitters around. They also have high-tech equipment, such as the Vector System, to help you choose the right club.

To be brutally honest, we were dubious about the Vector System and challenged Mark Wright, manager of the Chantilly store, to show us how it works. A mini driving range of sorts, the Vector System appears to use a camera, microphone, and fancy computer screen to evaluate your swing. We monitored the screen while Wright hit balls with several different clubs—all identical except for the shaft. After each swing, colorful circles on the computer screen would pop up to show the ball's speed, vertical angle, spin, distance, etc.

The screen also pictures a golf course, like the ones you see in video games. Hitting along a straight line between the two pools of water is the optimal shot. Wright's fifth shot was right on the money, but, of course, he knew that would happen because he was familiar with the club. "No two golf swings are the same," he said. The club he uses would be completely wrong for someone else.

Washington Golf can offer good prices because it does a large volume of business. Being golf novices, we asked what clubs we should buy. Although Washington Golf has clubs such as Honma irons for $3,699—add the woods at $1,530 apiece—we were shown a Jack Nicholas Golden Bear Box Set, complete with woods, irons, stand-bag, and head covers, regularly $299, on sale for $249.99. Some of the stores have a "bargain corner" featuring discontinued items, such as shoes, clothing, and even clubs at a big discount. We found last year's Adidas shoes for 30 percent off and some drivers for as little as half price.

Other locations: 6831 Wisconsin Avenue, Bethesda, MD, (301) OK2-GOLF; 9811 Washingtonian Boulevard, Gaithersburg, MD, (301) 948-

7888; 9709 Lee Highway, Fairfax, VA, (703) 352-7888; 14370 Sullyfield Circle, Chantilly, VA, (703) 631-7444.

In the neighborhood: If billiards is your game, check out **Champion Billiards Sports Café**, 2620 S. Shirlington Road, a spacious sports bar filled with Brunswick tables, TV screens, and some serious pool players. The restaurants of the **Village at Shirlington** (S. 28th and Quincy streets) are nearby, and we highly recommend stopping there for lunch or dessert. You'll find a variety of cuisines, from Mexican to Thai to Spanish to American steaks, seafood, and deli sandwiches, plus a good homegrown brewpub, **Capitol City Brewing Co.** Save room for a scoop with mix-ins at **Maggie Moo's**, a top-rate, premium ice cream parlor.

SELECTED SPECIALTY GOODS BY LOCATION

Golf and Tennis

Washington, D.C.

DRILLING TENNIS & GOLF
1040 17th Street NW
Washington, DC 20036
(202) 737-1100

Maryland

EAST COAST GOLF & TENNIS
10438 Auto Park Drive
Bethesda, MD 20817
(301) 469-7000

WASHINGTON GOLF CENTER
6831 Wisconsin Avenue
Bethesda, MD 20815(301)
(301) OK2-GOLF

9811 Washingtonian Boulevard
Gaithersburg, MD 20878
(301) 948-7888
www.washingtongolf.com

Virginia

GOLFDOM
8203 Watson Street
McLean, VA 22102
(703) 790-8844
www.golfdomgolf.com

REPLAY SPORTS
Leesburg Pike Plaza
3537 S. Jefferson Street
Falls Church, VA 22041
(703) 998-4231

TENNIS FACTORY
2500 Wilson Boulevard, Suite 100
Arlington, VA 22201
(703) 522-2700
www.tennisfactory.com

WASHINGTON GOLF CENTER
2625 S. Shirlington Road
Arlington, VA 22206
(703) 979-7888

9709 Lee Highway
Fairfax, VA 9709
(703) 352-7888

14370 Sullyfield Circle
Chantilly, VA 20151
(703) 631-7444
www.washingtongolf.com

Skates and Skis

Washington, DC

SKI CENTER
49th Street and Massachusetts
  Avenue NW
Washington, DC 20016
(202) 966-4474
www.skicenter.com

Maryland

SKI CHALET
203 Muddy Branch Road
Gaithersburg, MD 20878
(301) 948-5200
www.skichalet.com

Virginia

ALPINE SKI SHOP
45573 W. Church Road
Sterling, VA 20164
(703) 444-7844
www.alpineskishop.com

PRO-FIT SKI & SKATE
545 E. Market Street, #D
Leesburg, VA 20176
(703) 777-7547
www.ski-skate.com

SKI CHALET
8338 Leesburg Pike
Vienna, VA 22182
(703) 761-3040

2704 Columbia Pike
Arlington, VA 22204
(703) 521-1700

14130 Sullyfield Circle
Chantilly, VA 20151
(703) 631-7880
www.skichalet.com

Bikes

Washington, D.C.

BICYCLE PRO SHOP
3403 M Street NW
Washington, DC 20007
(202) 337-0311
www.bicycleproshop.com

BIG WHEEL BIKES
1034 33rd Street NW
Washington, DC 20007
(202) 337-0254
www.bigwheelbikes.com

CAPITOL HILL BIKES
709 Eighth Street SE
Washington, DC 20003
(202) 544-4234

CITY BIKES
2501 Champlain Street NW
Washington, DC 20009
(202) 265-1564
www.citybikes.com

REVOLUTION CYCLES
3411 M Street NW
Washington, DC 20007
(202) 965-3601
www.revolutioncycles.com

Maryland

BICYCLE PLACE INC
8313 Grubb Road
Silver Spring, MD 20910
(301) 588-6160
www.thebicycleplace.com

BIG WHEEL BIKES
6917 Arlington Road
Bethesda, MD 20814
(301) 652-0192
www.bigwheelbikes.com

CITY BIKES
8401 Connecticut Avenue, Suite 111
Chevy Chase, MD 20815
(301) 652-1777
www.citybikes.com

GRIFFIN CYCLE INC
4949 Bethesda Avenue
Bethesda, MD 20814
(301) 656-6188
www.griffincycle.com

Virginia

BIG WHEEL BIKES
3119 Lee Highway
Arlington, VA 22201
(703) 522-1110

2 Prince Street
Alexandria, VA 22314
(703) 739-2300
www.bigwheelbikes.com

BIKES @ VIENNA
128-A Church Street NW
Vienna, VA 22180
(703) 938-8900
www.bikesatvienna.com

REVOLUTION CYCLES
2731 Wilson Boulevard
Arlington, VA 22201
(703) 312-0007
www.revolutioncycles.com

SPOKES ETC.
224 Maple Ave East
Vienna, VA 22180
(703) 281-2004

1506 Belle View Boulevard
Alexandria, VA 22307
(703) 765-8005

1545 N. Quaker Lane
Alexandria, VA 22302
(703) 820-2200
www.spokesetc.com

Running and Walking

Washington, DC

FLEET FEET
1841 Columbia Road NW
Washington, DC 20009
(202) 387-3888
www.fleetfeetdc.com

GEORGETOWN RUNNING CO
3401 M Street NW
Washington, DC 20007
(202) 337-8626
www.dcrunningcompany.com

Maryland

METRO RUN & WALK
1776 E. Jefferson Street
Rockville, MD 20852
(301) 984-2900
www.runwalklive.com

Virginia

METRO RUN & WALK
7516 Leesburg Pike
Falls Church, VA 22043
(703) 790-3338

7251 Commerce Street
Springfield, VA 22150
(703) 913-0313
www.runwalklive.com

PACERS
1301 King Street
Alexandria, Virginia 22314
(703) 836-1463
www.runpacers.com

Camping and Hiking

Washington, DC

HUDSON TRAIL OUTFITTERS LTD.
4530 Wisconsin Avenue NW
Washington, DC 20016
(202) 363-9810
www.hudsontrail.com

Maryland

GALYAN'S
2 Grand Corner Avenue
Gaithersburg, MD 20878
(301) 947-0200
www.galyans.com

HUDSON TRAIL OUTFITTERS LTD
12085 Rockville Pike
Rockville, MD 20852
(301) 881-4955

401 N. Frederick Avenue
Gaithersburg, MD 20879
(301) 948-2474
www.hudsontrail.com

REI-RECREATIONAL EQUIPMENT INC
9801 Rhode Island Avenue
College Park, MD 20740
(301) 982-9681
www.rei.com

SUNNY'S
13718 Washington Boulevard
Laurel MD, 20706
(301) 604-5771
www.sunnyssurplus.com

Virginia

CASUAL ADVENTURE
3451 N. Washington Boulevard
Arlington, VA 22201
(703) 527-0600
www.casualadventure.com

EASTERN MOUNTAIN SPORTS
The Market Common
2800 Clarendon Boulevard
Arlington, VA 22201
(703) 248-8310
www.ems.com

GALYAN'S
12501 Fairlakes Circle
Fairfax, VA 22033
(703) 803-0300
www.galyans.com

HUDSON TRAIL OUTFITTERS LTD
Fair Oaks Mall
11743 Fair Oaks
Fairfax, VA 22033
(703) 385-3907

9488 Arlington Boulevard
Farifax, VA 22031
(703) 591-2950

Pentagon Row
1201 S. Joyce Street
Arlington, VA 22202
(703) 415-4861

Springfield Mall
6701 Loisdale Road
Springfield, VA 22150
(703) 922-0050
www.hudsontrail.com

PLAY IT AGAIN SPORTS
5750 Union Mill Road
Clifton, VA 20124
(703) 266-8677
www.playitagainsports.com

REI–RECREATIONAL EQUIPMENT INC.
3509 Carlin Springs Road
Falls Church, VA 22041
(703) 379-9400

11950 Grand Commons Avenue
Fairfax, VA 22030
(571) 522-6568
www.rei.com

SUNNY'S
370 S. Pickett Street
Alexandria, VA 22304
(703) 461-0088

11650 Sudley Manor Drive
Manassas VA 20110
(703) 257-7069
www.sunnyssurplus.com

CHAPTER 13

Potpourri

SHOPS SO GOOD, WE HAD TO FIND A PLACE TO TELL YOU

To be included in this chapter is a real honor. These shops didn't fit into any of our categories, but we felt they were so good, we had to find a place for them. Or you could say this is our cop-out chapter, full of the stuff we didn't know what to do with. Either way you look at it, these stores are worth a look.

IF YOU'RE looking for art supplies—sketch pads, oil or acrylic paints, brushes, easels, beautiful papers, journals, cute, colored notebooks—you'll find it's worthwhile to put up with Georgetown's traffic and parking so you can shop at the three-story Art Store, which has serious sales regularly. Although part of a twelve-shop chain, The Art Store's Georgetown location is the only one on the East Coast outside of New York and Boston. Even those with no artistic ability get excited over the

> **THE ART STORE**
> 3019 M Street NW
> Washington, DC 20007
> (202) 342-7030

shelves piled high with paper, the rows of paints, and the bins of pencils, kneadable erasers, and drawing pads.

This store has more paper than we've seen anywhere, with a terrific color selection of business and social stationery near the front. But the great array of artists' paper, arranged by type, weight, and size, is on the twenty or so shelves in the back. Printed sheets of paper suitable for gift wrap and heavier artistic paper hang on wooden rod racks.

The Art Store's second floor is almost exclusively dedicated to paints—oil, acrylic, watercolor—brushes, and the like. Pencils and some basic fun art media, such as Sculpey polymer clay products, are on the third floor.

Okay, so they have a lot of art stuff, but the real deal is the sale prices. We've found a tackle box-like supply container on sale for under $10 here; we've paid $20 for an identical one elsewhere. A deluxe studio easel with a manufacturer's suggested price of $449.95 was on sale for $189.98, while a tabletop box easel with a $79.95 price tag was on sale for $39.98. Even if you can't draw a stick figure, The Art Store will impress.

In the neighborhood: Since you're here anyway, you may as well stick around and window-shop in **Georgetown.** It's almost impossible to make only one store your destination anyway. Across M Street you'll find the **Georgetown Frame Shoppe,** with an enchanting collection of animation cels and limited edition lithographs from Chagall, Miró, and Warhol. Speaking of art, **Grafix** offers magazine covers designed when covers *were* art, from vintage copies of *Esquire* to the *New Yorker*. **Movie Madness,** full of posters in the basement at 1083 Thomas Jefferson Street NW, is a fun diversion for movie buffs. And, of course, there's **Bartleby's,** a first-rate antiquarian book seller (see chapter 6, Bookstores).

~~~~~

JOHN LOW had been a film student, actor, ski bum, stand-up comedian, and drive-time DJ for the Steamboat Springs, Colorado, country and western radio station (he hates country music), when he became a stockbroker so successful he won his firm's national sales award three years in a row. Then he quit it all to open banning+Low, a gallery selling vintage political paraphernalia, posters, photographs, and old campaign buttons.

BANNING+LOW
3730 Howard Avenue
Kensington, MD 20895
(301) 933-0700
www.banningandlow.com

The shop became a reality after Low's father and partner, Jack Banning, closed a photo and art gallery in Manhattan but still had inventory. A great space on Antique Row in Kensington, in an old building across from the train station, suited Low's vision for a venue that could double as a place to sell goods and a twenty-first-century salon where people meet, talk, and exchange ideas.

Sit on the cozy sofa among the framed, vintage political posters (many of them real works of art) and pet the two snoring French bulldogs that often accompany Low to work. Many of his posters are from the Vietnam era, a time when artistic people were wild with ideas for graphic expression. The "Silent Majority 1970" poster shows a crowd of people wearing identical Nixon masks. "Unconditional and Universal Amnesty" features a royal blue rifle sitting vaselike, with bright red daisies coming out of the barrel. "Fly Far Fareastern Airways this Vacation: Visit Beautiful Vietnam" features a drawing of GIs crawling through the jungle clutching their rifles.

Photo exhibits change frequently. On one visit we saw out-of-print promotional photos (issued during the launch of the Macintosh computer) of John and Yoko, Gandhi, and other iconoclasts as well as a month-long show of photos taken in Baghdad by photojournalist Scott Wallace. An original photo from a Ku Klux Klan postparade rally at the Washington Monument in 1925 is one of the more valuable—and frightening—images in the shop.

It's worth a trip to banning+Low just for conversation. Low's varied background and political knowledge make him an entertaining companion, no matter what your political persuasion (though he leans just a tad to the left). But don't leave until you make him do his "country DJ" voice—"Big Johnny on your Big Country"—as he sells you that "Kucinich for President" bumper sticker.

In the neighborhood: Pen Haven, www.penhaven.com, a tiny shop in the back of banning+Low, specializes in pens: buying, selling, and repair/restoration of fountain pens. The showroom is open only on weekends. After you leave, browse the antique and specialty shops on Howard Avenue.

BACK WHEN (and before) people watched shows with Ed Sullivan, Jackie Gleason, and Red Skelton, they also frequented places called "variety stores." Okay, so we're showing our age, but we remember with more than a little fondness looking at the

BRUCE VARIETY
6922 Arlington Road
Bethesda, MD 20814
(301) 656-7543

kaleidoscopes, yo-yos, and nerd or X-ray spectacles in the toy aisles while our mothers shopped for buttons, socks, or lampshades. Bruce Variety is a dinosaur in this arena—a big one—and has been in business for half a century.

A very narrow storefront hides what would be enough merchandise to stock several shops, from supplies for the seamstress (including fabric) to crafts, markers, crayons, glitter, and beads for holidays or parties. Backpacks and piñatas hang from the ceiling, hula hoops are looped over a high divider wall in the cookware department, and paperback classics such as *Little Women* and *Heidi* are shelved in the small toy room toward the back.

We rejected the lavender-scented mothballs on one of our recent visits, but could not resist Invisible Glass, a product that seems to have magical powers for cleaning windows and mirrors. And the $1.57 spent on a heavy, powerful magnet for our son was a good investment; now he can test his teacher's theory that some breakfast cereals contain iron particles.

In the neighborhood: In the Bradley Shopping Center, Bruce Variety is next to **Strosnider's Hardware**, one of the most magnificent hardware stores in the region (see chapter 8, Home and Garden). Parking in the small strip center's lot can be tough, but a visit to Bruce Variety and Strosnider's—and **Bradley Food and Beverage** for a pastry and coffee—is worth the wait for a space. You'll feel nostalgic, and your kids will love it.

~~~

CRAFT-IMPAIRED folks who long for a hand-smocked dress for their toddler, a knitted dress for a Barbie doll, or a handmade quilt for practically anyone will love Elder Crafters in Old Town. A not-for-profit store run by volunteers fifty-five years of age or older, each crafter (chosen by a selection committee) earns a commission on items sold. During the Christmas season, shoppers buy everything from hand-knit stroller blankets (clever little devices that fit right over a baby's head while he or she is being strolled), cute little crayon caddies, and hand-printed greeting cards. We've even wondered whether some buyers might be passing the work off as their own ("I made this just for you, dear.") Other noteworthy items include stained glass, fancy jackets made from sweatshirt material, and lots of well-made children's clothing.

> **ELDER CRAFTERS OF ALEXANDRIA, INC.**
> 405 Cameron Street
> Alexandria, VA 22314
> (703) 683-4338
> www.eldercrafters.com

In the neighborhood: Cameron Street in Old Town Alexandria (one block off of King) is full of interesting clothing boutiques for women. After you browse, head over to 208 Queen Street for lunch or sample sumptuous appetizers at the charming **Bilbo Baggins** restaurant (www.bilbobaggins.net), (703) 683-0300—but save room for some white chocolate bread pudding for dessert.

~~~~

WHETHER YOU'RE interested in the geology of the D.C. area or you just want to pick up an inexpensive souvenir from you trip to Old Town, this funky little shop a block off off King Street near the waterfront is a good bet. Operated by retired electrical engineer Marvin Young and his son, Mike, it's been a real-live, hands-on family business for three decades.

OLDE TOWNE GEMSTONES
6 Prince Street
Alexandria, VA 22314
(703) 836-1377

Olde Town Gemstones has seen many changes since it opened its doors in 1975, just in time for the country's bicentennial. Mike married a woman he hired to work in the shop, and they had a daughter who spent many of her formative years in the store. (Wife Pat, a teacher, and now college-age daughter Rebecca also have a hand in the business.) At one time, they sold lapidary (rock-polishing) equipment; during another phase, turquoise Indian jewelry was all the rage. They've also changed locations a couple of times, rolling their belongings across the street in a wheelbarrow.

Today the store has pretty rocks for good prices. Where else can you pick up a shark tooth necklace for your kid for around $5, a sparkling purple rock in a box for $7.50 or a handmade "tree" of your very own birthstone for $20 on up (depending on size)? Of course, the shop has many more expensive mineral specimens from all over the world as well. If you enjoy fossil hunting, pick Marvin's brain about the area's resources. He knows the best places to hunt for turritella fossils and shark's teeth.

To be honest, we checked out this shop because we were just plain nosy. What could be lurking in the little freestanding wooden structure next to the Potomac? Nice folks, nice rocks, good conversation, that's what.

In the neighborhood: Olde Town Gemstones is only a couple of blocks from the **Torpedo Factory Art Center**. In between are **Olsson's** bookstore, **Firehook Bakery**, and other worthy shops.

WOODCRAFT IS an absolute must-visit stop for any woodworker or wannabe. True, it's a national chain, but the locations in Springfield, Virginia, and Rockville, Maryland, are among the only four stores in the world that offer The Woodworkers Club, a full wood shop stocked with the very best table saws, lathes, jointers, and drill presses. They're available for an hourly or yearly fee.

> **WOODCRAFT**
> 6123 Backlick Road
> Springfield, VA 22150
> (703) 912-6727
> www.woodcraft.com

Founded in Boston in 1928, the Woodcraft Supply Corp. sells everything for the woodworker: carving tools from Switzerland, workbenches from Germany, turning tools from England, and sharpening stones from Japan. The store has a large selection of books with instructions for building bookcases, furniture, even guitars.

Woodworking has always been a dream of ours, but we have neither the funds nor the space for a full-scale wood shop. So we signed up for "Woodworking Fundamentals," a two-day class where we learned about cutting drying lumber, choosing wood, using tools, and refinishing. As part of the deal, each of the six students constructed a bookshelf out of oak and walnut, using every power tool imaginable and taking home a beautiful finished piece that looks like it was made by a master craftsman. Other classes include "Basic Pens and Pencils," carving, turning, and the much more involved "Cabinet and Furniture Making," taught at two levels.

While making our humble projects, we could admire members of the Woodworkers Club as they constructed striking humidors, colorful wooden boxes, bookshelves, and more intricate pieces, in a six-thousand-square-foot club facility. Staff stood by to assist with equipment—and are available to help with advice in the store as well. A lot of the customers can offer advice, too, since woodworkers really just like to hang out together.

Other Locations: 4950 Wyacond Road, Rockville, MD, (301) 984-9033.

In the neighborhood: Woodcraft is in the same shopping center as **Fisher's Hardware** (see chapter 8, Home and Garden).

CHAPTER 14

Getting to Great Shopping, A Neighborhood Guide

It would impossible at best, and confusing at least, to provide door-to-door directions to each store in this book, even though we believe they all are highly worthy of your visits. Greater Washington is big and, despite his best intentions, designer Pierre-Charles L'Enfant's plans for the city seem to have gone haywire as soon as they hit the suburbs. Even within the District of Columbia—sorry, Pierre, but it's true—an awful lot of people get lost without even leaving a single quadrant.

We don't intend to leave you lost. We've provided phone numbers for every entry, and store employees are generally eager to help if you call for directions. We've also provided the Web sites for most stores, many of which have directions. If they don't, popular, free Internet map and direction sites (such as MapQuest and Yahoo! Maps) make it easy to get from point A to point B. If you're just visiting the Washington area, ask your hotel or ask a stranger. Washingtonians like to help. (Our hats are off to you visitors, incidentally; there's no better way to get to know a city than to go exploring its greatest stores.)

Though not all of the area's best boutiques, markets, and other shops are in defined shopping districts such as Georgetown or Old Town Alexandria, plenty of them are. Use the following directions as a starting point if you're just looking for a neighborhood with interesting possibilities. But once you know your way around, branch out and you'll discover so much more.

GEORGETOWN

On the Potomac (but don't neglect to discover the uphill shops) in the city's Northwest quadrant, this is the most famous of Washington's shopping and dining destinations. The two primary roads are M Street and Wisconsin Avenue, and they intersect in the heart of the shopping district.

From downtown Washington, go west on Pennsylvania Avenue or M Street, beyond the Foggy Bottom/George Washington University neighborhood, and you'll wind up in Georgetown.

From Virginia, take the George Washington Parkway (from Alexandria), Lee Highway (from Arlington), or Interstate 66 (from Fairfax County) to the Rosslyn section of Arlington, paying attention to the signs for the Key Bridge. Cross Key Bridge and you're in Georgetown.

From Maryland or Northwest Washington, follow Wisconsin Avenue into town. When the road starts descending the hill, you'll know you're getting close.

Metro (the subway) does not stop in Georgetown, but it's only a five-block walk down Pennsylvania Avenue (to its intersection with M Street) from the Foggy Bottom stop (Orange or Blue line), or you can look for a shuttle or cab.

OLD TOWN ALEXANDRIA

From sites of historic settlers and cobblestone streets to some fine and fun shopping, Old Town is a local favorite and a must at Christmas, when it is delightfully festive. King Street is the primary shopping street, but don't neglect the others.

From Washington, cross the Potomac on any of the bridges to Virginia and take the George Washington Parkway or U.S. 1 south. Both roads intersect with King Street.

From elsewhere in **Virginia**, follow the directions from Washington—or, if you're coming from the west, take Route 7 (Leesburg Pike/King Street) or Route 236 (Little River Turnpike/Duke Street) east; either will land you in Old Town.

From Maryland, follow the directions from Washington; if coming from Prince George's County or beyond, take I-495 (the Capital Beltway) across the Wilson Bridge and get off at the first exit in Virginia, then head north about ten blocks.

Metro's Blue and Yellow lines stop on King Street; walk east and the shops will appear. Shoppers who don't want the exercise might want to take a cab from the Metro stop if they're headed to the galleries of the Torpedo Factory or other places nearest the river, though they'll miss some new and awfully neat shops.

WHEATON

This is a more specialized destination, great for those who love finding ethnic eateries and markets, magic, toys, and comic books. It's not funky, but with its 1960s-era Maryland suburban feel, it's not a big tourist destination, either.

From Washington, drive north on 16th Street NW until it ends and puts you on Georgia Avenue in Maryland (stay in the left lanes to turn north). Go north about two miles, just past Viers Mill Road, which veers off diagonally to the left. The best exploring is in the triangle bounded by George Avenue, Viers Mill Road, and University Boulevard.

From Virginia and other Maryland locations, take I-495 (the Capital Beltway) to the Georgia Avenue exit and drive north.

Metro's Red line has a stop in Wheaton that drops you off near the heart of it all.

U STREET AND ADAMS MORGAN

Urban hipsters love this Northwest Washington area steeped in local lore (Duke Ellington once walked these streets), which seems to get new boutiques, stylish stores (a number of them listed throughout this book), and restaurants constantly. If your idea of excitement is country-club living and a day at the spa, this area's edge might not suit your style, but it's great for any shopper who appreciates retail pioneers and loves discovering exciting new merchants. A side trip to nearby **Adams Morgan,** on 18th Street NW from Florida Avenue to Columbia Road, is in order for more funky chic.

From downtown Washington, drive north on 14th Street NW to U Street; turn left on U and park.

From Dupont Circle, take Connecticut Avenue to Florida Avenue, turn right on U Street.

CAPITOL HILL, EASTERN MARKET, AND EIGHTH STREET

The area around the U.S. Capitol is known among locals for its two sides—the House (south) and the Senate (north)—and the best shopping is unquestionably on the House side.

From Washington and other departure points: Pennsylvania Avenue SE has a couple blocks of shops near the Library of Congress. Several of the restaurants and bars bounded by First and Third streets are popular among congressional staffers. Heading east a few blocks, the Eastern Market is just off the north side of Pennsylvania Avenue near Seventh Street (on your left if you're coming from the Capitol). A block farther down Pennsylvania—but this time on the south side—is up-and-coming Eighth Street.

Metro's Orange and Blue lines share the Eastern Market stop.

DUPONT CIRCLE

The northwest portion of this neighborhood, especially on Connecticut Avenue, draws the biggest shopping and browsing crowds because of its cafés and interesting shops. But don't neglect the southwest side, across Massachusetts Avenue NW.

From Washington or Maryland, take Massachusetts or Connecticut avenue; they meet up briefly at Dupont Circle.

From Virginia, well, the directions can get a little tricky. Once you get into the District, find 18th Street—just west of the White House—and take it north to Connecticut (which comes in at an angle), turning left. Or take L Street to New Hampshire Avenue, turning northeast. New Hampshire will take you right to the circle.

On **Metro**, take the Red line to the Dupont Circle stop.

CLARENDON

Though long an Arlington, Virginia, enclave with good local shops, Clarendon has been picking up more trendy chain stores with a fairly new and attractive shopping center, Clarendon Market Common on Clarendon

Boulevard (Crate & Barrel, Pottery Barn, Barnes & Noble, etc.). It also attracts pioneering sole proprietors and is a hangout for young adults drawn to the neighborhood's cafés and ethnic dining options, from Peruvian to Vietnamese. The two main roads, Wilson and Clarendon boulevards, are one-way here, and don't neglect to check out the shopping on both.

From Washington and Maryland, take any bridge into Virginia and head to Arlington's Rosslyn neighborhood—the area with tall buildings across the Potomac River from Georgetown. In Rosslyn, look for Wilson Boulevard and turn right; Wilson will take you directly to Clarendon.

From Virginia: If you're coming from Alexandria, take the George Washington Parkway to Rosslyn, then follow the directions above. If you're coming from the south or southwest, take I-66 to the Glebe Road exit, which puts you on Fairfax Drive. Stay straight on Fairfax Drive for nearly a mile, turning slightly right—and very briefly—on E. Tenth Street. Turn immediately left onto Wilson Boulevard and continue until you see the shopping.

Metro's Orange line train has a Clarendon station, near all the shopping.

CHEVY CHASE AND BETHESDA

These are actually separate neighborhoods—Chevy Chase straddling the D.C. and Maryland border, Bethesda a mile farther out Wisconsin Avenue in Maryland. Chevy Chase is the glitzier of the two, with the intersection of Wisconsin and Western avenues marking the heart of a district featuring such retailers as Saks Fifth Avenue, Versace, Georgette Klinger, and Neiman Marcus; yet, you can also find bargains at Filene's Basement and standard mall fare at the Gap. Farther up Wisconsin Avenue, the shopping continues in downtown Bethesda with gift stores, shoes, dresses, tobacco, electronics, books, music—and a very good array of restaurants. Bethesda shopping isn't quite as concentrated as in Chevy Chase, but if you're willing to walk around a bit, you can amuse yourself for hours. Be sure to check out Bethesda's side streets, not only between Wisconsin and Woodmont avenues, but also between Wisconsin Avenue and Old Georgetown Road—a somewhat separate area—on the northern edge of downtown.

From Washington: Take Wisconsin Avenue through Chevy Chase, then continue to downtown Bethesda.

From Virginia: Take I-495 (the Capital Beltway) in the direction of

Rockville, making sure to stay on I-495 at the I-270 spilt. Exit at Old Georgetown Road and go south to Bethesda. Keep going and you'll find Wisconsin Avenue, where you can continue on to Chevy Chase.

Metro's Red line has stops in both neighborhoods: get off at Friendship Heights for Chevy Chase and Bethesda for downtown Bethesda.

CHAPTER 15

Where to Find It

THE BEST OF EVERYTHING BY LOCATION

Washington, D.C.

A LITTERI INC.
517-519 Morse Street NE
Washington, DC 20002
(202) 544-0183
www.litteris.com

A MANO
1677 Wisconsin Avenue NW
Washington, DC 20007
(202) 298-7200

ALL ABOUT JANE
24382 18th Street NW
Washington, DC 20009
Phone (202)797-9710
www.allaboutjane.com

ALVEAR STUDIO DESIGN AND IMPORTS
705 Eighth Street SE
Washington, DC 20003
(202) 546-8434
www.alvearstudio.com

AMERICAN STUDIO
2906 M Street NW
Washington, DC 20007
(202) 965-3274

THE ART STORE
3019 M Street NW
Washington, DC 20007
(202) 342-7030

ASMAN CUSTOM PHOTO
924 Pennsylvania Avenue SE
Washington, DC
(202) 547-7713

BACKSTAGE INC.
545 Eighth Street SE
Washington, DC 2003
(202) 544-5744
www.backstagebooks.com

BALDAQUIN
1413 Wisconsin Avenue NW
Washington, DC 20007
(202) 625-1600
www.baldaquin.com

BARTLEBY'S BOOKS
3034 M Street NW
Washington, DC 20007
(202) 298-0460
www.bartlebysbooks.com

BLUEMERCURY
3059 M Street NW
Washington, DC 20007
(202) 965-1300

1745 Connecticut Avenue NW
Washington, DC
(202) 462-1300
www.bluemercury.com

THE BRASS KNOB
2311 18th Street NW
Washington DC 20009
(202) 332-3370
www.thebrassknow.com

BRIDGE STREET BOOKS
2814 Pennsylvania Avenue NW
Washington, DC 20007
(202) 965-5200

CALVERT-WOODLEY LIQUORS
4339 Connecticut Avenue NW
Washington, DC 20008
(202) 966-4400
www.wineaccess.com/store/calvertwoodley

CHAPTERS A LITERARY BOOKSTORE
445 11th Street NW
Washington, DC 20004
(202) 737-5553
www.chaptersliterary.com

CHEVY CHASE WINE AND SPIRITS
5544 Connecticut Avenue NW
Washington, DC 20015
(202) 363-4000

CHILD'S PLAY
5536 Connecticut Avenue NW
Washington, DC 20015
(202) 244-3602

COMMANDER SALAMANDER
1420 Wisconsin Avenue NW
Washington, DC 20007
(202) 337-2265

THE COMPLEMENT
888 17th Street & I NW
Washington, DC 20006
(202) 785-9111

DAISY
1814 Adams Mill Road NW
Washington, DC 20009
(202) 797-1777

DEAN & DELUCA
3276 M Street NW
Washington, DC 20007
(202) 342-2500

EASTERN MARKET
225 Seventh Street SE
(near Capitol Hill)
Washington, DC 20003
www.easternmarket.net

ENCORE RESALE DRESS SHOP
3715 Macomb Street NW
Washington, DC 20016
(202) 966-8122

EVERLASTING LIFE
2928 Georgia Avenue NW
Washington, DC 20001
(202) 232-1700
www.everlastinglife.net

FILENE'S BASEMENT
5300 Wisconsin Avenue NW
Washington, DC 20015
(202) 966-0208

529 14th Street NW
Washington, DC 20045
(202) 638-4110
www.filenesbasement.com

FORNASH DESIGNS
3222 M Street NW, Suite W-025
Washington, DC 20007
(202) 338-0774

FRANZ BADER BOOKSTORE
19111 Eye Street NW
Washington, DC 20006
(202) 337-5440

GO MAMA GO
1809 14th Street NW
Washington, DC 20009
(202) 299-0850

GOOD EYE
4918 Wisconsin Avenue NW
Washington, DC 20016

(202) 244-8516
www.goodeyeonline.com

THE HATTERY
3222 M Street NW
Washington, DC 20007
(202) 364-HATS

HOME RULE
1807 14th Street NW
Washington, DC 20009
(202) 797-5544
www.homerule.com

IDLE TIME BOOKS
2467 18th Street NW
Washington, DC 20009
(202) 232-4774
www.idletime.com

INGA'S ONCE IS NOT ENOUGH
4830 MacArthur Boulevard NW
Washington, DC 20007
(202) 337-3072

KRAMERBOOKS AND AFTERWORDS CAFÉ AND GRILL
1517 Connecticut Avenue NW
Washington, DC 20036
(202) 387-1400
www.kramers.com

LAMBDA RISING BOOKSTORE
1625 Connecticut Avenue NW
Washington, DC 20009
(202) 462-6969

LOEHMANN'S
5333 Wisconsin Avenue NW
Washington, DC 20015
(202) 362-4733
www.loehmanns.com

LUSH
3066 M Street NW
Washington DC 20007
(202) 333-6950

MACARTHUR BEVERAGES
4877 MacArthur Boulevard NW
Washington, DC 20007
(202) 338-1433
www.bassins.com

MEEPS & AUNT NEENSIE'S VINTAGE CLOTHING
1520 U Street NW
Washington, DC 20009
(202) 265-6546
www.meepsonu.com

MELODY RECORD SHOP
1623 Connecticut Avenue NW
Washington, DC 20009
(202) 232-4002
www.melodyrecords.com

MILLENNIUM DECORATIVE ARTS
1528 U Street NW
Washington, DC 20009
(202) 483-1218

NANA
1534 U Street NW
Washington DC 20009
(202) 667-6955
www.nanadc.com

NATURALLY YOURS
2029 P Street NW
Washington, DC 20036
(202) 429-1718

THE NEWSROOM
1803 Connecticut Avenue NW
Washington, DC 20009
(202) 332-1489

OLSSON'S BOOKS & RECORDS
1307 19th Street NW
Washington, DC 20036
(202) 785-1133

418 Seventh Street NW
Washington, DC 20004
(202) 638-7610
ww.Olssons.com

PARK PLACE
2251 Wisconsin Avenue NW
Washington, DC 20007
(202) 342-6294

PEARSON'S
2436 Wisconsin Avenue NW
Washington, DC 20007
(202) 333-6666
www.pearsonswinewebsite.com

PENN CAMERA
840 E Street NW
Washington, DC 20004
(202) 347-5777

1015 18th St NW
Washington, DC 20036
(202) 785-7366
www.penncamera.com

THE PHOENIX
1514 Wisconsin Avenue NW
Washington, DC 20007
(202) 338-4404

PICCOLO PIGGIES
1533 Wisconsin Avenue NW
Washington, DC 20007
(202) 333-0123

PIRJO
1044 Wisconsin Avenue NW
Washington, DC 20007
(202) 337-1390

PLAID
715 Eighth Street SE
Washington, DC 20003
(202) 675-6900
www.plaidstore.com

POLITICS AND PROSE
5015 Connecticut Avenue NW
Washington, DC 20008
(202) 364-1919 or (800) 722-0790
www.politicsandprose.com

POP
1803a 14th Street NW
Washington, DC 20009
(202) 332-3312
www.shoppop.com

PRO PHOTO
1902 Eye Street NW
Washington, DC 20006
(202) 223-1292
www.prophotodc.com

PROPER TOPPER
3213 P Street NW
Washington, DC 20007
(202) 333-6200

1350 Connecticut Avenue NW
Washington, DC 20036
(202) 842-3055
www.propertopper.com

RAGE CLOTHING
1069 Wisconsin Avenue NW
Washington, DC 20007
(202) 333-1069
www.rageclothing.com

REITER'S SCIENTIFIC AND PROFESSIONAL BOOKS
2021 K Street NW
Washington, DC 20006
(202) 223-3327
www.reiters.com

RESTORATION HARDWARE
1222 Wisconsin Avenue NW
Washington, DC 20007
(202) 625-2771

RODMAN'S
5100 Wisconsin Avenue NW
Washington, DC 20016
(202) 363-3466
www.rodmans.com

SASSANOVA
1641 Wisconsin Avenue NW
Washington, DC 20007
(202) 471-4400

SCHNEIDER'S OF CAPITOL HILL
300 Massachusetts Avenue NE
Washington, DC 20002
(202) 543-9300
www.schneiderswine.com

SECOND STORY BOOKS
2000 P Street NW
Washington, DC 20036
(202) 659-8884
www.secondstorybooks.com

SECONDI INC.
1702 Connecticut Avenue NW
Washington, DC 20009
(202) 667-1122

SECRETS OF NATURE
3923 S. Capitol Street SW
Washington, DC 20032
(202) 562-0041

SHERMAN PICKEY
1647 Wisconsin Avenue NW
Washington, DC 20007
(202) 333-4212

SIXTEEN FIFTY-NINE
1659 Wisconsin Avenue NW
Washington, DC 20007
(202) 333-1480

SKI CENTER
49th Street & Massachusetts Avenue NW
Washington, DC 20016
(202) 966-4474
www.skicenter.com

SMITH & HAWKEN
1209 31st Street NW
Washington, DC 20007
(202) 965-2680
www.smithandhawken.com

SUGAR
1633 Wisconsin Avenue NW
Washington, DC 20007
(202) 333-5231

SULLIVAN'S TOY STORE
3412 Wisconsin Avenue NW
Washington, DC 20016
(202) 362-1343

SUTTON PLACE GOURMET/ BALDUCCI'S
3201 New Mexico Avenue NW
Washington, DC 20016
(202) 363-5800
www.suttongourmet.com

TEMPO BOOKSTORE
4905 Wisconsin Avenue NW
Washington, DC 20016
(202) 363-6683

TINY JEWEL BOX
1147 Connecticut Avenue NW
Washington, DC 20036
(202) 393-2747
www.tinyjewelbox.com

TREE TOP TOYS & BOOKS
3301 New Mexico Avenue NW
Washington, DC 20016
(202) 244-3500
www.treetopkids.com

WASHINGTON LAW AND PROFESSIONAL BOOKS
1900 G Street NW
Washington, DC 20006
(202) 223-5543
www.washingtonlawbooks.com

WATERWORKS
3314 M Street NW
Washington, DC 20007
(202) 333-7180

WILD WOMEN WEAR RED
1512 U Street NW
Washington, DC 20009
(202) 387-5700

YES NATURAL GOURMET
1825 Columbia Road NW
Washington, DC 20009
(202) 462-5150

YES ORGANIC MARKET
3425 Connecticut Avenue NW
Washington, DC 20008
(202) 363-1559

ZAWADI
1524 U Street NW
Washington, DC 20009
(202) 232-2214

Maryland

AFRICAN STARGINA COLLECTIONS
3500 East-West Highway
Hyattsville, MD 20782
(301) 559-8418

AMAZING SAVINGS
4816 Boiling Brook Parkway
Rockville, MD 20852
(301) 770-9022

ANGLO DUTCH POOL AND TOYS
5460 Westbard Avenue
Bethesda, MD 20816
(301) 951-0636

APPLE STORE
Westfield Shoppingtown Montgomery
7101 Democracy Boulevard
Bethesda, MD 20817
(301) 299-0723

ATOMIC MUSIC
9035 Baltimore Avenue
College Park, MD 20740
(301) 474-5752

BANNING+LOW
3730 Howard Avenue
Kensington, MD 20895
(301) 933-0709
www.banningandlow.com

BARRY'S MAGIC SHOP
11234 Georgia Avenue
Wheaton, MD 20902
(301) 933-0373
www.barrysmagicshop.com

BELINA
10215 Old Georgetown Road
Bethesda, MD 20814
(301) 897-2929

BETHESDA CO-OP
6500 Seven Locks Road
Bethesda, MD 20818
(301) 320-2530

BONIFANT BOOKS
11240 Georgia Avenue
Wheaton, MD 20902
(301) 946-1526
www.abebooks.com/home/bonifant

BRADLEY FOOD AND BEVERAGE
6904 Arlington Road
Bethesda, MD 20814
(301) 654-6966

BRUCE VARIETY
6922 Arlington Road
Bethesda, MD 20814
(301) 656-7543

BY BRAZIL
11335 Georgia Avenue
Wheaton, MD 20902
(301) 962-6686

CDEPOT
9039 Baltimore Ave.
College Park, MD 20740
(301) 982-3472
www.cdepot.com

CHUCK LEVIN'S WASHINGTON MUSIC CENTER
11151 Viers Mill Road
Wheaton, MD 20902
(301) 946-8808
www.washingtonmusic.com

THE COMPLEMENT
White Flint Plaza
5234 Nicholson Lane
Kensington, MD 20895
(301) 770-2700

CO-OP SUPERMARKET
121 Centerway
Greenbelt, MD 20770
(301) 474-0522

DAISY II
4940 St. Elmo Avenue
Bethesda, MD 20814
(301) 656-2280

DALE MUSIC CO.
8240 Georgia Avenue
Silver Spring, MD 20910
(301) 589-1459
www.dalemusic.com

EATZI'S
11503-B Rockville Pike
Rockville, Maryland 20852
(301) 816-2020
www.eatzis.com

EVERLASTING LIFE
Hampton Mall
9185 Central Avenue
Capitol Heights, MD 20743
(301) 324-6900
www.everlastinglife.net

G STREET FABRICS
Mid-Pike Plaza
11854 Rockville Pike
Rockville, Maryland 20852
(301) 231-8998

HOUSE OF MUSICAL TRADITIONS
7040 Carroll Avenue
Takoma Park, MD 20912
(301) 270-9090
www.musicaltraditions.com

IRRESISTIBLES
Wildwood Shopping Center
10301 Old Georgetown Road
Bethesda, MD 20814
(301) 897-2574

JS AUDIO
4919 Saint Elmo Avenue
Bethesda, MD 20814
(301) 656-7020
www.jsaudio.com

JOE'S RECORD PARADISE
1300 E. Gude Drive
Rockville, MD 20850
(301) 315-2235

K & G MEN'S MART
4955 Nicholson Court
Kensington, MD 20895
(301) 231-8140
www.kgmens.com

KARIBU
Prince George's Plaza
3500 East-West Highway
Hyattsville, MD 20782
(301) 559-1140

Bowie Town Center
15624 Emerald Way
Bowie, MD 20716
(301) 352-4110

Iverson Mall
3817 Branch Avenue
Hillcrest Heights, MD 20748
(301) 899-3730

Forest Village Park Mall
3393 Donnell Drive
Forestville, MD 20747
(301) 736-6170
www.karibubooks.com

KUGLER'S HOME FASHIONS
20 University Boulevard East
Silver Spring, MD 20902
(301) 593-8905
www.kuglers.com

LEMON TWIST
8534 Connecticut Avenue
Chevy Chase, MD 20815
(301) 986-0044

LOEHMANN'S
5230 Randolph Road
Rockville, MD 20852
(301) 770-0030
www.loehmanns.com

LUNA
7232 Woodmont Avenue
Bethesda, MD 20814
(301) 656-1111
www.shopluna.com

MONTGOMERY FARM WOMEN'S COOPERATIVE MARKET
7155 Wisconsin Avenue
Bethesda, MD 20814
(301) 652-2291

MY ORGANIC MARKET
9827 Rhode Island Avenue
College Park, MD 20740
(301) 220-1100

11711 Parklawn Drive
Rockville, MD 20852
(301) 816-4944

OLSSON'S BOOKS AND RECORDS
7647 Old Georgetown Road
Bethesda, MD 20814
(301) 652-3336

OUTLINE INC.
Prince George's Plaza
3500 East-West Hwy
Hyattsville, MD 20782
(301) 559-9000

PC RETRO
5031 Garrett Avenue
Beltsville, MD 20705
(301) 931-6630
www.pcretro.com/webstore

PEACH CREEK SHOPS
201 Main Street
Laurel, MD 20707
(301) 498-9071
www.peachcreekshops.com

PIRJO
4821 Bethesda Avenue
Bethesda, MD 20814
(301) 986-1870

POTOMAC TRADING COLLECTIBLES
3610 University Boulevard West
Kensington, MD 20895
(301) 949-5656

THE RITZ BOUTIQUE
5014 Nicholson Lane
Rockville, MD 20852
(301) 230-2167
www.ritzconsignment.com

RODMAN'S
5148 Nicholson Lane
Rockville, MD 20895
(301) 881-6253

4301 Randolph Road
Wheaton, MD 20906
(301) 946-3100
www.rodmans.com

SECOND CHANCE
7702 Woodmont Avenue, #205
Bethesda, MD 20814
(301) 652-6606

SECOND STORY BOOKS
12160 Parklawn Drive
Rockville, MD 20852
(301) 770-0477
www.secondstorybooks.com

SKI CHALET
203 Muddy Branch Road
Gaithersburg, MD 20878
(301) 948-5200
www.skichalet.com

SMITH & HAWKEN
8551 Connecticut Avenue
Chevy Chase, MD 20815
(301) 215-5960
www.smithandhawken.com

SOUND IMAGES
7700 Old Georgetown Road
Bethesda, MD 20817
(301) 718-2824
www.soundimagesusa.com

SOUTH MOON UNDER
Bethesda Wildwood Center
10247 Old Georgetown Road
Bethesda, MD 20814
(301) 564-0995
www.southmoonunder.com

SOUTHWORTH GUITARS
7845 Old Georgetown Road
Bethesda, MD 20814
(301) 718-1667
www.southworthguitars.com

SPRINGRIVER CORP.
5606 Randolph Road
Rockville, MD 20852
(301) 881-5694
www.springriver.com

STROSNIDER'S
6930 Arlington Road
Bethesda, MD 20814
(301) 654-5688

815 Wayne Avenue
Silver Spring, MD 20910
(301) 565-9150

10110 River Road
Potomac, MD 20854
(301) 299-6333
www.strosniders.com

TAKOMA PARK-SILVER SPRING FOOD CO-OP
201 Ethan Allen Avenue
Takoma Park, MD 20912
(301) 891-2667

8309 Grubb Road
Silver Spring, MD 20910
(240) 247-2667
www.tpss.org

THE TOY EXCHANGE
11265 Triangle Lane
Wheaton, Maryland 20902
(301) 929-0690
www.montgomerycountymd.com/
   shopping/toyexchange.htm

VALUE CITY
Iverson Mall
3701 Branch Avenue
Hillcrest Heights, MD 20748
(301) 899-5101

Beltway Plaza
6252 Greenbelt Road
Greenbelt, MD 20770
(301) 441-9588
www.valuecity.com

WASHINGTON GOLF CENTER
6831 Wisconsin Avenue
Bethesda, MD 20814
(301) OK2-GOLF

9811 Washingtonian Boulevard
Gaithersburg, MD 20878
(301) 948-7888
www.washingtongolf.com

WHEATON HEALTH FOODS INC.
2656 University Boulevard West
Wheaton, MD 20902
(301) 933-3066

WOODCRAFT
4950 Wyacond Road
Rockville, MD 20852
(301) 984-9033
www.woodcraft.com

YOUNG WORLD
3723 Branch Avenue
Temple Hills, MD 20748
(301) 423-0883

Virginia

A LIKELY STORY
1555 King Street
Alexandria, VA 22314
(703) 836-2498
www.alikelystory.com

ACTION MUSIC
Williamsburg Shopping Center
6501 N. 29th Street
Arlington, VA 22213
(703) 534-4801

ALADDIN'S LAMP BOOKS
Lee Harrison Shopping Center
2499 N. Harrison Street, Lower Level,
　Suite 10

Arlington, VA 22207
(703) 241-8281

ALL ABOUT JANE
2839 Clarendon Boulevard
Arlington, VA 22201
(703) 243-4424
www.allaboutjane.com

ALPINE SKI SHOP
45573 Church Road
Sterling, VA 20164
(703) 444-7844
www.alpineskishop.com

AN AMERICAN IN PARIS
1225 King Street
Alexandria, VA 22314
(703) 519-8234

ANIME PAVILLION
7395-B Lee Highway
Falls Church, VA 22042
(703) 204-1844
www.animepavillion.com

APHRODITE
5886 Leesburg Pike
Falls Church, VA 22041
(703) 931-5055

APPLE STORE
Market Common at Clarendon
2700 Clarendon Boulevard
Arlington, VA 22201

Tysons Corner
1961 Chain Bridge Road
McLean, VA 22102

ART TO WEAR
(703) 691-9000
NOTE: Call for current location.

ARTCRAFT COLLECTION
132 King Street
Alexandria, VA 22314
(703) 299-6616

11960 Market Street
Reston, VA 20190
(703) 964-0145
www.artcraftcollection.com

ARTS AFIRE
102 N. Fayette Street
Alexandria, VA 22314
(703) 838-9785

BACK DOOR
2499 N. Harrison Street
Arlington, VA 22207
(703) 237-6117
www.thebackdoorinc.com

BELLACARA
924 King Street
Alexandria, VA 22314
(703) 299-9652
www.bellacara.com

BESTWAY
3109 Graham Road
Falls Church, VA 22042
(703) 560-2101

690 Elden Street
Herndon, VA 20170
(703) 668-0323

BOOT HILL WESTERN
13231 Gordon Boulevard
Woodbridge, VA 22191
(703) 490-0090
www.boothill.us

CD CELLAR
709 W. Broad Street
Falls Church, VA 22046
(703) 534-6318

CHINOISERIE
1024 King Street
Alexandria, VA 22314
(703) 838-0520

COMP USA
5901 Stevenson Avenue
Alexandria, VA 22304
(703) 212-6610

Fair Lakes Promenade
12189 Fair Lakes Parkway
Fairfax, VA 22033
(703) 359-1401

8357 Leesburg Pike
Vienna, VA 22180
(703) 821-7700

14427 Potomac Mills Road
Woodbridge, VA 22192
(703) 492-6262
www.compusa.com

THE COMPLEMENT
656 S. Pickett Street
Alexandria, VA 22304
(703) 751-5600

COMPUTER WAREHOUSE
Tysons Station Shopping Center
7516 Leesburg Pike
Falls Church, VA 22043
(703) 821-1400
www.pcretro.com/webstore

COUNTRY CURTAINS
4805 N. First Street
Arlington, VA 22203

(703) 522-7111
www.countrycurtains.com

DAFFY'S
Potomac Mills
2700 Potomac Mills Circle
Woodbridge, VA 22192
(703) 494-3636
www.daffys.com

DÉJAVU AUDIO LTD.
1401 Chain Bridge Road, Suite 203
McLean, VA 22101
(703) 734-9391
www.dejavuaudio.com

DOMINION CAMERA
112 W. Broad Street
Falls Church, VA 22046
(703) 532-6700
www.dominioncamera.com

ELDER CRAFTERS OF ALEXANDRIA, INC.
405 Cameron Street
Alexandria, VA 22314
(703) 683-4338
www.eldercrafters.com

ENCORE
110 S. Union Street
Alexandria, VA 22314
(703) 683-1756

EXQUISITE ARTS GALLERY
45965 Nokes Boulevard, Suite 150
Sterling, VA 20166
(703) 433-2380
www.exquisitearts.com

FISCHER'S HARDWARE
Concord Centre Plaza
6129 Backlick Road

Springfield, VA 22150
(703) 451-3700

FOXES MUSIC CO.
416 S. Washington Street
Falls Church, VA 22046
(703) 533-7393 or (800) 446-4414
www.foxesmusic.com

FRENCH COUNTRY LIVING
10135 Colvin Run Road
Great Falls, VA 22066
(703) 759-2245
www.frenchcountry.com

G STREET FABRICS
Seven Corners Center
6250 Arlington Boulevard
Falls Church, VA 22044
(703) 241-1700

Potomac Mills
2700 Potomac Mills Circle
Woodbridge, VA 22192
(703) 494-5900

Sully Station
5077 Westfields Boulevard
Centreville, VA 20120
(703) 818-8090
www.gstreetfabrics.com

GAME PARLOR
14400 Smoketown Road
Woodbridge, VA 22192
(703) 551-4200

13936 Metrotech Drive
Chantilly, VA 20151
(703) 803-3114
www.gameparlor.com

GERMAN GOURMET
7185 Lee Highway
Falls Church, VA 22046
(703) 534-1908
www.german-gourmet.com

GOLFDOM
8203 Watson Street
McLean, VA 22102
(703) 790-8844
www.golfdomgolf.com

GRANDDAD'S HOBBY SHOP
5260-A Port Royal Road
Springfield, VA 22151
(703) 426-0700
www.granddadshobbyshop.com

GREY HOUSE POTTERS
5509 Wilson Boulevard North
Arlington, VA 22205
(703) 522-7738

IMAGINE ARTWEAR
1124 King Street
Alexandria, VA 22314
(703) 548-1461
www.imagineartwear.com

IMAGINATION STATION
4524 Lee Highway
Arlington VA 22201
(703) 522-2047

THE ITALIAN STORE
3123 Lee Highway
Arlington, VA 22201
(703) 528-6266

JUDY RYAN OF FAIRFAX
9565 Braddock Road
Fairfax, VA 22032
(703) 425-1855

K & G MENS MART
5832 Columbia Pike
Falls Church,VA 22041
(703) 931-1124
www.kgmens.com

KARIBU
Pentagon City
1100 S. Hayes Street
Arlington, VA 22202
(703) 415-1118

KINDER HAUS TOYS
4510 Lee Highway
Arlington, VA 22207
(703) 527-5929
www.kinderhaus.com

LA CASA BELLA
1213 King Street
Alexandria, VA 22314
(703) 684-1213

LEMON TWIST
4518 N. Lee Highway
Arlington, VA 22207
(703) 524-4680

L.L. BEAN
Tysons Corner Center
1961 Chain Bridge Road
McLean, Virginia 22102
(703) 288-4466
www.llbean.com

LOEHMANN'S
7241 Arlington Boulevard
Falls Church, VA 22042
(703) 573-1510

MADELEINE'S KIDS INC.
1521 King Street
Alexandria, VA 22314

(703) 836-9046
www.madeleineskids.com

MEDITERRANEAN BAKERY AND CAFÉ
352 S. Pickett Street
Alexandria, VA 22304
(703) 751-1702
www.eastwestmart.com

MICRO CENTER
Pan Am Plaza
3089 Nutley Street
Fairfax, VA 22031
(703) 204-8400
www.microcenter.com

MINIATURES FROM THE ATTIC
111 Park Avenue
Falls Church, VA 22046
(703) 237-0066
www.minis4u.com

MRS MCGREGOR'S GARDEN SHOP
4801 First Street North
Arlington, VA 22203
(703) 528-8773

MY FRIENDS AND ME
118 South Street SE
Leesburg, VA 20175
(703) 777-8222
www.myfriendsandme.com

MY ORGANIC MARKET
3831 Mount Vernon Avenue
Alexandria, VA 22305
(703) 535-5980

MY PLACE IN TUSCANY
1127 King Street
Alexandria, VA 22314
(703) 683-8882
www.myplaceintuscany.com

NEW TO YOU
125 N. Washington Street
Falls Church, VA 22046
(703) 533-1251
www.newtoyou.net

NORDSTROM RACK
Potomac Mills
2700 Potomac Mills Circle
Woodbridge, VA 22192
(703) 490-1440
www.nordstrom.com/ourstores/
  rackstores

NORM'S BEER AND WINE
136 Branch Road SE
Vienna, VA 22180
(703) 242-0100

OLD LUCKETT'S STORE
42350 Lucketts Road (Route 15)
Leesburg, VA 20176
(703) 779-0268
www.luckettstore.com

OLD TOWNE GEMSTONES
6 Prince Street
Alexandria, VA 22314
(703) 836-1377

OLD TOWN NEWS
721 King Street
Alexandria, VA 22314
(703) 739-9024

OLSSON'S BOOKS AND RECORDS
(See yellow pages for locations.)

ORPHEUS RECORDS
3173 Wilson Boulevard
Arlington, VA 22201
(703) 294-6774

PLAY IT AGAIN SPORTS
5750 Union Mill Road
Chifton, VA 20214
(703) 266-8677

THE RED APPLE
2922 Chain Bridge Road
Oakton, VA 22124
(703) 281-1701

REPLAY SPORTS
Leesburg Pike Plaza
3537 S. Jefferson Street
Falls Church, VA 22041
(703) 998-4231
www.tennisracketpros.com

RESTORATION HARDWARE
614 King Street
Alexandria, VA 22314
(703) 299-6220

Tyson's Corner Center
1961 Chain Bridge Road
McLean, VA 22102
(703) 821-9655
www.restorationhardware.com

REUNIONS
1709 Centre Plaza
Alexandria, VA 22302
(703) 931-8161

THE RUSSIAN GOURMET
1396 Chain Bridge Road
McLean, VA 22101
(703) 760-0280

SHOE FLY
2618 Wilson Boulevard
Arlington, VA 22201
(703) 243-6290

SKI CHALET
2704 Columbia Pike
Arlington, VA 22204
(703) 521-1700

14130 Sullyfield Circle
Chantilly, VA 20151
(703) 631-7880

8338 Leesburg Pike
Tysons Corner, VA 22182
(703) 761-3040
www.skichalet.com

SMITH & HAWKEN
6705 Whittier Avenue
McLean, VA 22101
(703) 506-0065
www.smithandhawken.com

SOUND IMAGES
6541 Arlington Boulevard
Falls Church, VA 22042
(703) 534-1733
www.soundimagesusa.com

SOUTH MOON UNDER
Reston Town Center
11950 Market Street
Reston, VA 20190
(703) 435-0605

2700 Clarendon Boulevard, Suite R-440
Arlington, VA 22201
(703) 807-4083
www.southmoonunder.com

SPOKES ETC.
224 Maple Avenue East
Vienna, VA 22180
(703) 281-2004

1506 Belle View Boulevard
Alexandria, VA 22307
(703) 765-8005

1545 N. Quaker Lane
Alexandria, VA 22302
(703) 820-2200
www.spokesetc.com

SPRINGRIVER CORP.
2757 Summerfield Road
Falls Church, VA 22042
(703) 241-2818

**STABLER-LEADBETTER
APOTHECARY SHOP**
Museum Store
105–107 Fairfax Street
Alexandria, VA 22314
(703) 836-3713

SUPER H MART
10780 Lee Highway
Fairfax, VA 22030
(800) 427-9870
www.superhmart.com

TALKING BOOK WORLD
Sugarland Crossing
47010 Community Plaza (Route 7)
Sterling, VA 20164
(703) 433-2400
www.talkingbookworld.com

TENNIS FACTORY
2500 Wilson Boulevard, Suite 100
Arlington, VA 22201
703-522-2700
www.tennisfactory.com

TORPEDO FACTORY ART CENTER
105 N. Union Street
Alexandria, VA 22314
(703) 838-4565
www.torpedofactory.org

TOTAL WINE AND MORE
1451 Chain Bridge Road
McLean, VA 22101
(703) 749-0011
www.totalwine.com
(See Website or check yellow pages for other locations.)

TRAKSIDE
14457 Potomac Mills Road
Woodbridge, VA 22192
(703) 497-8725

TREE TOP TOYS
1382 Chain Bridge Road
McLean, VA 22101
(703) 356-1400
www.treetopkids.com

TROUSSEAU
306 Maple Avenue West
Vienna, VA 22180
(703) 255-3300
www.trousseaultd.com

UNIVERSAL BEAUTY SUPPLY
1055 W. Broad Street
Falls Church, VA 22046
(703) 534-8882

UPSCALE RESALE
8100 Lee Highway
Falls Church, VA 22042
(703) 698-8100
www.upscale-resale.com

WASHINGTON GOLF CENTER
2625 S. Shirlington Road
Arlington, VA 22206
(703) 979-7888

9709 Lee Highway
Fairfax, VA 22030
(703) 352-7888

14370 Sullyfield Circle
Chantilly, VA 20151
(703) 631-7444
www.washingtongolf.com

WHAT'S IN
1101 S. Joyce Street
Arlington, VA 22202
(703) 414-3353

WHY NOT
200 King Street
Alexandria, VA 22314
(703) 548-4420

WOODBURNERS TWO
6600 Arlington Boulevard
Falls Church, VA 22042
(703) 241-1400
www.woodburnerstwo.com

WOODCRAFT
6123 Backlick Road
Springfield, VA 22150
(703) 912-6727
www.woodcraft.com

YVES DELORME
125 King Street
Alexandria, VA 22314
(703) 549-6600

McLean Square Shopping Center
6651A Old Dominion Drive
McLean, VA 22101
(703) 356-3085
www.yvesdelorme.com

CHAPTER 16

A Directory of Even More Noteworthy Stores

ACCESSORIES

COACH LEATHERWARE
3259 M Street NW
Washington, DC 20007
(202) 333-3005

1100 S, Hayes Street
Arlington, VA 22202
(703) 418-6787

Westfield Shoppingtown Montgomery
7101 Democracy Boulevard
Bethesda, MD 20817
(301) 469-6602
www.coach.com

*FORNASH DESIGNS
3222 M Street NW
Washington, DC 20007
(202) 338-0774

PROPER TOPPER
3213 P Street NW
Washington, DC 20007
(202) 333-6200

1350 Connecticut Avenue NW
Washington, DC 20036
(202) 842-3055
www.propertopper.com

---

*Denotes stores included in the book.   **Denotes stores in our Top Ten.

KATE SPADE INC.
3061 M Street NW
Washington, DC 20007
(202) 333-8302

ARTS AND CRAFTS

APPALACHIAN SPRING
50 Massachusetts Avenue NE
Washington, DC 20002
(202) 682-0505

1415 Wisconsin Avenue NW
Washington, DC 20007
(202) 337-5780

102 W. Jefferson Street
Falls Church, VA 22046
(703) 533-0930

1641 Rockville Pike
Rockville, MD 20852
(301) 230-1380

Reston Town Center
11877 Market Street
Reston, VA 20190
(703) 478-2218

*ART TO WEAR
10455 North Street
Fairfax, VA 22030
(703) 691-9000

**ARTCRAFT COLLECTION
132 King Street
Alexandria, VA 22314
(703) 299-6616

11960 Market Street
Reston, VA 20190

(703) 964-0145
www.artcraftcollection.com

ARTISANS
Langley Shopping Center
1368 Chain Bridge Road
McLean, VA 22101
(703) 506-0158
www.artisansofmclean.com

AS KINDRED SPIRITS
1101 S. Joyce Street
Arlington, VA 22202
(703) 415-9898

Congressional Plaza
1611 Rockville Pike
Rockville, MD 20852
(301) 984-0102

*ELDER CRAFTERS OF ALEXANDRIA, INC.
405 Cameron Street
Alexandria, VA 22314
(703) 683-4338
www.eldercrafters.com

GAZELLE LIMITED
5335 Wisconsin Avenue NW
Washington, DC 20015
(202) 686-5656

*GREY HOUSE POTTERS
5509 Wilson Boulevard North
Arlington, VA 22205
(703) 522-7738

*IMAGINE ARTWEAR
1124 King Street
Alexandria, VA 22314

---

*Denotes stores included in the book.   **Denotes stores in our Top Ten.

(703) 548-1461
www.imagineartwear.com

MAGICAL ANIMAL
The Shops at Georgetown Park
3222 M Street NW
Washington, DC 20007
(202) 337-4476

RED ORCHARD
10217 Old Georgetown Road
Bethesda, MD 20814
(301) 571-7333

*TORPEDO FACTORY ART CENTER
The Shops at Georgetown Park
105 N. Union Street
Alexandria, VA 22314
(703) 838-4565

Arts and Crafts Supplies

*THE ART STORE
3019 M Street NW
Washington, DC 20007
(202) 342-7030

COLOR WHEEL
1374 Chain Bridge Road
McLean, VA 22101
(703) 356-8477

PEARL ART & CRAFT SUPPLIES INC.
5695 Telegraph Road,
Alexandria, VA 22303
(703) 960-3900

12266 Rockville Pike
Rockville, MD 20852
(301) 816-2900

SULLIVAN'S ART SUPPLIES
3412 Wisconsin Avenue NW
Washington, DC 20016
(202) 362-1343

UTRECHT ART & DRAFTING SUPPLIES
1250 Eye Street NW
Washington, DC 20005
(202) 898-0555

AUDIO EQUIPMENT

*DÉJAVU AUDIO LTD.
1401 Chain Bridge Road, Suite 203
McLean, VA 22101
(703) 734-9391
www.dejavuaudio.com

*JS AUDIO
4919 Saint Elmo Avenue
Bethesda, MD 20814
(301) 656-7020
www.jsaudio.com

*SOUND IMAGES
6541 Arlington Boulevard
Falls Church, VA 22042
(703) 534-1733
www.soundimagesusa.com

BICYCLES

BICYCLE PLACE INC.
8313 Grubb Road
Silver Spring, MD 20910
(301) 588-6160
www.thebicycleplace.com

---

*Denotes stores included in the book.

**Denotes stores in our Top Ten.

BICYCLE PRO SHOP
3403 M Street NW
Washington, DC 20007
(202) 337-0311
www.bicycleproshop.com

BIG WHEEL BIKES
1034 33rd Street NW
Washington, DC 20007
(202) 337-0254

3119 Lee Highway
Arlington, VA 22201
(703) 522-1110

2 Prince Street
Alexandria, VA 22314
(703) 739-2300

6917 Arlington Road
Bethesda, MD 20814
(301) 652-0192
www.bigwheelbikes.com

BIKES @ VIENNA
128 Church Street NW
Vienna, VA 22180
(703) 938-8900

CAPITOL HILL BIKES
709 Eighth Street SE
Washington, DC 20003
(202) 544-4234

CITY BIKES
2501 Champlain Street NW
Washington, DC 20009
(202) 265-1564
www.citybikes.com

GRIFFIN CYCLE INC.
4949 Bethesda Avenue
Bethesda, MD 20814
(301) 656-6188
www.griffincycle.com

REVOLUTION CYCLES
3411 M Street NW
Washington, DC 20007
(202) 965-3601

2731 Wilson Boulevard
Arlington, VA 22201
(703) 312-0007
www.revolutioncycles.com

***SPOKES ETC.**
224 Maple Avenue East
Vienna, VA 22180
(703) 281-2004

1506 Belle View Boulevard
Alexandria, VA 22307
(703) 765-8005

1545 N. Quaker Lane
Alexandria, VA 22302
(703) 820-2200
www.spokesetc.com

BOOKS

ADC MAP & TRAVEL CENTER
1636 Eye Street NW
Washington, DC 20006
(202) 628-2608

***BARTLEBY'S BOOKS**
3034 M Street NW
Washington, DC 20007

*Denotes stores included in the book.   **Denotes stores in our Top Ten.

(202) 298-0486
www.bartlebysbooks.com

*BONIFANT BOOKS
11240 Georgia Avenue
Wheaton, MD 20902
(301) 946-1526
www.abebooks.com/home/bonifant

*BRIDGE STREET BOOKS
2814 Pennsylvania Avenue NW
Washington, DC 20007
(202) 965-5200

*CHAPTERS A LITERARY BOOKSTORE
445 11th Street NW
Washington DC 20004
(202) 737-5553
www.chaptersliterary.com

*FRANZ BADER
19111 Eye Street, NW
Washington, DC 20006
(202) 337-5440

GLOVER BOOKS & MUSIC
2319 Wisconsin Avenue NW
Washington, DC 20007
(202) 338-8100

*IDLE TIME BOOKS
2467 18th Street NW
Washington, DC 20009
(202) 232-4774
www.idletime.com

*KARIBU
Prince George's Plaza
3500 East-West Highway
Hyattsville, MD 20782
(301) 559-1140

Bowie Town Center
15624 Emerald Way
Bowie, MD 20716
(301) 352-4110

Iverson Mall
3817 Branch Avenue
Hillcrest Heights, MD 20748
(301) 899-3730

Forest Village Park
3393 Donnell Drive
Forestville, MD 20747
(301) 736-6170

Pentagon City
1100 S. Hayes Street
Arlington, VA 22202
(703) 415-1118
www.karibu.com

*KRAMERBOOKS AND AFTERWORDS
 CAFÉ AND GRILL
1517 Connecticut Avenue NW
Washington, DC 20036
(202) 387-1400
www.kramers.com

LAMBDA RISING BOOKSTORE
1625 Connecticut Avenue NW
Washington, DC 20009
(202) 462-6969

*OLSSON'S BOOKS & RECORDS
1307 19th Street NW
Washington, DC 20036
(202) 785-1133

418 7th Street NW
Washington, DC 20004
(202) 638-7610

---

*Denotes stores included in the book.   **Denotes stores in our Top Ten.

Reagan Washington
   National Airport
Terminal C
Arlington, VA 20001
(703) 417-1087

1735 N. Lynn Street
Arlington, VA 22209
(703) 812-2103

2111 Wilson Boulevard
Arlington, VA 22201
(703) 525-4227

106 S. Union Street
Alexandria, VA 22314
(703) 684-0077

7647 Old Georgetown Road
Bethesda, MD 20814
(301) 652-3336
www.olssons.com

*POLITICS AND PROSE
5015 Connecticut Avenue, NW
Washington, DC 20008
(202) 364-1919 or (800) 722-0790
www.politicsandprose.com

***REITER'S SCIENTIFIC AND
   PROFESSIONAL BOOKS**
2021 K Street NW
Washington, DC 20006
(202) 223-3327
www.reiters.com

**SECOND STORY BOOKS
12160 Parklawn Drive
Rockville, MD 20852
(301) 770-0477

2000 P Street NW
Washington, DC 20036
(202) 659-8884

*TALKING BOOK WORLD
Sugarland Crossing
47010 Community Plaza (Route 7)
Sterling, VA 20164
(703) 433-2400
www.talkingbookworld.com

*TEMPO BOOKSTORE
4905 Wisconsin Avenue NW
Washington, DC 20016
(202) 363-6683

TROVER SHOP
1270 F Street NW
Washington, DC 20004
(202) 347-6460

VERTIGO BOOKS
7346 Baltimore Avenue
College Park, MD 20740
(301) 779-9300

***WASHINGTON LAW AND
   PROFESSIONAL BOOKS**
1900 G Street NW
Washington, DC 20006
(202) 223-5543
www.washingtonlawbooks.com

Newstands

*THE NEWSROOM
1803 Connecticut Avenue NW
Washington DC 20009
(202) 332-1489

---

*Denotes stores included in the book.   **Denotes stores in our Top Ten.

*OLD TOWN NEWS
721 King Street
Alexandria, VA 22314
(703) 739-9024

Children's

*A LIKELY STORY
1555 King Street
Alexandria, VA 22314
(703) 836-2498
www.alikelystory.com

*ALADDIN'S LAMP BOOKS
Lee Harrison Shopping Center
2499 N. Harrison Street, Lower Level, Suite 10
Arlington, VA 22207
(703) 241-8281

*IMAGINATION STATION
4524 Lee Highway
Arlington VA 22201
(703) 522-2047

CAMERAS

*DOMINION CAMERA
112 W. Broad Street
Falls Church, VA 22046
(703) 532-6700
www.dominioncamera.com

*PENN CAMERA
840 E Street NW
Washington, DC 20004
(202) 347-5777

1015 18th Street NW
Washington, DC 20036
(202) 785-7366
www.penncamera.com

*PRO PHOTO
1902 Eye Street NW
Washington, DC 20006
(202) 223-1292
www.prophotodc.com

CAMPING AND HIKING GEAR

CASUAL ADVENTURE
3451 N. Washington Boulevard
Arlington, VA 22201
(703) 527-0600
www.casualadventure.com

EASTERN MOUNTAIN SPORTS
The Market Common
2800 Clarendon Boulevard, Suite R550
Arlington, VA 22201
(703) 248-8310
www.ems.com

GALYANS
2 Grand Corner Avenue
Gaithersburg, MD 20878
(301) 947-0200

12501 Fairlakes Circle
Fairfax, VA 22033
(703) 803-0300
www.galyans.com

---

*Denotes stores included in the book.   **Denotes stores in our Top Ten.

HUDSON TRAIL OUTFITTERS LTD
4530 Wisconsin Avenue NW
Washington, DC 20016
(202) 363-9810

12085 Rockville Pike
Rockville, MD 20852
(301) 881-4955

401 N. Frederick Avenue
Gaithersburg, MD 20879
(301) 948-2474

Pentagon Row
1201 S. Joyce Street, Suite B29
Arlington, VA 22202
(703) 415-4861

Springfield Mall #F-11
6701 Loisdale Road
Springfield, VA 22150
(703) 922-0050

Fair Oaks Mall
11743 Fair Oaks
Fairfax, VA 22033
(703) 385-3907

9488 Arlington Boulevard
Fairfax, VA 22031
(703) 591-2950
www.hudsontrail.com

*L.L. BEAN
Tysons Corner Center
1961 Chain Bridge Road
McLean, VA 22102
(703) 288-4466

REI-RECREATIONAL EQUIPMENT INC.
9801 Rhode Island Avenue
College Park, MD 20740
(301) 982-9681

3509 Carlin Springs Road
Falls Church, VA 22041
(703) 379-9400

11950 Grand Commons Avenue
Fairfax, VA 22030
(571) 522-6568
www.rei.com

SUNNY'S
370 S. Pickett Street
Alexandria, VA 22304
(703) 461-0088

11650 Sudley Manor Drive
Manassas, VA 20110
(703) 257-7069

13718 Washington Boulevard
Laurel MD 20707
(301) 604-5771
www.sunnyssurplus.com

CDS AND RECORDS

*CD CELLAR
709 W. Broad Street
Falls Church, VA 22046
(703) 534-6318

*CDEPOT
9039 Baltimore Avenue
College Park, MD 20740
(301) 982-3472
www.cdepot.com

*JOE'S RECORD PARADISE
1300 E. Gude Drive
Rockville, MD 20850
(301) 315-2235

*Denotes stores included in the book.   **Denotes stores in our Top Ten.

*MELODY RECORD SHOP
1623 Connecticut Avenue NW
Washington, DC 20009
(202) 232-4002
www.melodyrecords.com

*ORPHEUS RECORDS
3173 Wilson Boulevard
Arlington, VA 22201
(703) 294-6774

CLOTHING

Mens'

**BOOT HILL WESTERN
13231 Gordon Boulevard
Woodbridge, VA 22191
(703) 490-0090
www.boothill.us

BROOKS BROTHERS
8009-U Tysons Corner Centerr
McLean, VA 22102
(703) 556-6566

5504 Wisconsin Avenue
Chevy Chase, MD 20815
(301) 654-8202

1201 Connecticut Avenue NW
Washington, DC 20036
(202) 659-4650
www.brooksbrothers.com

BURBERRY'S LIMITED
1155 Connecticut Avenue NW
Washington, DC 20036
(202) 463-3000
www.burberry.com

*COMMANDER SALAMANDER
1420 Wisconsin Avenue NW
Washington, DC 20007
(202) 337-2265

EVERETT HALL DESIGNS
1250 Connecticut Avenue NW
Washington, DC 20036
(202) 467-0003

Chevy Chase Pavilion
5345 Wisconsin Avenue NW
Washington, DC 20015
(202) 362-0191
www.everetthalldesigns.com

*L.L. BEAN
Tysons Corner Center
1961 Chain Bridge Road
McLean, VA 22102
(703) 288-4466
www.llbean.com

*OUTLINE INC.
Prince George's Plaza
3500 East-West Hwy
Hyattsville, MD 20782
(301) 559-9000

POLO RALPH LAUREN
3222 M Street NW
Washington, DC 20007
(202) 965-0904
www.poloralphlauren.com

*POP
1803a 14th Street NW
Washington DC 20009
(202) 332-3312
www.shoppop.com

---

*Denotes stores included in the book.   **Denotes stores in our Top Ten.

*SHERMAN PICKEY
1647 Wisconsin Avenue NW
Washington, DC 20007
(202) 333-4212

*SOUTH MOON UNDER
10247 Old Georgetown Road
Bethesda, MD 20814
(301) 564-0995

Reston Town Center
11950 Market Street
Reston, VA 20190
(703) 435-0605

2700 Clarendon Boulevard
Arlington, VA 22307
(703) 807-4083
www.southmoonunder.com

URBAN OUTFITTERS
3111 M Street NW
Washington, DC 20007
(202) 342-1012
www.urbanoutfitters.com

Women's

*ALL ABOUT JANE
2438½ 18th Street NW
Washington DC 20009
(202) 797-9710

2839 Clarendon Boulevard
Arlington, VA 22201
(703) 243-4424
www.allaboutjane.com

*AN AMERICAN IN PARIS
1225 King Street
Alexandria, VA 22314
(703) 519-8234

*ART TO WEAR
(703) 691-9000
NOTE: Call for current location.

*BELINA
10215 Old Georgetown Road
Bethesda, MD 20814
(301) 897-2929

BETSY FISHER
1224 Connecticut Avenue NW
Washington, DC 20036
(202) 785-1975

**BOOT HILL WESTERN STORE
13231 Gordon Boulevard
Woodbridge, VA 22191
(703) 490-0090
www.boothill.us

CHANEL BOUTIQUE
1455 Pennsylvania Avenue NW
Washington, DC 20004
(202) 638-5055
www.chanel.com

*COMMANDER SALAMANDER
1420 Wisconsin Avenue NW
Washington, DC 20007
(202) 337-2265

*DAISY
1814 Adams Mill Road NW
Washington, DC 20009
(202) 797-1777

*DAISY II
4940 St. Elmo Avenue
Bethesda, MD 20814
(301) 656-2280

*Denotes stores included in the book.　　**Denotes stores in our Top Ten.

FORECAST
218 Seventh Street SE
Washington, DC 20003
(202) 547-7337

FRENCH CONNECTION
1229 Wisconsin Avenue NW
Washington, DC 20007
(202) 965-4690

*IRRESISTIBLES
Wildwood Shopping Center
10301 Old Georgetown Road
Bethesda, MD 20814
(301) 897-2574

*JUDY RYAN OF FAIRFAX
9565 Braddock Road
Fairfax, VA 22032
(703) 425-1855

*LEMON TWIST
4518 N. Lee Highway
Arlington, VA 22207
(703) 524-4680

8534 Connecticut Avenue
Chevy Chase, MD 20815
(301) 986-0044

*L.L. BEAN
Tysons Corner Center
1961 Chain Bridge Road
McLean, Virginia 22102
(703) 288-4466
www.llbean.com

LUNA
7232 Woodmont Avenue
Bethesda, MD 20814
(301) 656-1111
www.shopluna.com

MICMAC BIS
5301 Wisconsin Avenue NW
Washington, DC 20015
(202) 362-6834

*NANA
1534 U Street NW
Washington, DC 20009
(202) 667-6955
www.nanadc.com

*OUTLINE INC.
Prince George's Plaza
3500 East-West Hwy
Hyattsville, MD 20782
(301) 559-9000

*THE PHOENIX
1514 Wisconsin Avenue NW
Washington, DC 20007
(202) 338-4404

*PIRJO
1044 Wisconsin Avenue NW
Washington, DC 20007
(202) 337-1390

4821 Bethesda Avenue
Bethesda, MD 20814
(301) 986-1870

*PLAID
715 Eighth Street SE
Washington, DC 20003
(202) 675-6900
www.plaidstore.com

RIZIK BROTHERS INC.
1100 Connecticut Avenue NW
Washington, DC 20036
(202) 223-4050
www.riziks.com

*Denotes stores included in the book.   **Denotes stores in our Top Ten.

SAKS-JANDEL
Watergate
2522 Virginia Avenue NW
Washington, DC 20037
(202) 337-4200

5510 Wisconsin Avenue
Chevy Chase, MD 20815
(301) 652-2250

*SHERMAN PICKEY
1647 Wisconsin Avenue NW
Washington, DC 20007
(202) 333-4212

*SOUTH MOON UNDER
Bethesda Wildwood Center
10247 Old Georgetown Road
Bethesda, MD 20814
(301) 564-0995

Reston Town Center
11950 Market Street
Reston, VA 20190
(703) 435-0605

2700 Clarendon Boulevard
Arlington, VA 22307
(703) 807-4083
www.southmoonunder.com

*SUGAR
1633 Wisconsin Avenue NW
Washington, DC 20007
(202) 333-5231

URBAN OUTFITTERS
3111 M Street NW
Washington, DC 20007

(202) 342-1012
www.urbanoutfitters.com

*WHAT'S IN
1101 S. Joyce Street
Arlington, VA 22202
(703) 414-3353

Children's

KID'S CLOSET
1226 Connecticut Avenue NW
Washington, DC 20036
(202) 429-9247

*MADELEINE'S KIDS INC.
1521 King Street
Alexandria, VA 22314
(703) 836-9046
www.madeleineskids.com

*PICCOLO PIGGIES
1533 Wisconsin Avenue NW
Washington, DC 20007
(202) 333-0123

*THE RED APPLE
Oakton Shopping Center
2922 Chain Bridge Road
Oakton, VA 22124
(703) 281-1701

*WHY NOT
200 King Street
Alexandria, VA 22314
(703) 548-4420

*YOUNG WORLD
3723 Branch Avenue
Temple Hills, MD 20748
(301) 423-0883

*Denotes stores included in the book.   **Denotes stores in our Top Ten.

OFF-PRICE

A. J. WRIGHT
7844 Richmond Highway
Alexandria, VA 22306
(703) 704-9161

Smoketown Road & Gideon Drive
Woodbridge, VA 22192
(703) 490-2314
www.tjx.com/about/ajwright.html

BURLINGTON COAT FACTORY
(Check Web site yellow pages for location nearest you.)

*DAFFY'S
Potomac Mills Mall
2700 Potomac Mills Circle
Woodbridge, VA 22192
(703) 494-3636
www.daffys.com

FILENE'S BASEMENT
5300 Wisconsin Avenue NW
Washington, DC 20015
(202) 966-0208

529 14th Street NW
Washington, DC 20045
(202) 638-4110

*K & G MENS WEAR
5832 Columbia Pike
Falls Church, VA 22041
(703) 931-1124

4955 Nicholson Court
Kensington, MD 20895
(301) 231-8140
www.kgmens.com

LOEHMANN'S
5333 Wisconsin Avenue NW
Washington, DC 20015
(202) 362-4733

7241 Arlington Boulevard
Falls Church, VA 22042
(703) 573-1510

5230 Randolph Road
Rockville, MD 20852
(301) 770-0030
www.loehmanns.com

MARSHALLS
www.marshallsonline.com
(See yellow pages for location nearest you.)

*NORDSTROM RACK
Potomac Mills
2700 Potomac Mills Circle
Woodbridge, VA 22192
(703) 490-1440

T. J. MAXX
www.tjmaxx.com
(See yellow pages for mulitple locations)

*VALUE CITY
Iverson Mall
3701 Branch Avenue
Temple Hills, MD 20748
(301) 899-5101

Beltway Plaza
6252 Greenbelt Road
Greenbelt, MD 20770
(301) 441-9588
www.valuecity.com

---

*Denotes stores included in the book.   **Denotes stores in our Top Ten.

Swimwear

BIKINI SHOP
741 15th Street NW
Washington, DC 20005
(202) 331-8372
www.bikinishop.com

*SOUTH MOON UNDER
Bethesda Wildwood Center
10247 Old Georgetown Road
Bethesda, MD 20814
(301) 564-0995

Reston Town Center
11950 Market Street
Reston, VA 20190
(703) 435-0605

2700 Clarendon Boulevard
Arlington, VA 22307
(703) 807-4083
www.southmoonunder.com

Lingerie

ABRIELLE
3301 New Mexico Avenue NW
Washington, DC 20016
(202) 364-6118

*TROUSSEAU
306 Maple Avenue West
Vienna, VA 22180
(703) 255-3300
www.trousseaultd.com

Consignment Boutiques

*ENCORE
110 S. Union Street
Alexandria, VA 22314
(703) 683-1756

*ENCORE RESALE DRESS SHOP
3715 Macomb Street NW
Washington, DC 20016
(202) 966-8122

*INGA'S ONCE IS NOT ENOUGH
4830 MacArthur Boulevard NW
Washington, DC 20007
(202) 337-3072

*NEW TO YOU
125 N. Washington Street,
Falls Church, VA 22046
(703) 533-1251
www.newtoyou.net

*THE RITZ BOUTIQUE
5014 Nicholson Lane
Rockville, Maryland 20852
(301) 230-2167
www.ritzconsignment.com

*SECOND CHANCE
7702 Woodmont Avenue, # 205
Bethesda, MD 20814
(301) 652-6606

SECONDHAND ROSE
1516 Wisconsin Avenue NW
Washington, DC 20007
(202) 337-3378

*SECONDI INC.
1702 Connecticut Avenue NW
Washington, DC 20009
(202) 667-1122

Vintage

BOUTIQUE UNIQUE
2499 N. Harrison Street
Arlington, VA 22207

---

*Denotes stores included in the book.   **Denotes stores in our Top Ten.

(703) 538-4850
www.boutique-unique.com

MEEPS & AUNT NEENSIE'S VINTAGE CLOTHING
1520 U Street NW
Washington, DC 20009
(202) 265-6546
www.meepsonu.com

*RAGE CLOTHING
1069 Wisconsin Avenue NW
Washington, DC 20007
(202) 333-1069
www.rageclothing.com

COMPUTERS

APPLE STORE
Market Common at Clarendon
2700 Clarendon Boulevard
Arlington, VA 22201
(703) 875-9880

*COMPUTER WAREHOUSE
Tyson's Station Shopping Center
7516 Leesburg Pike
Falls Church, VA 22043
(703) 821-1400
www.pcretro.com/webstore

COMP USA
Alexandria:
5901 Stevenson Avenue
Alexandria, VA 22304
703) 212-6610

Fairfax:
12189 Fair Lakes Parkway
Fair Lakes Promenade
Fairfax, VA 22033
(703) 359-1401

Gaithersburg:
500 Perry Parkway
Gaithersburg, MD 20877
(301) 947-0001

Rockville:
1776 E. Jefferson, #203
Rockville, MD 20852
(301) 816-8963

Vienna:
8357 Leesburg Pike
Vienna, VA 22180
(703) 821-7700

Woodbridge:
14427 Potomac Mills Road
Woodbridge, VA 22192
(703) 492-6262
www.compusa.com

*MICRO CENTER
Pan Am Plaza
3089 Nutley Street
Fairfax, VA 22031
(703) 204-8400
www.microcenter.com

*PC RETRO
5031 Garrett Avenue
Beltsville, MD 20705
(301) 931-6630
www.pcretro.com/webstore

COSMETICS

*BELLACARA
924 King Street
Alexandria, VA 22314
(703) 299-9652
www.bellacara.com

---

*Denotes stores included in the book.   **Denotes stores in our Top Ten.

*BLUEMERCURY
3059 M Street NW
Washington, DC 20007
(202) 965-1300

1619 Connecticut Avenue NW
Washington, DC 20009
(202) 462-1300
www.bluemercury.com

*LUSH
3066 M Street NW
Washington DC 20007
(202) 333-6950

PERFUMANIA
Fashion Centre at Pentagon City
1100 S. Hayes Street
Arlington, VA 22202
(703) 418-0877

Potomac Mills
2700 Potomac Mills Circle
Prince William, VA 22192
(703) 497-4773
www.perfumania.com

*RODMAN'S
5100 Wisconsin Avenue NW
Washington, DC 20016
(202) 363-3466

5148 Nicholson Lane
Rockville, MD 20895
(301) 881-6253

4301 Randolph Road
Wheaton, MD 20906
(301) 946-3100
www.rodmans.com

*UNIVERSAL BEAUTY SUPPLY
1055 W. Broad Street
Falls Church, VA 22046
(703) 534-8882

COSTUMES

ARTISTIC DANCE FASHIONS INC.
4915 Cordell Avenue
Bethesda, MD 20814
(301) 652-2323

**BACKSTAGE INC.
545 Eighth Street SE
Washington, DC 20003
(202) 544-5744
www.backstagebooks.com

STEIN'S THEATRICAL AND
    DANCE SUPPLY
3100 Clarendon Boulevard
Arlington, Virginia 22201
(703) 522-2660
www.steins-theatrical.com

CURTAINS

COUNTRY CURTAINS
4805 First Street North
Arlington, VA 22203
(703) 522-7111

DISCOUNT

(See also Clothing, Off-Price)

*AMAZING SAVINGS
4816 Boiling Brook Parkway
Rockville, MD 20852
(301) 770-9022

---

*Denotes stores included in the book.   **Denotes stores in our Top Ten.

*THE COMPLEMENT
656 S. Pickett Street
Alexandria, VA 22304
(703) 751-5600

DOLLHOUSE SUPPLIES

*MINIATURES FROM THE ATTIC
111 Park Avenue
Falls Church, VA 22046
(703) 237-0066
www.minis4u.com

FABRIC

*G STREET FABRICS
Potomac Mills
2700 Potomac Mills Circle
Woodbridge, VA 22192
(703) 494-5900

Seven Corners Center
6250 Arlington Boulevard
Falls Church, VA 22044
(703) 241-1700

Sully Station
5077 Westfield Boulevard
Centreville, VA 20120
(703) 818-8090

Mid-Pike Plaza
11854 Rockville Pike
Rockville, MD 20852
(301) 231-8998
www.gstreetfabrics.com

FIREPLACE

OFFENBACHER'S
(See Garden and Patio Below)

*WOODBURNERS TWO
6600 Arlington Boulevard
Falls Church, VA 22042
(703) 241-1400
www.woodburnerstwo.com

FOOD

Gourmet and Produce

*BRADLEY FOOD AND BEVERAGE
6904 Arlington Road
Bethesda, MD 20814
(301) 654-6966

*DEAN AND DELUCA
3276 M Street NW
Washington, DC 20007
(202) 342-2500

*EASTERN MARKET
225 Seventh Street SE (near
    Capitol Hill)
Washington, DC 20003
www.easternmarket.net

**EATZI'S
11503-B Rockville Pike
Rockville, Maryland 20852
(301) 816-2020
www.eatzis.com

*MONTGOMERY FARM WOMEN'S
    COOPERATIVE MARKET
7155 Wisconsin Avenue
Bethesda, MD 20814
(301) 652-2291

*RODMAN'S DISCOUNT GOURMET
White Flint Plaza
5148 Nicholson Lane
Rockville, MD 20895

---

*Denotes stores included in the book.   **Denotes stores in our Top Ten.

(301) 881-6253
www.rodmans.com

*SUTTON PLACE
   GOURMET/BALDACCI'S
3201 New Mexico Avenue NW
Washington, DC 20016
(202) 363-5800
www.suttongourmet.com
(See yellow pages for other
   locations)

Italian

*A LITTERI
517–519 Morse Street NE
Washington, DC 20002
(202) 544-0183

*THE ITALIAN STORE
3123 Lee Highway
Arlington, VA 22201
(703) 528-6266

Latin American

*BESTWAY
3109 Graham Road
Falls Church, VA 22042
(703) 560-2101

690 Elden Street
Herndon, VA 20170
(703) 668-0323

*BY BRAZIL
11335 Georgia Avenue
Wheaton, MD 20902
(301) 962-6686

Middle Eastern

*APHRODITE
5886 Leesburg Pike
Falls Church, VA 22041
(703) 931-5055

*MEDITERRANEAN BAKERY AND CAFÉ
352 S. Pickett Street
Alexandria, VA 22304
(703) 751-1702
www.eastwestmart.com

German

*GERMAN GOURMET
7185 Lee Highway
Falls Church, VA 22046
(703) 534-1908
www.german-gourmet.com

Russian

*THE RUSSIAN GOURMET
1396 Chain Bridge Road
McLean, VA 22101
(703) 760-0680
www.russian-gourmet.com

Asian

*SUPER H MART
10780 Lee Highway
Fairfax, VA 22030
(800) 427-9870
www.superhmart.com

FURNITURE

(See also, HOME ACCESSORIES AND
   FURNISHINGS below.)

---

*Denotes stores included in the book.   **Denotes stores in our Top Ten.

APARTMENT ZERO
406 Seventh Street NW
Washington, DC 20004
(202) 628-4067
www.apartmentzero.com

ARHAUS
4213 Fairfax Corner East Avenue
Fairfax Corner, VA 22030
(703) 968-9688
www.arhaus.com

BAKER GEORGETOWN
3330 M Street NW
Washington, DC 20007
(202) 342-7080

COLONY HOUSE
1700 Lee Highway
Arlington, VA 22209
(703) 524-1700

13818 Braddock Road
Centreville, VA 20121
(703) 266-7777

CONTEMPORARIA
4926 Del Ray Avenue
Bethesda, MD 20814
(301) 913-9602
www.contemporaria.com

DANKER FURNITURE
1211 S. Fern Street
Arlington, VA 22202
(703) 416-0200

120 Halpine Road
Rockville, MD 20852
(301) 881-6010

1582 Rockville Pike
Rockville, MD 20852
(301) 881-6010

10431 Lee Highway
Fairfax, VA 22030
(703) 218-5422

ETHAN ALLEN
www.ethanallen.com
(See yellow pages or Web site for locations)

*FRENCH COUNTRY LIVING
10135 Colvin Run Road
Great Falls, VA 22066
(703) 759-2245
www.frenchcountry.com

IKEA
Potomac Mills
2901 Potomac Mills Circle
Woodbridge, VA 22192
(703) 494-4532

10100 Baltimore Avenue
College Park, MD 20740
(301) 345-6552
www.ikea.com

KREISS COLLECTION
5215 Wisconsin Avenue NW
Washington, DC 20015
(202) 537-7333

KELLOGG COLLECTION
3424 Wisconsin Avenue NW
Washington, DC 20016
(202) 363-6879

---

*Denotes stores included in the book.   **Denotes stores in our Top Ten.

10241 Old Georgetown Road
Bethesda, MD 20814
(301) 897-9102

1353 Chain Bridge Road
McLean, VA 22101
(703) 506-0850
www.kelloggcollection.com

MASTERCRAFT INTERIORS
www.mastercraftinteriors.com
(See yellow pages or web for location near you)

MULEH HOME FURNISHINGS
4731 Elm Street
Bethesda, MD 20814
(301) 941-1174

1831 14th Street NW
Washington, DC 20009
(202) 667-3440
www.muleh.com

SKYNEAR & CO.
2122 18th Street NW
Washington, DC 20009
(202) 797-7160

THOS. MOSER CABINETMAKERS
3300 M Street
Washington, DC 20007
(202) 338-4292

TIMOTHY WILLIAMS
101 N. Union Street
Alexandria, VA 22314
(703) 739-4285
www.timothywilliamsonline.com

VASTU
1829 14th Street NW
Washington, DC 20009
(202) 234-8344
www.vastudc.com

GAMES

*GAME PARLOR
14400 Smoketown Road
Woodbridge, VA 22192
(703) 551-4200

13936 Metrotech Drive
Chantilly, VA 20151
(703) 803-3114
www.gameparlor.com

GOLF

DRILLING TENNIS & GOLF
1040 17th Street NW
Washington, DC 20036
(202) 737-1100

EAST COAST GOLF & TENNIS
10438 Auto Park Avenue
Bethesda, MD 20817
(301) 469-7000

*GOLFDOM
8203 Watson Street
McLean, VA 22102
(703) 790-8844
www.golfdomgolf.com

*WASHINGTON GOLF CENTER
6831 Wisconsin Avenue
Bethesda, MD 20815
(301) OK2-GOLF

---

*Denotes stores included in the book.   **Denotes stores in our Top Ten.

9811 Washingtonian Boulevard
Gaithersburg, MD 20878
(301) 948-7888

2625 S. Shirlington Road
Arlington, VA 22206
(703) 979-7888

9709 Lee Highway
Fairfax, VA 22031
(703) 352-7888

14370 Sullyfield Circle
Chantilly, VA 20151
(703) 631-7444

HATS

*THE HATTERY
3222 M Street, NW
Washington, DC 20007
(202) 364-HATS

PROPER TOPPER
3213 P Street NW
Washington, DC 20007
(202) 333-6200

HARDWARE

FISCHER'S HARDWARE
Concord Centre Plaza
6129 Backlick Road
Springfield, VA 22150
(703) 451-3700

RESTORATION HARDWARE INC.
1222 Wisconsin Avenue NW
Washington, DC 20007
(202) 625-2771

614 King Street
Alexandria, VA 22314
(703) 299-6220

Tysons Corner Center
1961 Chain Bridge Road
McLean, VA 22102
(703) 821-9655
www.restorationhardware.com

*STROSNIDER'S
6930 Arlington Road
Bethesda, MD 20814
(301) 654-5688

815 Wayne Avenue
Silver Spring, MD 20910
(301) 565-9150

10110 River Road
Potomac, MD 20854
(301) 299-6333
www.strosniders.com

HOBBY SHOPS

ANIME PAVILION
7395-B Lee Highway
Falls Church, VA 22042
(703) 204-1844
animepavilion.com/animepavilion.html

*GRANDDAD'S HOBBY SHOP
5260-A Port Royal Road
Springfield, VA 22151
(703) 426-0700
www.granddadshobbyshop.com

*PEACH CREEK SHOPS
201 Main Street
Laurel, MD 20707
(301) 498-9071
www.peachcreekshops.com

---

*Denotes stores included in the book.   **Denotes stores in our Top Ten.

*POTOMAC TRADING COLLECTIBLES
3610 University Boulevard West
Kensington, MD 20895
(301) 949-5656

**THE TOY EXCHANGE
11265 Triangle Lane
Wheaton, Maryland 20902
(301) 929-0690
www.montgomerycountymd.com/
   shopping/toyexchange

*TRAKSIDE
14457 Potomac Mills Road
Woodbridge, VA 22192
(703) 497-8725

HOME FURNISHINGS AND ACCESSORIES

(See also, FURNITURE.)

*AFRICAN STARGINA COLLECTIONS
3500 East-West Highway
Hyattsville, MD 20782
(301) 559-8418

***ALVEAR STUDIO DESIGN
   AND IMPORTS**
705 Eighth Street SE
Washington, DC 20003
(202) 546-8434
www.alvearstudio.com

*AMERICAN STUDIO
2906 M Street NW
Washington, DC 20007
(202) 965-3273

*BACK DOOR
2499 N. Harrison Street
Arlington, VA 22207

(703) 237-6117
www.thebackdoorinc.com

BEEKEEPER'S COTTAGE
43738 Hay Road
Ashburn, VA 20147
(703) 726-9411

42350 Lucketts Road
Lucketts, VA 20176
(703) 771-9006
www.beekeeperscottage.com

*CHINOISERIE
1024 King Street
Alexandria, VA 22314
(703) 838-0520

GEORGETOWN FRAME SHOPPE
2902½ M Street NW
Washington, DC 20007
(202) 338-1097
www.georgetownframeshoppe.com

*GO MAMA GO
1809 14th Street NW
Washington, DC 20009
(202) 299-0850

HOME RULE
1807 14th Street NW
Washington, DC 20009
(202) 797-5544
www.homerule.com

*ZAWADI
1524 U Street NW
Washington, DC 20009
(202) 232-2214

---

*Denotes stores included in the book.   **Denotes stores in our Top Ten.

Garden

GARDEN DISTRICT
1801 14th Street NW
Washington, DC 20009
(202) 797-9005

***MRS MCGREGOR'S GARDEN SHOP**
4801 First Street North
Arlington, VA 22203
(703) 528-8773

***PARK PLACE**
2251 Wisconsin Avenue NW
Washington, DC 20007
(202) 342-6294

PLOW & HEARTH COUNTRY STORE AND CATALOG OUTLET
Route 29 North
Madison, VA 22727
(540) 948-3659
www.plowhearth.com

***SMITH & HAWKEN**
1209 31st Street NW
Washington, DC 20007
(202) 965-2680

8551 Connecticut Avenue
Chevy Chase, MD 20815
(301) 215-5960

6705 Whittier Avenue
McLean, VA 22101
(703) 506-0065
www.smithandhawken.com

Patio

OFFENBACHER'S
1120-D W. Broad Street
Falls Church, VA 22046
(703) 532-2883

6123-A Backlick Road
Springfield, VA 22150
(703) 569-5700

46262-115 Cranston Street
Sterling, VA 20165
(703) 444-8882

5500 Randolph Road
Rockville, MD 20852
(301) 881-8565
www.offenbachers.com

***PARK PLACE**
2251 Wisconsin Avenue NW
Washington, DC 20007
(202) 342-6294

Glassware and Pottery

***A MANO**
1677 Wisconsin Avenue NW
Washington, DC 20007
(202) 298-7200

***GREY HOUSE POTTERS**
5509 Wilson Boulevard North
Arlington, VA 22205
(703) 522-7738

***MY PLACE IN TUSCANY**
1127 King Street
Alexandria, VA 22314
(703) 683-8882

QUIMPER FAIENCE
1121 King Street
Alexandria, VA 22314
703 519-8339

*Denotes stores included in the book.

**Denotes stores in our Top Ten.

Vintage

**GOOD EYE
4918 Wisconsin Avenue NW
Washington, DC 20016
(202) 244-8516
www.goodeyeonline.com

GOOD WOOD INC.
1428 U Street NW
Washington, DC 20009
(202) 986-3640

MILLENNIUM DECORATIVE ARTS
1528 U Street NW
Washington, DC 20009
(202) 483-1218

**OLD LUCKETT'S STORE
42350 Lucketts Road (Route 15)
Leesburg, VA 20176
(703) 779-0268
www.luckettstore.com

*REUNIONS
1709 Centre Plaza
Alexandria, VA 22302
(703) 931-8161

*SIXTEEN FIFTY-NINE
1659 Wisconsin Avenue NW
Washington, DC 20007
(202) 333-1480

*UPSCALE RESALE
8100 Lee Highway
Falls Church, VA 22042
(703) 698-8100
www.upscale-resale.com

JEWELRY

*ALL ABOUT JANE
2438½ 18th Street NW
Washington DC 20009
(202) 797-9710
www.allaboutjane.com

*ARTCRAFT COLLECTION
132 King Street
Alexandria, VA 22314
(703) 299-6616
www.artcraftcollection.com

*ARTS AFIRE
102 N. Fayette Street
Alexandria, VA 22314
(703) 838-9785

*ART TO WEAR
(703) 691-9000
NOTE: Call for current location.

*IMAGINE ARTWEAR
1124 King Street
Alexandria, VA 22314
(703) 548-1461
www.imagineartwear.com

*THE PHOENIX
1514 Wisconsin Avenue NW
Washington, DC 20007
(202) 338-4404

*PIRJO
1044 Wisconsin Avenue NW
Washington, DC 20007
(202) 337-1390

---

*Denotes stores included in the book.   **Denotes stores in our Top Ten.

*PLAID
715 Eighth Street SE
Washington, DC 20003
(202) 675-6900
www.plaidstore.com

*TINY JEWEL BOX
1147 Connecticut Avenue NW
Washington, DC 20036
(202) 393-2747
www.tinyjewelbox.com

*WHAT'S IN
1101 S. Joyce Street
Arlington, VA 22202
(703) 414-3353

LAMPS

ANNAPOLIS LIGHTING CO.
6533 Arlington Boulevard
Falls Church, VA 22042
(703) 536-6220

1616-A Rockville Pike
Rockville, MD 20852
(301) 231-4994

ARTISAN LAMP
3331 Connecticut Avenue NW
Washington, DC 20008
(202) 244-8900

GAYLORD LAMPS & SHADES
4620 Leland Street
Chevy Chase, MD 20815
(301) 986-9680

ILLUMINATIONS
3323 Cady's Alley NW
Washington, DC 20007

(202) 965-4888
www.illuminations.com

Tysons Corner Center
1961 Chain Bridge Road
McLean, VA 22102
(703) 790-8610

Westfield Shoppingtown Montgomery
7101 Democracy Boulevard
Bethesda, MD 20817
(301) 365-8848

LAMPS UNLIMITED
1362 Chain Bridge Road
McLean, VA 22101
(703) 827-0090

LINENS

*BALDAQUIN
1413 Wisconsin Avenue NW
Washington, DC 20007
(202) 625-1600
www.baldaquin.com

*KUGLER'S HOME FASHIONS
20 University Boulevard West
Silver Spring, MD 20902
(301) 593-8905
www.kuglers.com

*LA CASA BELLA
1213 King Street
Alexandria, VA 22314
(703) 684-1213

*WATERWORKS
3314 M Street NW
Washington, DC 20007
(202) 333-7180

---

*Denotes stores included in the book. **Denotes stores in our Top Ten.

MAGIC SHOPS

*BARRY'S MAGIC SHOP
11234 Georgia Avenue
Wheaton, MD 20902
(301) 933-0373
www.barrysmagicshop.com

MUSICAL INSTRUMENTS

*ACTION MUSIC
6501 N. 29th Street
Arlington, VA 22213
(703) 534-4801

*ATOMIC MUSIC
9035 Baltimore Avenue
College Park, MD 20740
(301) 474-5752

*CHUCK LEVIN'S WASHINGTON MUSIC CENTER
11151 Viers Mill Road
Wheaton, MD 20902
(301) 946-8808
www.washingtonmusic.com

*DALE MUSIC CO.
8240 Georgia Avenue
Silver Spring, MD 20910
(301) 589-1459
www.dalemusic.com

*FOXES MUSIC CO.
416 S. Washington Street
Falls Church, VA 22046
(703) 533-7239 or (800) 446-4414
www.foxesmusic.com

*HOUSE OF MUSICAL TRADITIONS
7040 Carroll Avenue
Takoma Park, MD 20912

(301) 270-9090
www.musicaltraditions.com

**SOUTHWORTH GUITARS
7845 Old Georgetown Road
Bethesda, MD 20814
(301) 718-1667

SHOES

PRINCE & PRINCESS
1400 Wisconsin Avenue NW
Washington, DC 20007
(202) 337-4211

*SASSANOVA
1641 Wisconsin Avenue NW
Washington, DC 20007
(202) 471-4400

SHAKE YOUR BOOTY INC.
2439 18th Street NW
Washington, DC 20009
(202) 518-8205

*SHOE FLY
2618 Wilson Boulevard
Arlington, VA 22201
(703) 243-6490

SHOES BY LARA
1139 18th Street NW
Washington, DC 20036
(202) 331-5002

913 19th Street NW
Washington, DC 20006
(202) 659-9420

703 14th Street NW
Washington, DC 20005
(202) 637-9787

*Denotes stores included in the book.   **Denotes stores in our Top Ten.

1622 Crystal Square Arcade
Arlington, VA 22202
(703) 416-4162

*WILD WOMEN WEAR RED
1512 U Street NW
Washington, DC 20009
(202) 387-5700

Athletic

FLEET FEET
1841 Columbia Road NW
Washington, DC 20009
(202) 387-3888
www.fleetfeetdc.com

GEORGETOWN RUNNING CO.
3401 M Street NW
Washington, DC 20007
(202) 337-8626
www.dcrunningcompany.com

METRO RUN & WALK
1776 E. Jefferson Street
Rockville, MD 20852
(301) 984-2900

7516 Leesburg Pike
Falls Church, VA 22043
(703) 790-3338

7251 Commerce Street
Springfield, VA 22150
(703) 913-0313
www.runwalklive.com

PACERS
1301 King Street
Alexandria, VA 22314
(703) 836-1463
www.runpacers.com

Children's

JEANNE'S SHOES
5110 Ridgefield Road, #203
Bethesda, MD 20816
(301) 654-3877

RAMER'S STRIDE RITE FOR CHILDREN
3810 Northampton Street NW
Washington, DC 20015
(202) 244-2288

SPORTING GOODS

GALYAN'S
2 Grand Corner Avenue
Gaithersburg, MD, 20878
(301) 947-0200

12501 Fairlakes Circle
Fairfax, VA 22033
(703) 803-0300
www.galyans.com

***PLAY IT AGAIN SPORTS**
5750 Union Mill Road
Clifton, VA 20124
(703) 266-8577
www.playitagainsports.com

***REPLAY SPORTS (SPORT PROS)**
Leesburg Pike Plaza
3537 S Jefferson Street
Falls Church, VA 22041
(703) 998-4231
www.tennisracketpros.com

SPRINGRIVER CORP.
5606 Randolph Road
Rockville, MD 20852
(301) 881-5694

---

*Denotes stores included in the book.   **Denotes stores in our Top Ten.

2757 Summerfield Road
Falls Church, VA 22042
(703) 241-2818
www.springriver.com

Skis and Skates

*ALPINE SKI SHOP
45573 Church Road
Sterling, VA 20164
(703) 444-7844
www.alpineskishop.com

PRO-FIT SKI & SKATE
545-D E. Market Street
Leesburg, VA 20176
(703) 777-7547
www.ski-skate.com

SKI CENTER
49th Street & Massachusetts Avenue NW
Washington, DC 20016
(202) 966-4474
www.skicenter.com

*SKI CHALET
2704 Columbia Pike
Arlington, VA 22204
(703) 521-1700

8338 Leesburg Pike
Tysons Corner, VA 22182
(703) 761-3040

14130 Sullyfield Circle
Chantilly, VA 20151
(703) 631-7880

203 Muddy Branch Road
Gaithersburg, MD 20878
(301) 948-5200
www.skichalet.com

TENNIS

EAST COAST GOLF & TENNIS
10438 Auto Park Avenue
Bethesda, MD 20817
(301) 469-7000

*TENNIS FACTORY
2500 Wilson Boulevard, Suite 100
Arlington, VA 22201
(703) 522-2700
www.tennisfactory.com

TOYS

*ANGLO DUTCH POOL AND TOYS
5460 Westbard Avenue
Bethesda, MD 20816
(301) 951-0636

*CHILD'S PLAY
5536 Connecticut Avenue NW
Washington, DC 20015
(202) 244-3602

KINDER HAUS TOYS
4510 Lee Highway
Arlington, VA 22207
(703) 527-5929
www.kinderhaus.com

*MY FRIENDS AND ME
118 South Street SE
Leesburg, VA 20175
(703) 777-8222
www.myfriendsandme.com

*SULLIVAN'S TOY STORE
3412 Wisconsin Avenue NW
Washington, DC 20016
(202) 362-1343

---

*Denotes stores included in the book. **Denotes stores in our Top Ten.

**THE TOY EXCHANGE
11265 Triangle Lane
Wheaton, Maryland 20902
(301) 929-0690
www.montgomerycountymd.com/
  shopping/toyexchange.htm

TREE TOP TOYS & BOOKS
3301 New Mexico Avenue NW
Washington, DC 20016
(202) 244-3500

1382 Chain Bridge Road
McLean, VA 22101
(703) 356-1400
www.treetopkids.com

VITAMINS

*BETHESDA CO-OP
6500 Seven Locks Road
Bethesda, MD 20818
(301) 320-2530

*CO-OP SUPERMARKET
121 Centerway
Greenbelt, MD 20770
(301) 474-0522

*EVERLASTING LIFE
Hampton Mall
9185 Central Avenue
Capitol Heights, MD 20743
(301) 324-6900

2928 Georgia Avenue NW
Washington, DC 20001
(202) 232-1700
www.everlastinglife.net

*MY ORGANIC MARKET
3831 Mount Vernon Avenue
Alexandria, VA 22305
(703) 535-5980

9827 Rhode Island Avenue
College Park, MD 20740
(301) 220-1100

11711 Parklawn Drive
Rockville, MD 20852
(301) 816-4944

*NATURALLY YOURS
2029 P Street NW
Washington, DC 20036
(202) 429-1718

*SECRETS OF NATURE
3923 S. Capitol Street SW
Washington, DC 20032
(202) 562-0041

*TAKOMA PARK-SILVER SPRING FOOD CO-OP
201 Ethan Allen Avenue
Takoma Park, MD 20912
(301) 891-2667

8309 Grubb Road
Silver Spring, MD 20910
(240) 247-2667
www.tpss.org

THE VITAMIN SHOPPE
www.thevitaminshoppe.com
(See Website or check the yellow pages
  for the locations nearest you.)

*WHEATON HEALTH FOODS INC.
2656 University Boulevard W
Wheaton, MD 20902
(301) 933-3066

---

*Denotes stores included in the book.   **Denotes stores in our Top Ten.

WHOLE FOODS MARKET
www.wholefoods.com
(See Website or check the yellow pages
   for the locations nearest you.)

*YES! NATURAL GOURMET
1825 Columbia Road NW
Washington, DC 20009
(202) 462-5150

*YES! ORGANIC MARKET
3425 Connecticut Avenue NW
Washington, DC 20008
(202) 363-1559

WINE AND BEER

*CALVERT-WOODLEY LIQUORS
4339 Connecticut Avenue NW
Washington, DC 20008
(202) 966-4400

*CHEVY CHASE WINE AND SPIRITS
5544 Connecticut Avenue NW
Washington, DC 20015
(202) 363-4000

*MACARTHUR BEVERAGES
4877 MacArthur Boulevard NW
Washington, DC 20007
(202) 338-1433
www.bassins.com

*NORM'S BEER AND WINE
136 Branch Road SE
Vienna, VA 22180
(703) 242-0100

*PEARSON'S
2436 Wisconsin Avenue NW
Washington, DC 20007
(202) 333-6666
www.pearsonswinewebsite.com

*SCHNEIDER'S OF CAPITOL HILL
300 Massachusetts Avenue NE
Washington, DC 20002
(202) 543-9300

*TOTAL WINE AND MORE
1451 Chain Bridge Road
McLean, VA 22101
(703) 749-0011
www.totalwine.com
(See Website or check yellow pages or
   web for other locations.)

*Denotes stores included in the book.   **Denotes stores in our Top Ten.

CHAPTER 17

To the Mall

A DIRECTORY OF AREA SHOPPING MALLS

Washington, D.C.

CHEVY CHASE PAVILION
5335 Wisconsin Avenue NW
Washington, DC 20015
(202) 686-5335
www.ccpavillion.com

Metro: Red Line to Friendship Heights
Details: **Pottery Barn, J. Crew, Ann Taylor Loft, Cheesecake Factory** restaurant, cool decorative art and craftware at **Gazelle**, and much more.

MAZZA GALLERIE
5300 Wisconsin Avenue NW
Washington, DC 20015
(202) 966-6114
www.mazzagallerie.net

Metro: Red Line to Friendship Heights
Details: Upscale indoor mall with **Neiman Marcus, Saks Fifth Avenue Men's Store**, and our favorite for tableware, **Villeroy & Boch**.

SHOPS AT GEORGETOWN PARK
3222 M Street NW
Washington, DC 20007
(202) 298-5577
www.shopsatgeorgetownpark.com

Metro: Not directly Metro accessible, but if you are feeling energetic, take the Orange or Blue Line to Foggy Bottom and walk, or take the Georgetown Metro Connection shuttle
Details: Indoor mall, on the upscale side, in the heart of Georgetown. **The Hattery** and **Fornash Designs** are among the stores.

SHOPS AT NATIONAL PLACE
1331 Pennsylvania Avenue NW
Washington, DC 20004
(202) 662-1250

Metro: Orange, Blue, or Red Line to Metro Center
Details: Filene's Basement is the anchor tenant.

UNION STATION
50 Massachusetts Avenue NE
Washington, DC 20002
(202) 289-1908
www.unionstationdc.com

Metro: Red Line to Union Station
Details: Indoor mall inside the train station, has a large food court and specialty shops.

PAVILION AT THE OLD POST OFFICE
1100 Pennsylvania Avenue NW
Washington, DC 20004
(202) 289-4224
www.oldpostofficedc.com

Metro: Blue or Orange Line to Federal Triangle
Details: Near the Smithsonian and the Mall, the food court is the big drawing card. Don't forget to take the elevator to the top before you leave. The view is great and it's free.

Maryland

BELTWAY PLAZA MALL
6000 Greenbelt Road
Greenbelt MD 20770
(301) 345-1500
www.beltwayplazacenter.com

Metro: If you want some exercise, take the Green Line to the Greenbelt exit. The mall is a half-mile away.
Details: Indoor mall with **Value City** and **Burlington Coat Factory** as major tenants.

CITY PLACE MALL
8661 Colesville Road
Silver Spring, MD 20910
(301) 589-1091

Metro: Red Line to Silver Spring
Details: Urban outlet center with **Marshalls, Ross Dress for Less,** and **Burlington Coat Factory,** among others.

IVERSON MALL
3737 Branch Avenue
Hillcrest Heights, MD 20748
(301) 423-7400
www.iversonmall.com

Details: Indoor mall with **Value City** and **Young World.**

LAKEFOREST
701 Russell Avenue
Gaithersburg, MD 20877
(301) 840-5840
wwwshoplakeforest.com

Details: Indoor mall with all the right mall stuff, including **Hecht's, JC Penney, Lord & Taylor,** and **Sears.**

PRINCE GEORGE'S PLAZA
3500 East-West Highway
Hyattsville, MD 20782
(301) 559-8844

Metro: Green Line to Prince George's Plaza
Details: Indoor mall with **African Stargina Collections**, **Karibu** bookstore, **Outline Inc.**, and chains such as **The Gap**.

WESTFIELD SHOPPINGTOWN MONTGOMERY MALL
7101 Democracy Boulevard
Bethesda, MD 20817
(301) 469-6025
www.westfield.com/us/centres/maryland/montgomery

Details: **Nordstrom, Hecht's,** and all the right mall shops.

WESTFIELD SHOPPINGTOWN WHEATON
11160 Veirs Mill Road
Silver Spring, MD 20902
(301) 946-3200
www.westfield.com/us/centres/maryland/wheaton

Metro: Red Line to Wheaton
Details: **Hecht's, JC Penney, Giant** supermarket, movie theaters, and a food court.

WHITE FLINT MALL
11301 Rockville Pike
North Bethesda, MD 20895
(301) 468-5777
www.shopwhiteflint.com

Details: Home of **Bloomingdale's** and **Dave & Buster's**, the video arcade where kids can play while their dads drink beer.

Virginia

BALLSTON COMMON MALL
4238 Wilson Boulevard
Arlington, VA 22203
(703) 243-6346
www.ballston-common.com

Metro: Orange Line to Ballston-GMU Station
Details: **Hecht's** and an **Official Washington Redskins Store**.

THE CRYSTAL CITY SHOPS
1600 Crystal Square Arcade
(between 15th and 23rd streets)
Arlington, VA 22202
(703) 922-4636
www.thecrystalcityshops.com

Metro: Blue or Yellow Line directly to the Crystal City Station
Details: Very cool maze of underground shops. Pay close attention to where you park; all the buildings aboveground look alike.

DULLES TOWN CENTER
21100 Dulles Town Circle
Dulles, VA 20166
(703) 404-7120
www.shopdullestowncenter.com

Details: Suburban indoor mall.

FAIR OAKS MALL
11750 Fair Oaks
Fairfax, VA 22033
(703) 359-8300
www.shopfairoaksmall.com

Details: Suburban indoor shopping mall with **Macy's** and **Mastercraft Interiors** furniture.

FASHION CENTRE AT PENTAGON CITY
1100 S. Hayes Street
Arlington, VA 22202
(703) 415-2400
www.fashioncentrepentagon.com

Metro: Yellow or Blue Line to the Pentagon City Station
Details: Indoor mall with **Macy's** and **Nordstrom**.

LANDMARK MALL
5801 Duke Street
Alexandria, VA 22304
(703) 354-8405
www.landmarkmall.com

Details: Indoor mall with **Lord and Taylor**, **Hecht's**, and **Sears**.

LEESBURG CORNER PREMIUM OUTLETS
241 Fort Evans Road NE
Leesburg, VA 20176
(703) 737-3071
www.premiumoutlets.com

Details: Outlet mall with outlets for **Barney's New York, Brooks Brothers, Burberry, Kenneth Cole, Polo Ralph Lauren,** and more.

RESTON TOWN CENTER
New Dominion Parkway
Reston, VA 22090
(703) 689-4699
www.restontowncenter.com

Details: Outdoor shopping area with winter skating rink, upscale specialty shops, and restaurants.

POTOMAC MILLS
2700 Potomac Mills Circle
Woodbridge, VA 22192
(703) 643-1855
www.potomacmills.com

Details: Huge indoor outlet mall with **Daffy's, Nordstrom Rack,** and **Van's Skatepark** (indoor in-line skating/skateboarding/BMXing facility with ramps, pools, half-pipes, and rails and fun boxes for street skating, too).

SPRINGFIELD MALL
Franconia and Loisdale Road.
Springfield, VA 22150
(703) 971-3000
www.springfieldmall.com

Details: Suburban indoor mall with **JC Penney, Macy's,** and **Target.**

TYSONS CORNER CENTER
1961 Chain Bridge Road
McLean, VA 22102
(703) 893-9400
www.shoptysons.com

Details: Indoor shopping mall with **Bloomingdale's, Lord and Taylor, Nordstrom, Restoration Hardware,** and **L.L. Bean.**

TYSONS CORNER II, THE GALLERIA
2001 International Drive
McLean, VA 22102
(703) 827-7700
www.shoptysonsgalleria.com

Details: Very upscale indoor shopping mall. Stores include: **Neiman Marcus, Anthropologie, Betsey Johnson, Cartier, Coach, Eileen Fisher, Koffi Aguso, M*A*C, Saks Fifth Avenue, Thomas Pink, Tommy Bahama,** and **Versace Jeans Couture.**